KIDS DO THE WEB

Kids do the Web

by Cynthia Overbeck Bix
with Mary Anne Petrillo,
and Tom Morgan and John Miller of the Interactive Bureau

Adobe Press
San Jose, California

Library of Congress Catalog No.: 96-77651

ISBN: 1-56830-315-7

10 9 8 7 6 5 4 3 2 First Printing: October 1996

Published by Adobe Press, Adobe Systems Incorporated, http://www.adobe.com.

Text and cover design by Tom Morgan and John Miller, Interactive Bureau.

Designed and produced using Adobe PageMaker and Adobe Photoshop. Pre-press and printing by Shepard Poorman Communications Corporation, Indianapolis, IN, using Adobe PostScript computer-to-plate (filmless process) technology. Soy-based inks were used to eliminate releasing harmful chemicals into the environment. Printed in the United States of America.

Published simultaneously in Canada.

Adobe Press books are published and distributed by Macmillan Computer Publishing USA. For individual, educational, corporate, or retail sales accounts, call 1-800-428-5331, or 317-581-3500. For information address Macmillan Computer Publishing USA, 201 West 103rd Street, Indianapolis, IN 46290. Macmillan's World Wide Web page URL is http://www.mcp.com.

Dedicated to the students, teachers, educators,

and volunteers who are creating a new digital world.

Preface

Welcome to the special world of kids and the Web. What you are about to read and see is extraordinary—technology in the hands of young adults.

Here it is immediately evident that the Web is really about kids. It is youthful, vital, dynamic, and inquisitive. The Web is instant access to the world's knowledge and libraries; it is about learning and communicating and exploring. Nobody understands this at a more basic level than the youth of the world. It is their medium, and they are grabbing at it instinctively. They are creating their world view, and it is uplifting and inspirational. This book begs to represent those phenomena.

Creating your own Web site was once confined to software programmers and computer experts. No longer. This book attempts to show all of its readers how easy it is. Sprinkled throughout are software tips on how to create better Web sites, faster and easier. No matter your age, if you can move a mouse you can participate.

Any paper book about the Web will ultimately fail. It is impossible to show the thousands of sites kids have created. Each one is unique and creative and worth visiting. We sincerely apologize that everyone couldn't be included. In addition, Web sites often change their appearance. We heartily apologize to those who have recently advanced their Web sites only to have an older picture of it appear in this book. And finally we apologize to our readers if some sites have recently changed their Web addresses (URLs) since publication.

This book is a paper snapshot of an energetic, youthful world that changes daily. I'm sure you'll agree—we need the world's youthful minds and their creative insights to fully participate.

Patrick Ames, Publisher

Adobe Press, Adobe Systems Incorporated

C O N T E N T S

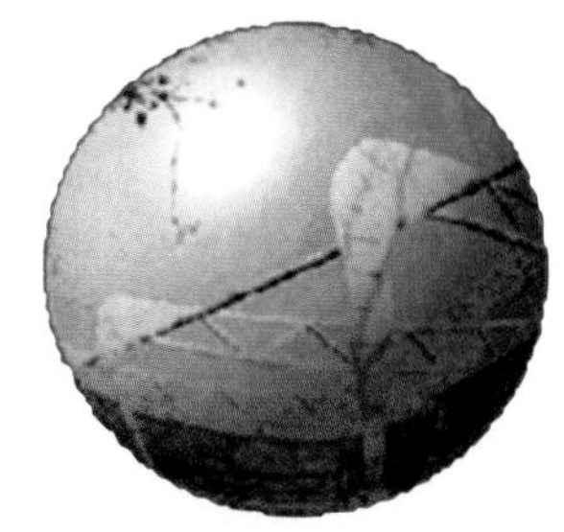

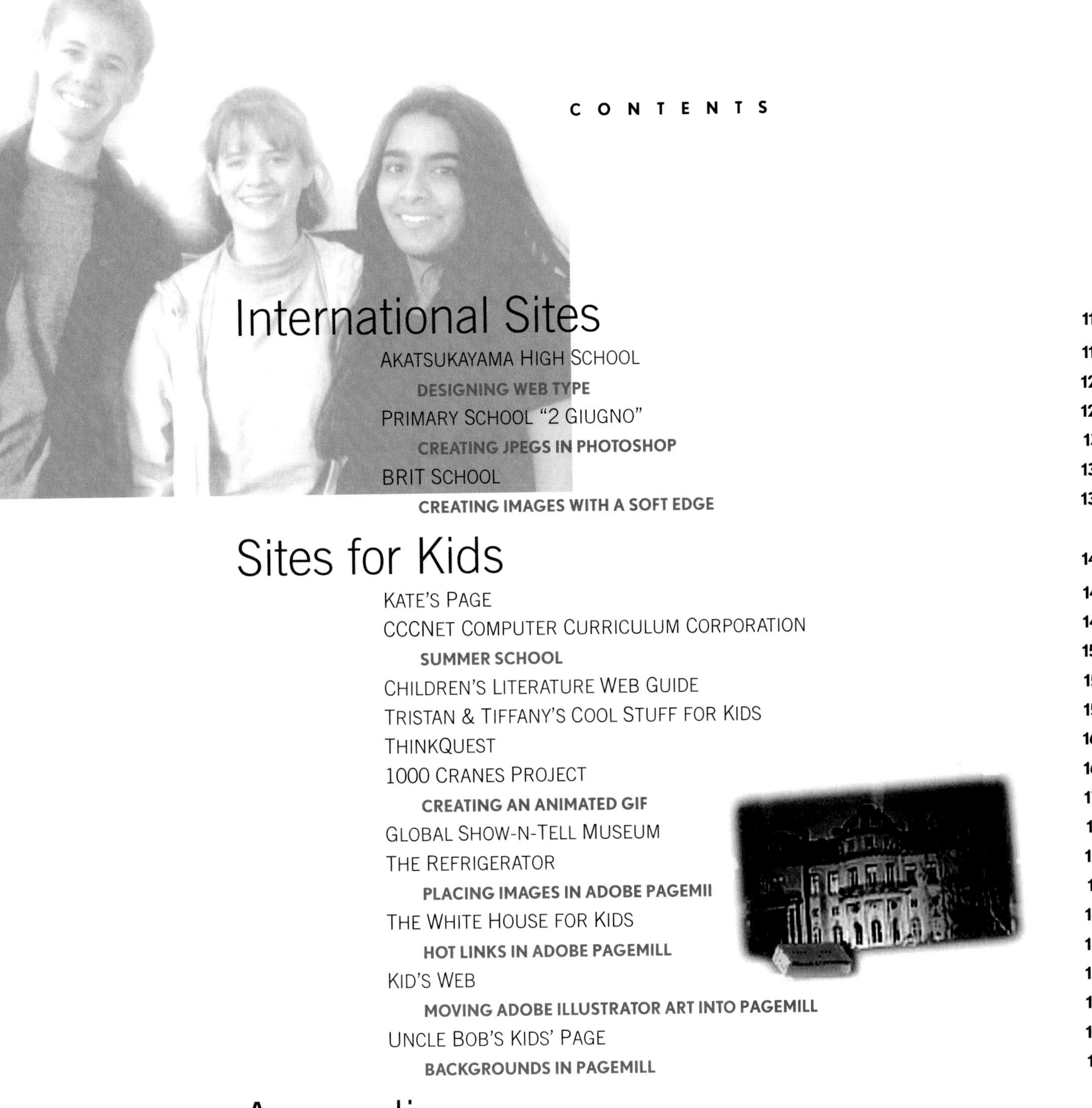

CONTENTS

Introduction

Travels on the World Wide Web

Whether you've been "logging on" to the World Wide Web for a while or are just beginning to explore it, you've probably already discovered that it's great territory for kids. The Web is a place where you can read stories or study world-famous paintings, "talk" to someone halfway across the globe or take a virtual climb on Mount Everest.

And you can do more than browse the Web: you can create your own site! In this book you'll see what many of those students and teachers, both in the United States and around the world, are doing on the Web.

A mini-guide to the Web

Whether you're familiar with the Web or not, its best to start off your explorations supplied with a few basic facts about the Web. Simply defined, the World Wide Web (WWW) is the part of the Internet that includes graphics—color pictures, charts, movies, and sound—along with text. It was developed beginning in 1990 at CERN, the European Particle Physics Laboratory in Geneva, Switzerland. Researchers there were looking for a way to help scientists share documents with graphic elements that couldn't be seen over the all-text Internet. They came up with HTML, a language that brings together all kinds of media, from text to images to video or audio files, in one document.

Users of the Web need a browser, like Netscape or Mosaic, to travel around. Each site, or destination on the Web, has an address, or URL (Universal Resource Locator). A typical URL would be that of Adobe Systems: http://www.adobe.com. Entering the URL brings you to the site's home page. From there, you use the links provided to access other pages in the site, as well as other sites.

Mapping your own paths on the Web

The Web is a great resource for finding any kind of information you can think of. When you research a topic, the secret of success is focus. By now, there are hundreds of thousands of Web sites on-line. Trying to find your way around in this endless maze of sites can be pretty confusing. That's why when you're researching a topic, it's essential to have a specific idea in mind—to know just what you're looking for and to stick to that search.

As great as the Web is for research, the most fun is to create your own site. It's fun to put up pages that tell people about your favorite books or music, about your pets, or about your school. But what really sets the Web apart from print or television is that it's interactive. Setting up a dialog, or conversation, with other people and other groups from near and far. When you put out your ideas, you get feedback—sometimes immediately—from people "out there" who read and see it. It's all part of creating a world-wide network of ideas that breaks through the boundaries of language and geography.

Safe traveling on the Web: a note for kids and parents

The Web is a mirror of the world we live in. As such, it is full of all kinds of people—some you want to know, and some you should avoid. For the most part, being on-line is a friendly and positive experience, and most of the people you'll communicate with are honest, well-intentioned people like you. But if you ever run across something that feels wrong—someone who says things you don't feel comfortable with, or a site that isn't right for kids—you should tell your parents or teacher and immediately exit from that site.

Teachers are aware of what's appropriate for their students and take steps to make sure kids' journeys on the Web are safe. At home, parents should exercise the same caution by paying attention to what their kids are looking at on the Web and helping them to make the right choices. Following a few simple rules will help you travel safely and enjoy your time spent on the Web.

- *Never give out personal information such as your last name, address, phone number, or school to anyone on the Web.*
- *If you come across something or someone on the Web that bothers you or just doesn't feel right, let your parents or teacher know right away.*
- *Never give out your password or your parents' password. No one needs to know it!*
- *Always treat people you "meet" on the Web with the same respect and courtesy you'd use when meeting face to face.*

The Web is part of your world

The sites in this book are examples of the originality and energy that kids have put into creating pages for the Web. Perhaps looking at these examples will be the inspiration you need to start a site of your own at home or at school, or to get a collaborative project going from within your classroom.

There's no reason to wait! You can begin right now, to create, learn, and enjoy on the Web and beyond!

How this book works

This book is divided into three sections: School Sites; International Sites; and Sites for Kids. For each site, some of the actual Web pages you'd see on the computer screen are reproduced at a reduced size. Captions below or next to these pages point out elements of special interest; you can locate these by noting the grid references in the captions (like 1a or 2c) that correspond to the numbers and letters along the top and sides of the book pages.

For each site, there's also a Special Features section that shows you unique pages of the site. And scattered throughout are step-by-step directions for creating some of the elements you'll see in the pages. For more detailed information about ways to create Web site elements, see the manuals for Adobe software such as Photoshop®, PhotoDeluxe®, PageMill®, SiteMill®, and Acrobat®.

Kids do the Web

Chances are, if you haven't already, you'll get your first glimpse of the Web at school. That's not surprising. For a lot of kids, this is where it's all happening. It's where they'll find the equipment and the know-how they need to get started. And some of the best Web sites come out of schools like yours. Look through these pages to see how kids across the country are having a great time creating a group identity.

School Sites

http://www.chsn.org

Clarkstown North High School

Clark County School District
New City, Rockland County, New York

Clarkstown North High School—CNHS—is a public school in what the students call "that little place north of New York City." The school's 1,500 students are famous for placing in the top percentiles of the state's academic ratings. Now some of that energy is also being funneled into the Clarkstown Web site.

One Internet provider has called the CNHS site "the best high school Web site in the U.S." Under the rubric @North, juniors Ian Nieves (Webmaster), Adam Berson, Adam Koniak, and Seth Mandel created this Web site in 1995. The torch is being quickly picked up by a new class of juniors and seniors.

"This site has been completely conceptualized and designed by a small group of students. They've done an incredible job of bringing our community closer together."

—John Krouskoff, English Instructor

Organize your site. If you have great graphics, but people can't find their way around, it's useless.

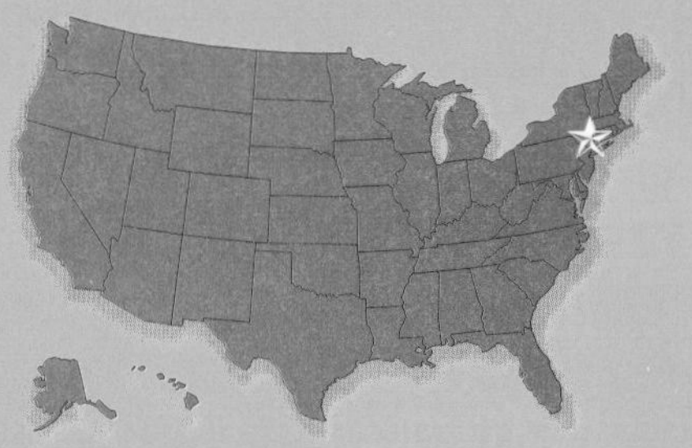

CNHS is in New City, New York, 20 miles north of New York City. In the 1950s, a lot of New Yorkers left the city for these quiet neighborhoods; it's been popular ever since.

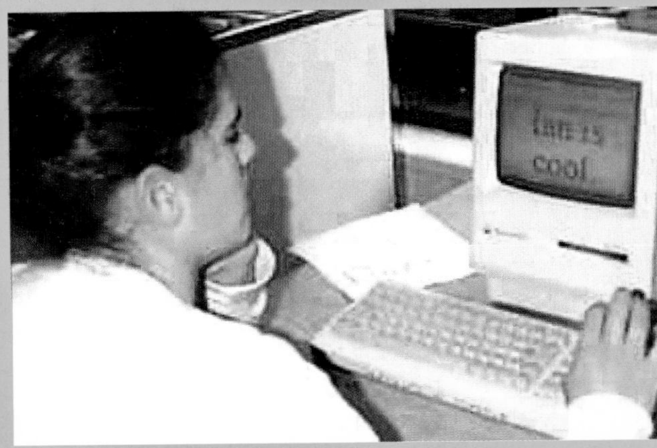

Jessica Blatt finishes a story for the school paper in the @North Writing Lab. *See pages 44-45 for a how-to.*

Lively and always changing, the site features three separate publications, an art gallery, and the "Internet Cafe." It started as a way to feature the student newspaper and literary creations, but now it's grown into a strong working link between the school and the community with campus maps, an e-mail address book…even up-to-the-minute weather reports!

Seth Mandel imports today's images into the Internet Cafe.

1 2 3 4

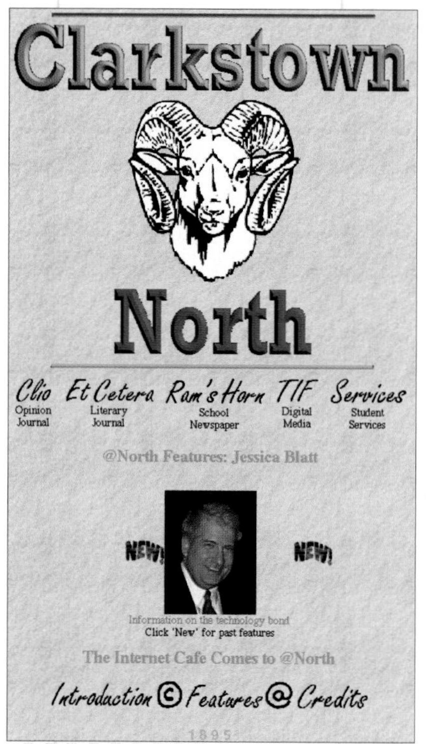

Students used Photoshop to assemble the home page background. (1a) *Small GIF images make the page links more interesting.* (1b) *Attention-getting animated GIFs for "New...New"* (1c) *were created in GIF Construction Set. See pages 170–173 for a how-to on animated GIFs.*

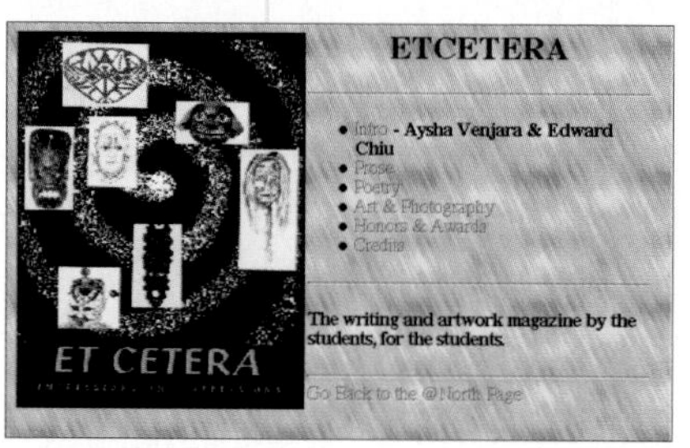

(1b) *Clicking "TIF-Digital Media" takes you to a page of digital artwork submitted by students called "Planet T.I.F."* (3a) *Originally the brainchild of junior Kevin Liu, it was brought onto the site by teamwork among members of @North team.*

Clicking on "Et Cetera" (1b) *brings visitors to the CNHS literary journal;* (3e) *here's a page from a story with the author's original art work. As Ian Nieves says, "Every student can become a full-fledged journalist or artist with an on-line portfolio."*

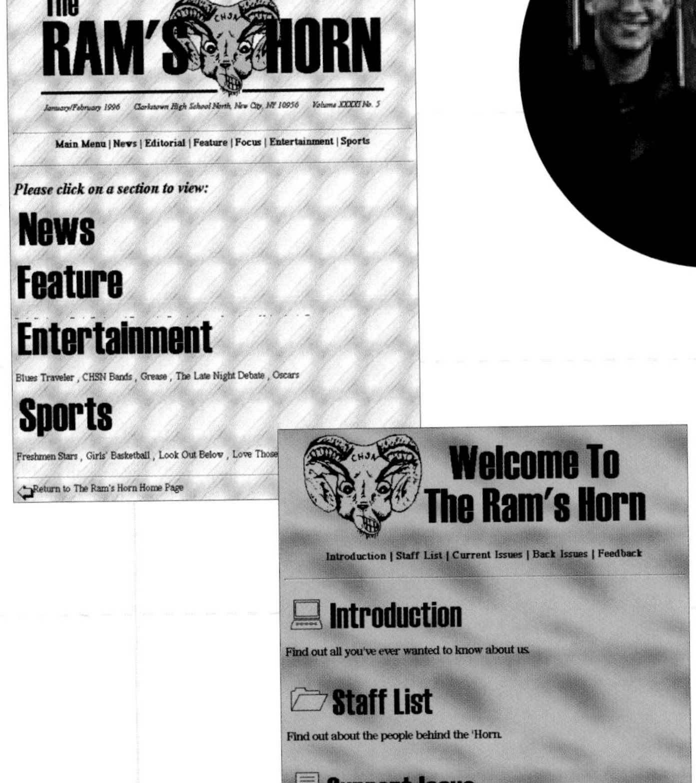

(1a) *A home page link leads to the* Ram's Horn, *the student newspaper,* (6a) *which comes out eight times yearly. It's a rich mix of school and community news; you can read back issues in the archives.* (6d) *Notice the way the CNHS mascot displays another side of its personality—an example of the clever way themes and images are carried through in this site.*

Here the site promotes a CD-ROM of the students' 1996 Writer's Workshop trip to London with their teacher, Mr. Holbrook. This multimedia presentation features stories, poems, and pictures by the students. Note the @ logo; (8b) *it refers to @North and it appears throughout the pages to direct visitors around the site.* *See Web Tip page 19.*

a b c d e

Clarkstown North High School Site Map

Special Features

Page 1

The CNHS Web site finds all sorts of creative ways of reaching out to the community. One strong link is the Student Services feature. This page includes the E-Mail Address Book (very popular with students and the community at large); the Year Calendar; an Extra Help Sessions schedule to help students connect with teachers and tutors; and even Campus Maps. During the fierce winter of 1996, people all over Rockland County depended on the site's Weather Center for accurate, up-to-the-minute reports.

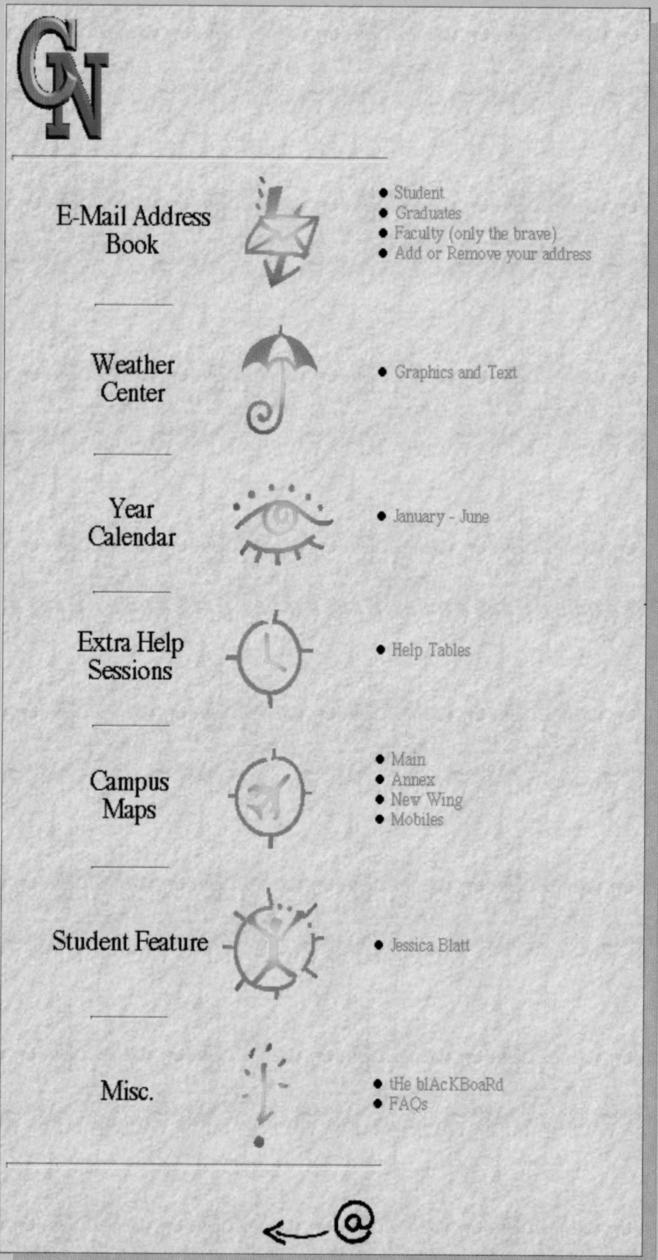

"When I hear a freshman walking down the hallway mentioning our site, or hear that a physics student found our online physics department crucial to their study efforts, I smile in a sigh of relief. All of the work was NOT FOR NOTHING!*"* — **IAN NIEVES, WEBMASTER**

web tip

Digital camera pictures look best when color corrected in Adobe Photoshop or Adobe PhotoDeluxe. For maximum rebuilding speed, these were saved as small GIF files (18k each). Experiment to get the smallest file possible without degrading the quality.

Page 2

The site's creators find ways to get involved person-to-person. For the "Internet Cafe" program, a local senior citizens group came to CNHS to learn how to "surf the Web" from the experts—the @North team. The event was recorded with a digital camera, as the students presented an overview of their site and how to get around on the Web.

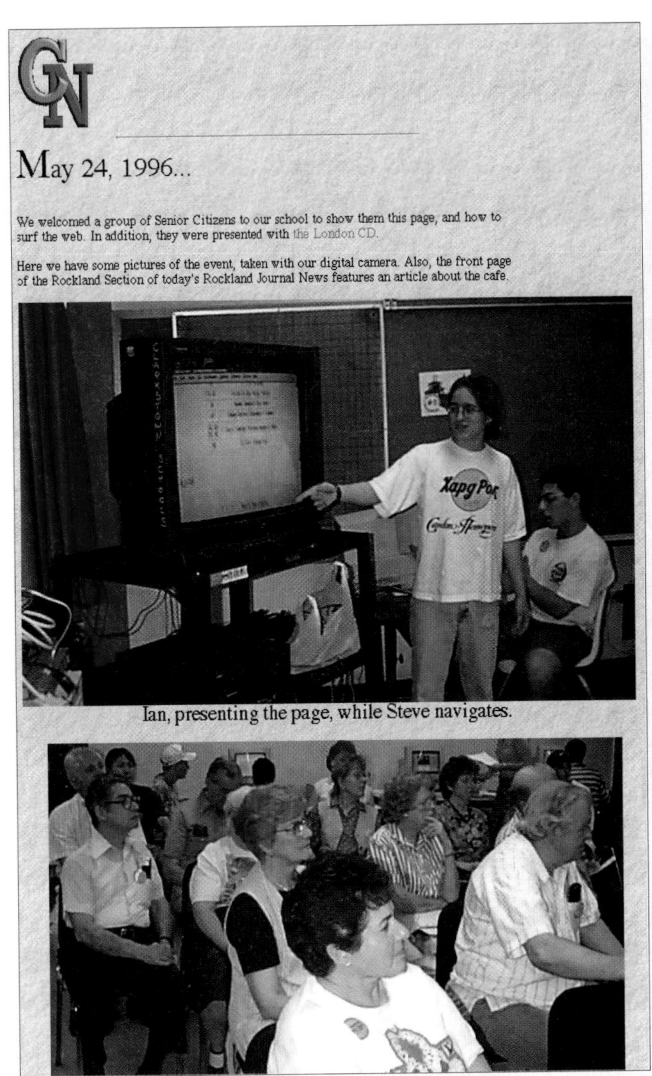

CN

May 24, 1996...

We welcomed a group of Senior Citizens to our school to show them this page, and how to surf the web. In addition, they were presented with the London CD.

Here we have some pictures of the event, taken with our digital camera. Also, the front page of the Rockland Section of today's Rockland Journal News features an article about the cafe.

Ian, presenting the page, while Steve navigates.

Clarkstown North High School

http://bob.coe.uga.edu/~bbiddle/bshoals/welcome.html

Barnett Shoals Elementary

Athens, Georgia

"Over the last three years Barnett Shoals has focused on technology. Now our students are on computers every day, using the Web, graphing programs, time line software and desktop publishing programs."

—Principal Ray W. Clark

Barnett Shoals, a public school in Athens, was named a 1991 Georgia School of Excellence. This is a school that makes a point of keeping up with the latest technology: it runs its own television broadcasting studio and has now developed a Web site. The site was created in the summer and fall of 1995 by teachers Christine Fuentes (3rd grade) and Lynn Gatachell (3rd to 5th grades).

Rather than dumping old pages when new ones are posted, group them into an "archives" section. Give visitors an opportunity to explore your site.

Barnett Shoals is located in Athens, Georgia, a small college town filled with southern charm and a very hip music scene.

The site does a great job of reporting on all of the school's classes. Here, science students examine dirt for microscopic wasps.

The site keeps everybody up-to-date on school projects, including the library's new bee collection.

"People-friendly" describes the Barnett Shoals site. Unlike many "high-tech" sites, these pages give a feeling of welcome. Every page exudes the school's energy, with hundreds of pictures and reports on students and their projects. The design is friendly, with small, fast-loading GIF and JPEG images, and is very easy to navigate. The creators have also included links to city- and state-created Web sites that provide community history, as well as information for visitors about local hotels, attractions, restaurants.

WELCOME TO
BARNETT SHOALS ELEMENTARY

A Georgia School of Excellence

Ray Clark, Principal

It's a Small World after all!

Pictured are some of our Barnett Shoals International students. As we anticipate the 1996 Olympic events in our midst, our students are researching and communicating with the world. We invite you to write to us and share something about your country. Do see our Olympic page.

ABOUT OUR SCHOOL...

Information about our school
A Welcome from our Principal
Staff Surfers
Current Student Projects
Student Projects Winter 1995
Barnett Shoals' Commitment to Technology

ABOUT OUR STATE...

Georgia Web Servers
State of Georgia Information
Guide to the 1996 Olympic Games
It's Atlanta - a guide to the Olympics
Georgia Legislative Information

CURRENT STUDENT PROJECTS

Bees are buzzing at Barnett Shoals. In a corner of our library is a real bee observation hive. Students can observe the queen laying eggs and the workers attending her. This has been a very popular place for our students to gather and read and observe these important pollinators first hand.

Mary IS a little lamb and she came to live at Barnett Shoals when she was 5 days old. She weighed 11 pounds. Mary drinks from a bottle 4 times a day, and she is gaining weight fast. Mary is a suffolk breed of sheep and so her body color will turn white but her lead and legs will remain black. Mary lives in a pen by the herb garden where she can visit with boys and girls on their way to classes.

Fifth graders examining nests of dirt daubers to discover Melittobia digitata (microscopic wasps). Investigation reveals their parasitic relationship to the dirt dauber larvae.

This page is being updated and maintained by Barnett Shoals Students Jaime and Stuwart.

Back to Welcome Page

Clicking on Current Student Projects (1c) *brings visitors to the heart of the school's site.* (3b) *Here, visitors get up-to-date reports on what's happening at Barnett Shoals. Roving reporters Jaime and Stuwart write stories, take classroom pictures, scan the images as JPEG files, (see pages 60–61) and assemble the complete pages.*

(1a) *The site's friendly feeling comes from photos of students and their projects. But the pages have more to* (1c) *offer: links to community and state-wide sites makes it useful for everyone in Athens. Especially popular were the pages and links about the 1996 Summer Olympics,* (1d) *held in the nearby Atlanta Metro area.*

Save image files as JPEG for drastic size compression. **See pages 60–61.**

(1c) *The Student Projects link also features a* (6d) *section of past classroom activities. Soon all of these pages will be available in a single "archives" section.*

STUDENT PROJECTS - WINTER 1995

Second and third grade Spectrum program students have been involved in global research as they prepare for our 1996 Olympics in Georgia. They have gathered information about big cities of the world and presented their research as travel guides. These books were typed and illustrated with various computer software programs.

To encourage kindergartners to read and to celebrate National Children's Book Week, we recently got all the kindergartners to come to the library to read. They brought their favorite books, their stuffed animals, and their pillows and blankets. Parents and teachers read to these students for about one and one-half hours. The children enjoyed it very much.

Our third graders are animal keepers. These classes have 2 rabbits, 2 gerbils, 1 guinea pig, and 1 bird. The students have to feed and give water to these pets daily. They also clean their cages once a week. In addition to their keeping of animals, they have been researching animals and presenting their research in programs using HyperStudio.

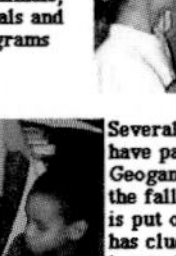

Several classes at our school have participated in the Geogame which takes place in the fall and spring. This game is put out over the Internet and has clues to help students locate 20 cities around the world. They send in their answers to be evaluated. Students can also participate in creating clues about their own

Back to Welcome Page

Clarke County's Commitment to Technology

Over the last three years our school has written and implemented our Technology Plan. After much research, school visitation, and faculty input, we formulated and prioritized our school's technology goals. These goals addressed three main areas - the securing of appropriate hardware and software, on-going staff development, and most importantly the integration of this technology into our curricula.

We continue to gain new insights into the use of technologies as classroom tools. Our students are now on computers daily. Students use computers in their classrooms, in our Josten's Lab, and in our Micro Society. Some of the many classroom projects have included using HyperStudio to produce student authored media presentations, graphing programs to present students' statistical findings, time line software to illustrate concepts of time in many units, and desktop publishing programs to enhance classroom curricula. Many of the student projects that we will exhibit on this page are the results of integrated technologies.

Our most recent endeavor has been the establishment of a television broadcasting studio. These news and feature broadcasts are written and produced by the 5th grade students for viewing by the student body on a daily basis. As part of a TCI grant, these broadcasts will soon be viewed in the homes of our community.

Pictured above are Christine Fuentes and Lynn Gatchell attending the Georgia Center for Advanced Telecommunications Technology conference where they were recognized for their efforts in integrating technology and telecommunications into the classroom.

Back to Welcome Page

School news feature pages are reached from the home (1c) *page. This page* (8a) *highlights the increasing use of technology in the school. In the photo, teachers Christine Fuentes and Lynn Gatachell receive special recognition by the Georgia Center for Advanced Telecommunications Technology for their efforts in bringing Web technology into the classroom.*

Special Features

This site has a strong link to its community—the city of Athens—and the students' home state of Georgia. 1996 was the year their state hosted the Summer Olympics, so they created a section of their site dedicated to the games, with a link to the official Olympic homepage.

OLYMPICS AT BARNETT SHOALS

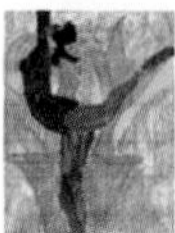

Olympic art work by Ali, a Barnett Shoals fifth grader.

Olympic mascot Izzy and University of Georgia's Hairy Dog visit Barnett Shoals students to kick off our Olympic studies. Our Athens community will be hosting the 1996 Soccer, Volleyball, and Rhythmic Gymnastics.

The Olympic Torch

The Olympic torch will come to the Athens, Georgia area around July 15, 1996. Several people in our community were selected to be torchbearers. Ms. Lisa Voigt's 4th grade class has been interviewing some of these Athens area Olympic torchbearers to find out what makes a community hero. Click here to meet our community torchbearing heroes.

Page 1

The students created original Olympic artwork, took photos of special events (such as the Olympic mascot's visit to the school), and scanned them all into PhotoDeluxe, quickly color-corrected them, and posted them in PageMill. A link to the Community Torchbearing Heroes takes viewers to the next page .

web tip

Adding hot links to other parts of the Web (like the Olympics home page) is fast and easy in Adobe PageMill. These links make your site interesting and useful to more people. A program such as Adobe SiteMill can keep those links current and organized. See pages 30 – 31.

"I take the e-mail off the computer in the morning, print it out, and deliver it. We get e-mail from other countries for our classroom pen pals. And we get e-mail for teachers and for students."

—**ELIZABETH RARRICK**

Page 2

Students from the 4th grade interviewed local people who were selected to be Olympic torchbearers because of their service to the community. Rather than running straight text, the students presented the interviews in a more interesting, magazine-style layout.

Mr. Paul Dorsey is a retired Athens, Georgia businessman. He is 81 years old and he has been named an Olympic torchbearer. A team of 4th grade students recently interviewed him.

Doug Hatch is a math teacher from Watkinsville, Georgia. He is 47. Doug has been involved in several community projects to help others. He serves on the board of Community Connection, ESP (Extra Special People, Inc.) and Georgia Options. As a young child, Doug had polio.

Janice Mathis

Jonathan Wilbanks

Back to Welcome Page

Barnett Shoals Elementary

Linking Pages

The key to helping visitors navigate successfully through your site is to create a series of logical, workable links from one page (the source) to another (the destination). The destination can be on the same page or another page in your site, or anywhere else on the Web. Links can lead to the top of the destination page, or to a specific place on a page, called an anchor. Here's how to create a basic link in Adobe PageMill.

Select a source and a destination

1 **Determine the destination** for your link. If necessary, create an anchor as your destination. You can do this by dragging the page icon to somewhere within its own page. After creating an anchor, you can drag the anchor to another page or to another location on the same page.

2 **Select the source of the link**—the text or image the reader will click to get to the destination.

Create a link

1 **Drag something representing** the destination (a page icon, image icon, anchor, etc.) to the text or image selected as the source and drop it. (You can also type the URL directly into the Link Location Bar.)

2 **To test your links,** click on Preview mode (the globe at the upper right corner of the page).

Updating Links

With Adobe SiteMill, making changes to your site's links is quick, easy, and efficient. SiteMill will automatically track all of your links, so that when you replace a link, it's updated throughout your site. This is especially helpful when you used a link in many pages.

1 **Choose Site>Load Site** and locate the root folder for your entire site; click Open.

2 **With the Site window** and External References window open, review the display of incoming and outgoing links. To see a list of incoming links to a file, click and hold the Incoming Links button. To see outgoing links, click and hold the Outgoing button.

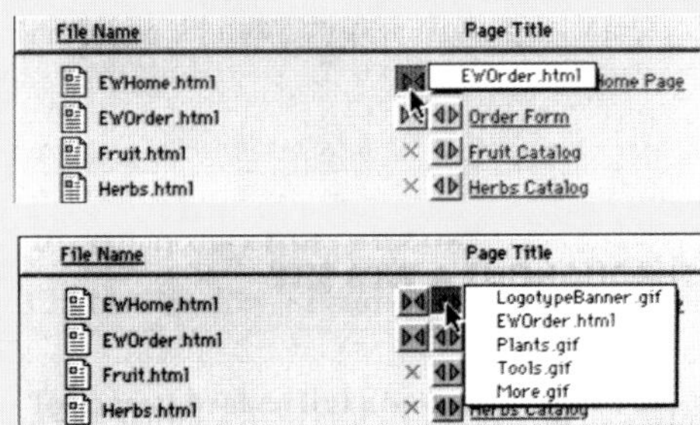

3 **To find and replace all instances** of a link, choose Site>Replace Links.

4 **Drag the link you want** to replace from the Site window or External References window into the Find Every Link To option, or type the URL.

5 **Drag the replacement link** from the Site window or External References window into the And Replace With A Link To option.

6 **Click Replace All.** Site Mill will ask you if it should update the references in the other files to reflect the new file name. Click OK.

ncia.net/schools/berlin/

Berlin High School

Berlin School District (SAU #3)
Berlin, New Hampshire

In this public high school of 600 students, grades 9 to 12, there wasn't enough equipment available for creating a Web site. But math teacher Tom Sweeny, along with a very supportive administration, was not deterred. They got help from Jeff Schall and others at nearby New Hampshire Technical College ("The Tech"), where they learned to write HTML and were given use of the facilities and a place to store their home page for free.

"The site exposes youngsters to the latest technology, which is what teaching is all about—preparing kids for the future."

—Tom Sweeny, Math Teacher and Technology Coordinator

David Montgomery posts new pages on the site's Alumni section.

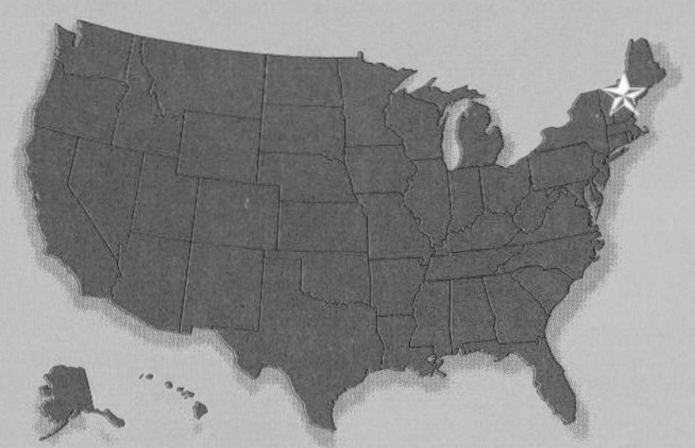

BHS is in an old paper-milling town—"the city that trees built"—in the White Mountains of New Hampshire, only 65 miles from Canada. French is spoken here as a second language.

The school's computers all default to the site's home page.

Team spirit and school pride are bonuses that emerged from the experience of building the site. Tom Sweeny says, "The kids who got involved in the creation of pages have a lot more pride in their school. A feeling of a team has developed, and there's even an increased communication between teachers and students."

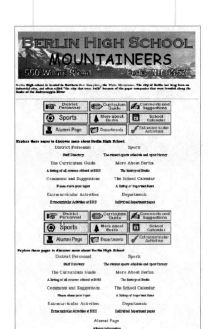

1 2 3 4

(1a) *This home page avoids slow, complicated graphics and presents everything in a clear, simple layout, with nice backgrounds (made of fast-building 2k GIFs). Practical features include a School Calendar;* (2b) (4d) *Curriculum Guide which the students edited;* (2c) *and a link to the town of Berlin.*

(1b) *Clicking on Sports brings visitors to the students' favorite pages.* (4e) *"That's where they have the most fun," says Sweeny. Note that the logo is large, but because it is just two colors, it was able to be highly compressed to build quickly.*

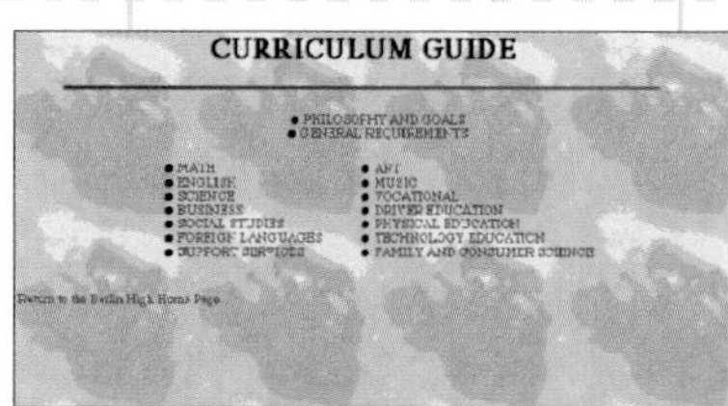

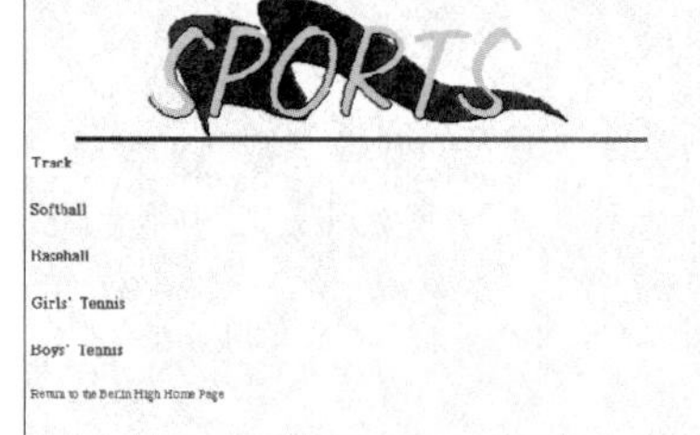

4e *Simple links to Track and Field lead to popular features such as BHS Girls' Track Record Holders.* 5e *This table format is easily created in the new version of PageMill.*

1b *Home page links also lead to the Alumni pages, which are used regularly by former* 6d *students. The pages feature an address book, alumni news, and nominations to the BHS Athletic Hall of Fame.* 8a

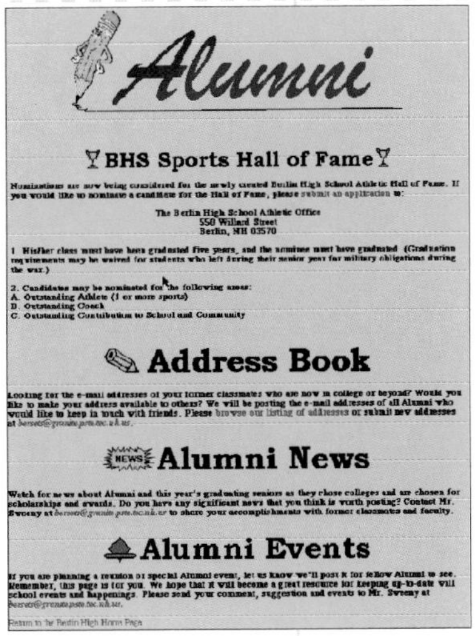

TRACK AND FIELD

Spring 1996 Schedule

The Coaches

The Team

BHS Girls' Track Record Holders

BHS Boys' Track Record Holders

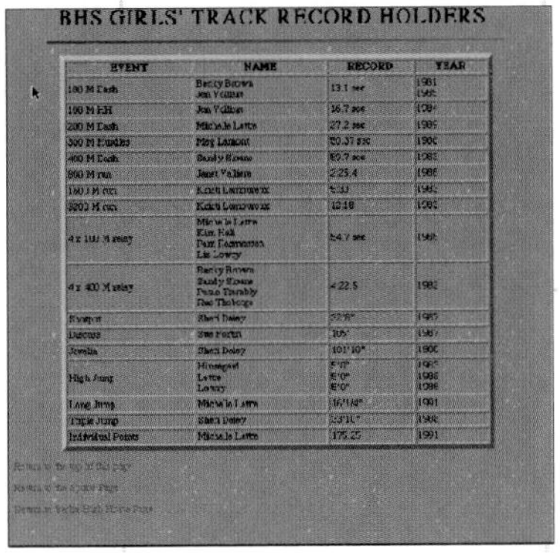

BHS GIRLS' TRACK RECORD HOLDERS

Alumni

BHS Sports Hall of Fame

Address Book

Alumni News

Alumni Events

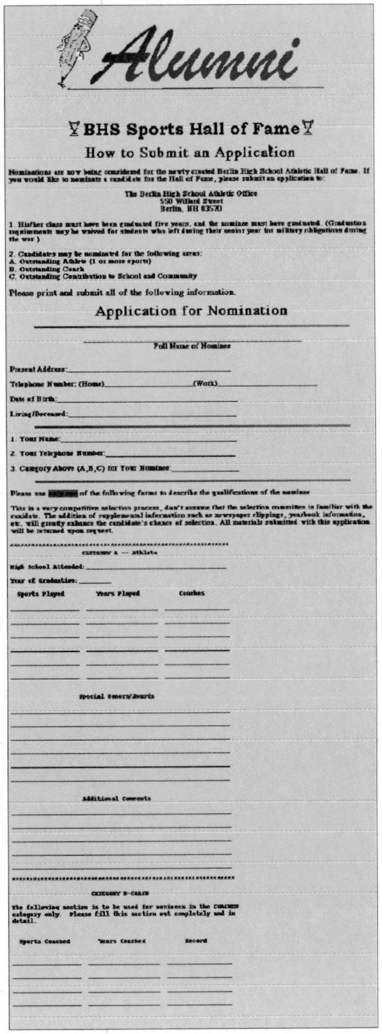

Alumni

BHS Sports Hall of Fame

How to Submit an Application

Application for Nomination

a b c d e

The Web is active! Change your site often! If people keep seeing the same thing over and over they won't come back...

Special Features

Future Plans

The computer team at BHS has lots of plans for the future of their site. They want to expand their sports pages to include the next year's programs, and to add more about extracurricular activities. The students understand that it's important for a site to keep changing. In fact, they're planning to totally reorganize the site to create a page for each department in the school.

Finally, they want to add more graphics—but nothing that slows down the pages too much. Tom Sweeny says, "Now we'd like to get small—but interesting—images up, and add more photos of the people at the school."

"I enjoy working with GIF files. We try to make each one unique and interesting, because pictures are what most people see first." — STACY BEAUDOIN, 10TH GRADE

"When I first started working on our home page, I had no knowledge of Web construction. But now I'm quite proficient." —MEG DOHERTY, 10TH GRADE

"I first discovered the Internet on my home computer and I said, 'Boy! There's a lot of great information out there.' And best of all it's fun, interesting, and very graphic." —TOM SWEENY

Creating GIF Images in Photoshop

Small images build more quickly on the Web. The way to make an image smaller is by compressing the number of colors used to create it. Here's how:

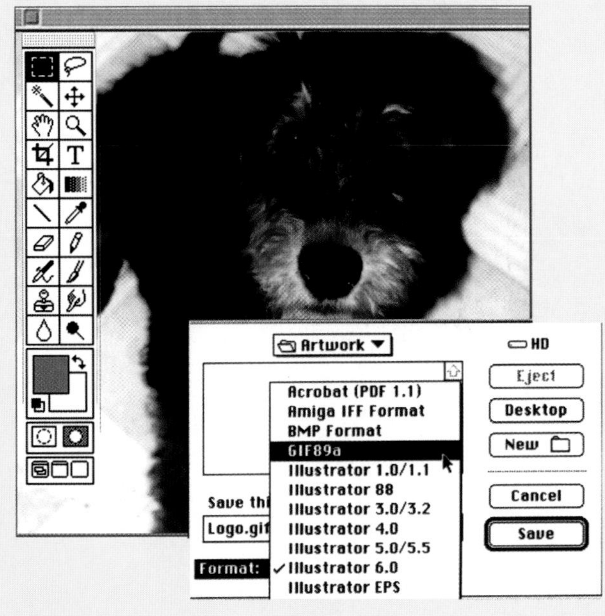

1 Open your artwork in Adobe Photoshop. Make sure that it's in RGB mode and 72 ppi.

2 Next, choose Mode>Indexed color. Choose the lowest bit resolution (number of colors) that give you good results. (You may need to experiment with a few settings using the Revert command.) Choose an Adaptive Palette and a Dither of None.

3 Click OK. If the image does not look as good as you like or if you think you can still reduce the number of colors used, choose File>Revert and repeat step 2. Otherwise, choose Save As, name the file with a .gif extension, and choose GIF89a from the Format menu.

http://168.216.210.13/index.htm

Oak Glen Middle School

Hancock County School District
Chester, West Virginia

"Students here don't have access to a lot of cultural activities and educational opportunities. Our Web site has given us a window on the world that the students would never have had."

—LOU CASINI, INTERNET COORDINATOR

Having a Web site has really put Oak Glen Middle School on the map. Located way out in a rural area, in the oldest building in Hancock County, Oak Glen now connects with the world through the World Wide Web.

Band teacher and founder of the Internet Class, Lou Casini says they didn't even intend to put up a site. "We stumbled into it! While we were requesting funds for our computer lab, we found it was cheap and easy to put up a server—and set up a site."

Rick, Maureen, and David were all instrumental in developing the site's hot links.

With 410 students, OGMS is in the tiny rural city of Chester, in the Northern Panhandle of West Virginia.

The pride of this site is the original home page design created by the students by special request for the governor of West Virginia. Also featured are many of the students' own home pages.

One great feature of the school's site is that it links the Magellan search engine into its home page, so users can do comprehensive searches of the Web—right from the Oak Glen site!

Oak Glen has just developed an e-mail pen pal program with Chester School in England.

1 2 3 4

The OGMS home page offers a great directory of other recommended sites to visit, including the NBC weather page.

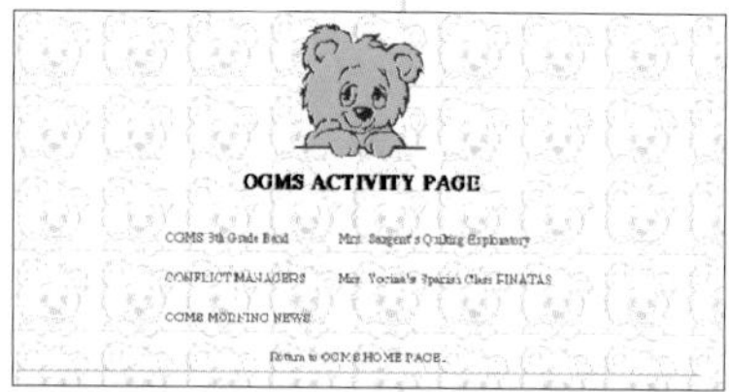

Oak Glen Middle School 8th Grade Band

West Virginia Music Educators Honor Finalist
1981, 1984, 1986, 1988, 1990
Mid East Instrumental Conference Honor Group 1993
West Virginia Student Music Educators Honor Group 1993
Music Festivals Grand Champion, 1995

Return to OGMS ACTIVITY PAGE.
Return to OGMS HOME PAGE.

(1c) *The page also has the Magellan search engine built right in, so users can search the entire web from the site. Clicking on* (3b) *Activities brings up school pages like 8th Grade Band.*

(1b) *The home page also links to school news. "What we try to do with the pages is to document school events as they happen," says* (4e) *Lou Casini. Here's an example of their reporting: photos were taken with a Casio digital camera using QVPC software.*

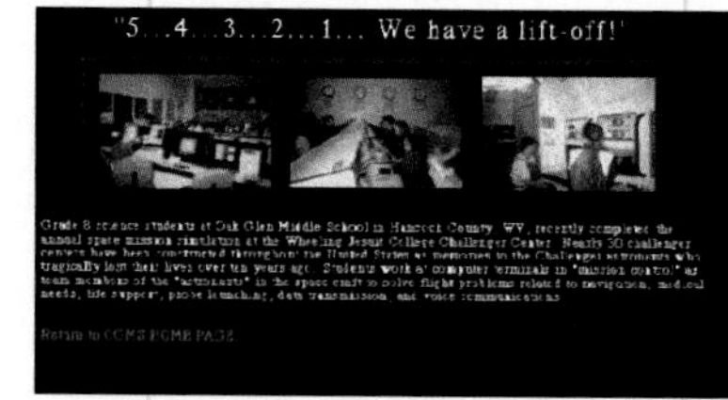

5 6 7 8

a b c d e

One very popular page is the OGMS Internet Exploratory Class; clicking on that link brings up a simple portrait page (8c) *featuring the geniuses behind the school's site.*

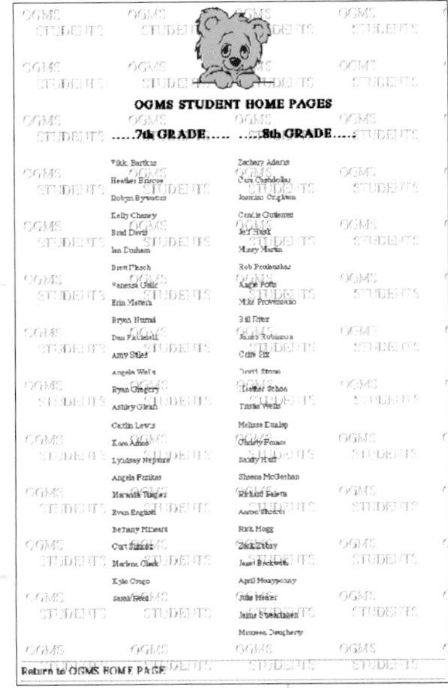

Clicking on Student Home (1c) *Pages brings up a listing of* (6b) *names to choose from. Rick's* (5d) *and* (6e) *Dave's home pages both use custom GIF backgrounds (images are 3k). Dave's is dedicated to his favorite football team—the Steelers.*

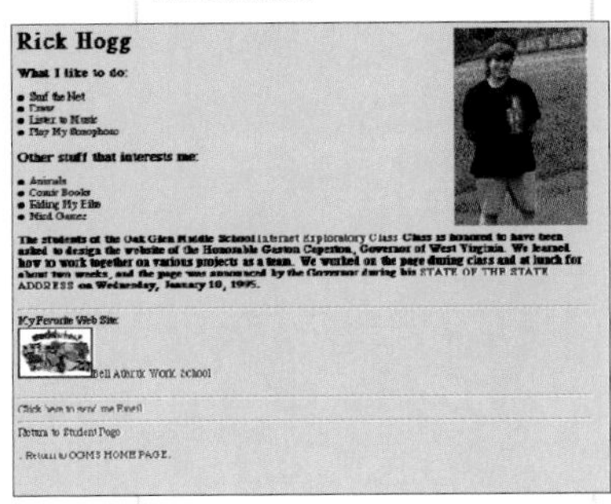

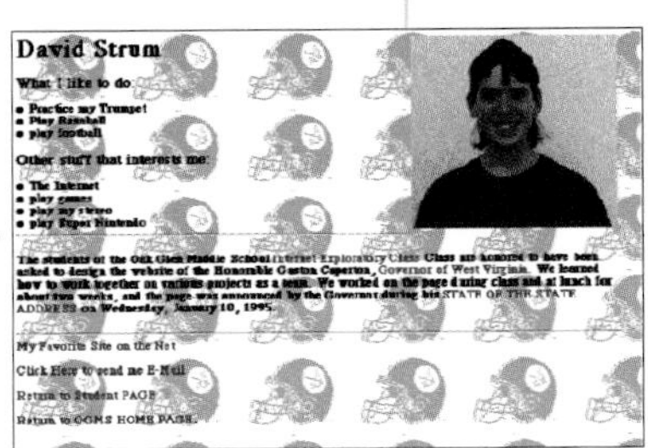

Oak Glen Middle School Site Map

Custom backgrounds can be created with one small GIF file. PageMill automatically repeats the image to create one big background that loads fast and looks great.

Special Features

Page 1

The feather in the cap of the OGMS Internet Exploratory Class is the home page designed by the kids for West Virginia Governor Gaston Caperton. During a campaign to get all the state's schools equipped with computers, the governor spotted the OGMS Web site. Lou Casini says, "Based on what he saw, he asked for a small group of students from OGMS to design a governor's home page." The eight kids in Casini's class designed the page, using custom backgrounds, lots of hot links, and tables.

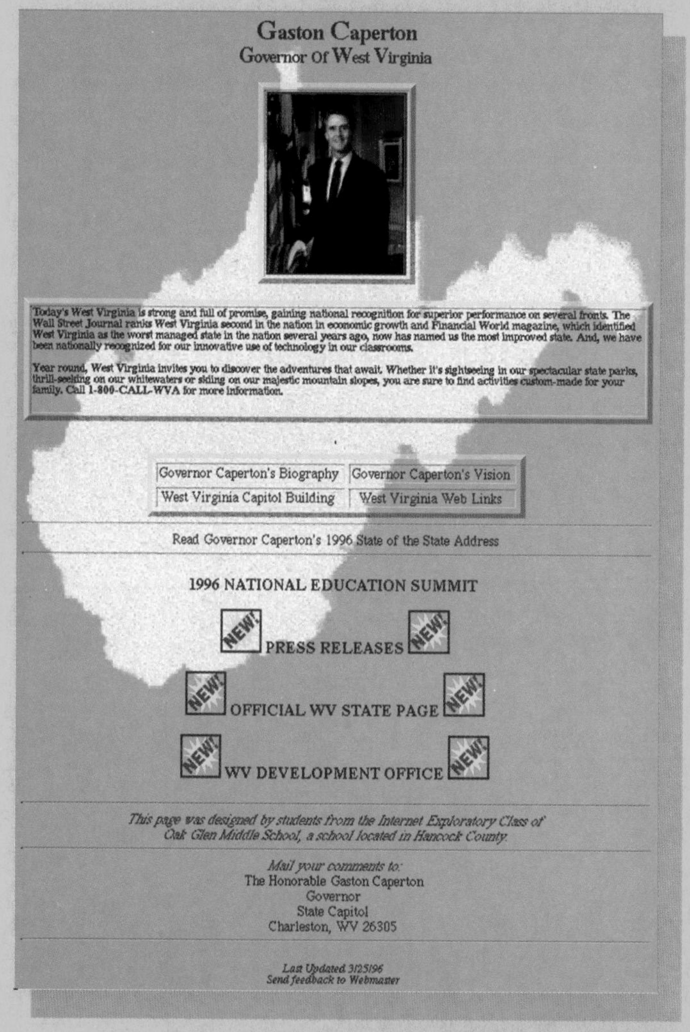

Gaston Caperton
Governor Of West Virginia

Today's West Virginia is strong and full of promise, gaining national recognition for superior performance on several fronts. The Wall Street Journal ranks West Virginia second in the nation in economic growth and Financial World magazine, which identified West Virginia as the worst managed state in the nation several years ago, now has named us the most improved state. And, we have been nationally recognized for our innovative use of technology in our classrooms.

Year round, West Virginia invites you to discover the adventures that await. Whether it's sightseeing in our spectacular state parks, thrill-seeking on our whitewaters or skiing on our majestic mountain slopes, you are sure to find activities custom-made for your family. Call **1-800-CALL-WVA** for more information.

Governor Caperton's Biography	Governor Caperton's Vision
West Virginia Capitol Building	West Virginia Web Links

Read Governor Caperton's 1996 State of the State Address

1996 NATIONAL EDUCATION SUMMIT

NEW! PRESS RELEASES NEW!

NEW! OFFICIAL WV STATE PAGE NEW!

NEW! WV DEVELOPMENT OFFICE NEW!

This page was designed by students from the Internet Exploratory Class of Oak Glen Middle School, a school located in Hancock County.

Mail your comments to:
The Honorable Gaston Caperton
Governor
State Capitol
Charleston, WV 26305

Last Updated 3/25/96
Send feedback to Webmaster

"This is a lot more fun than just sitting at a desk, looking at a book." — **DAVE, 8TH GRADE**

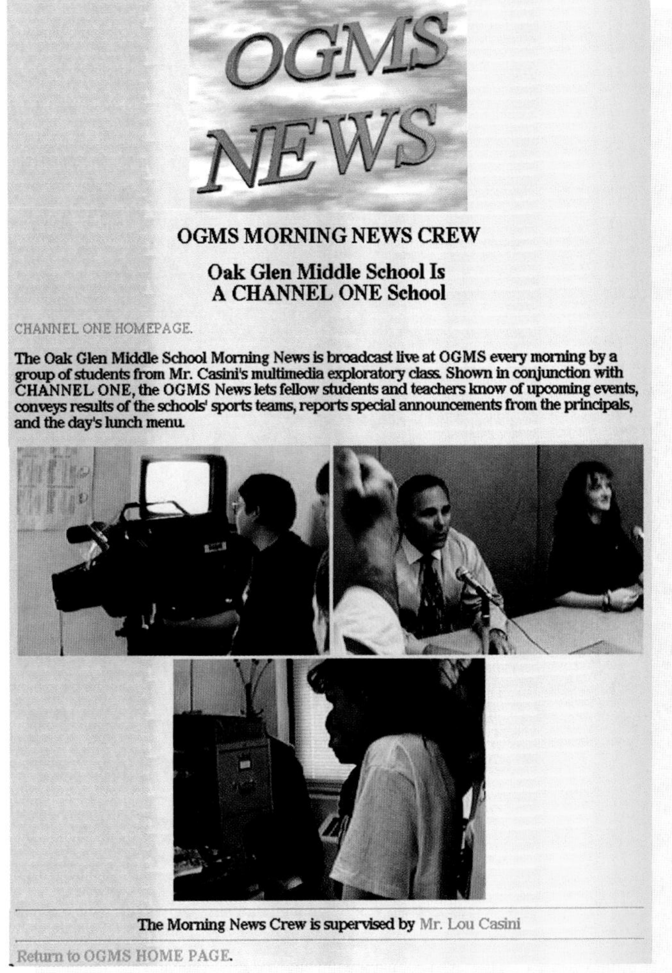

OGMS NEWS

OGMS MORNING NEWS CREW

Oak Glen Middle School Is A CHANNEL ONE School

CHANNEL ONE HOMEPAGE.

The Oak Glen Middle School Morning News is broadcast live at OGMS every morning by a group of students from Mr. Casini's multimedia exploratory class. Shown in conjunction with CHANNEL ONE, the OGMS News lets fellow students and teachers know of upcoming events, conveys results of the schools' sports teams, reports special announcements from the principals, and the day's lunch menu.

The Morning News Crew is supervised by Mr. Lou Casini

Return to OGMS HOME PAGE.

Page 2

Casini and the kids at OGMS have new pages in the works for next year. The OGMS Morning News Crew page gives an interesting hint of things to come. Students broadcast their own daily newscast over Channel 1, which is installed in their classroom. Updates of the broadcasts will appear regularly on this page.

The students would like to see daily updating of pages and even more links. To manage all of this, they'll be setting everything up in Adobe SiteMill, which manages the pages automatically. As Casini says, "I think the students will be able to be more creative when they can let the software do more of the work."

Adobe PageMill Page Layout

Before designing your Web pages, you should have a basic idea of how you want them to look and how they will link together. Remember that the actual appearance of your page depends on the browser used to view it, but you can control the location of elements and some type styles. You'll soon learn how to work with the natural limits of HTML to make pages that will get across what you want to show. To begin, draw a rough sketch of each page, blocking out general areas for text and images. Decide where you'll place your links, and what tools you'll provide for navigating among the pages. Be sure to save your work often as you go.

1 **Open a new page by choosing the Open command.** Make sure you are in the Edit mode (the pen and paper icon should be displayed at the upper right corner of the window).

2 **Select the text you have created** from the Pasteboard and drag it onto the new page. (Remember that using text styles like bold or italic, especially for headings, adds interest to your page and helps readers to find their way around it more easily.) Try to use horizontal rules as dividers so the page doesn't look too dense. Keep the page simple—if there's too much text, divide the topics into separate pages and link them.

3 **Select the images you want to use** and place them on the page. Remember that in addition to using images as static pictures to enhance your pages, you can use them as links or as buttons on forms. To work with an image, click on it and drag it to the location you want. You can resize it by dragging the selection handles or proportionally scale it by holding down the Shift key while you resize.

4 **Create links** to other pages in your site, to various parts of the same page, or to sites somewhere else on the Web. Select the text or image you want use as the source of the link and link it to the destination where you want it to lead.

5 **Finally, give your page extra** "pizzazz" by changing the text color and adding an interesting page background. Use the Attributes Inspector to select colors and make backgrounds that feature images of your choice.

6 **To get an idea of how your page** will look and behave when viewed in a Web browser, click on Preview mode (the globe at the upper right corner of the window).

http:chico.rice.edu/armadillo/Rice/Rice_home.html

Rice School (La Escuela Rice)

Houston Independent School District
Houston, Texas

"We said, let's put up stuff that's pertinent world-wide but that is anchored in our own backyard. You have to use your local history and culture as much as possible."

—Donald Perkins, Internet Services and Resources

Rice School is a computer lover's dream. The school, which serves students kindergarden through 8th grade, was developed as a collaboration between Rice University and the Houston School District. Donald Perkins, one of the site's creators, says, "Our idea is that the school is fueled by technology. The Rice University Center for Technology was instrumental from the start."

GIF cartoons advertise the school's new Internet survival class, starting this fall.

Rice School/La Escuela Rice is in Houston, Texas. The student body is made up of all income levels from diverse school neighborhoods around the city.

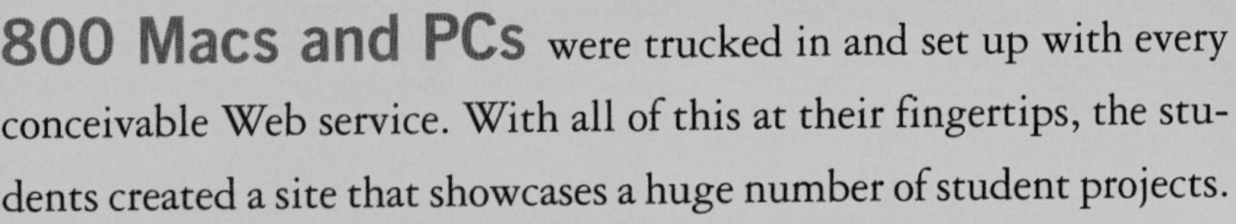

800 Macs and PCs were trucked in and set up with every conceivable Web service. With all of this at their fingertips, the students created a site that showcases a huge number of student projects. Both platforms (Mac and PC) were used for creation and reviewing pages once they were posted.

But a visitor to the site doesn't feel overwhelmed. The projects are categorized by year and topic, and the site's design is simple — everything is easily accessed.

Taft Architects created this floor plan, which was scanned into Adobe Photoshop and saved as a 21k GIF file.

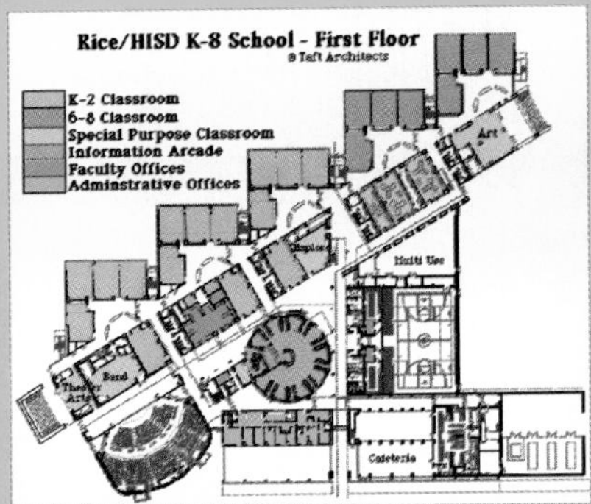

1 2 3 4

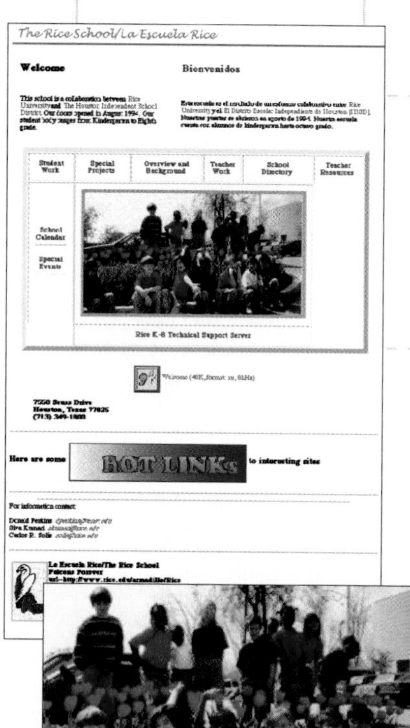

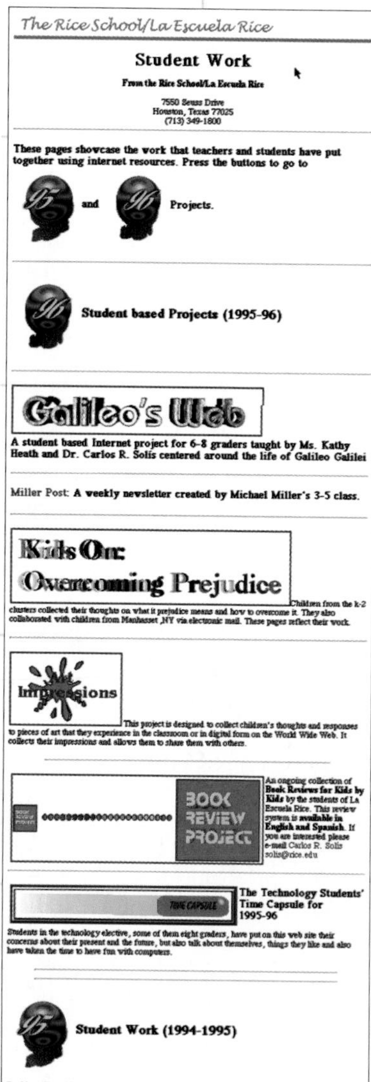

(1a) Starting from the home page, Rice School's site features an amazing array of choices. A clean grid design allows the viewer to not be confused by all of the hot links. English and Spanish are side by side. (1a) Click the home page link to go to Student Work, then to (2b) buttons for student projects from 1995 and 1996. There's also a bright, graphical listing of special projects, such as Galileo's Web (2c) and (2d) Impressions.

(2c) *One link leads to Galileo's Web, an* (8a) *ambitious ongoing project by the 6th, 7th, and 8th grade students. Using Rice's History of Science course pages as a jumping-off point, the kids tackled projects like The Villa Project,* (6b) *where they created blueprints of a new home for Galileo.*

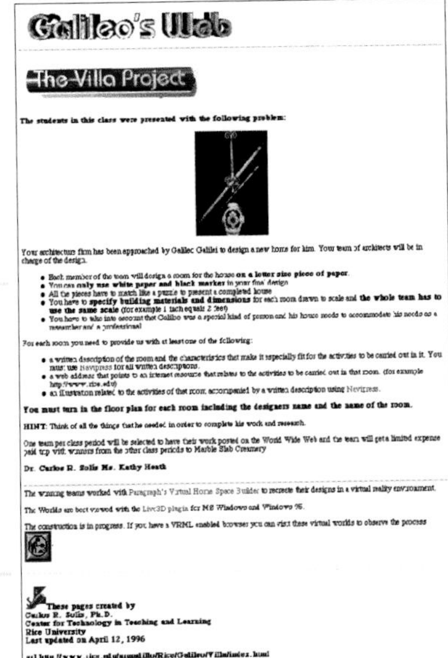
Galileo's Web

The Villa Project

The students in this class were presented with the following problem:

Welcome to the WebNaissance

Objectives

Activities in the WebNaissance

Visitors

Life Line

Experiments

Lesson Plans

WWW Resources

Sample Work

The Villa Project

Forms and questionnaires get viewers involved in your site. They're simple to add in PageMill or in Adobe Acrobat 3.0.

Special Features

Page 1

One of the most popular student projects is Book Reviews for Kids by Kids. This project collects students' comments and opinions on books they read for class or fun, then lists them in a simple, well-organized page.

At the Starting Point, a user presses the appropriate Review Form for the grade level (K–2, 3–5, or 6–8). Up comes the correct form, in English or Spanish. Students enter basic book information and their review; then press an icon to give the book a rating, and then send it off for others to consider.

The Rice School/La Escuela Rice

Book Reviews for Kids by Kids

This is the K-2 Section

Please enter the following information:

- Your Name:
- Your Teachers Name
- Your cluster ○ B ○ C ○ D

Your grade ○ K ○ 1 ○ 2

Your age

- Todays date: Day Month Year
- Book Title
- Author
- Illustrated by

Who is(are) the main character(s)?

What is the setting of this story?

This story is ○ Fiction or ○ Non-Fiction

The Genre is

○ Adventure ○ Biography ○ Fairy Tale ○ Folk tale/Legend ○ Horror ○ Humor/Jokes ○ Information ○ Mystery ○ Poetry ○ Romance ○ Science Fiction

Your Book Review goes here.

Please give the book a final rating

Send Review to my Teacher | Clear Form

These forms created and maintained by Carlos R. Solis solis@rice.edu

url http www rice edu/armadillo/Rice

"The most rewarding thing about working with VRML was to see how fast the students got into it; how quickly they understood it."—**CARLOS R. SOLIS**

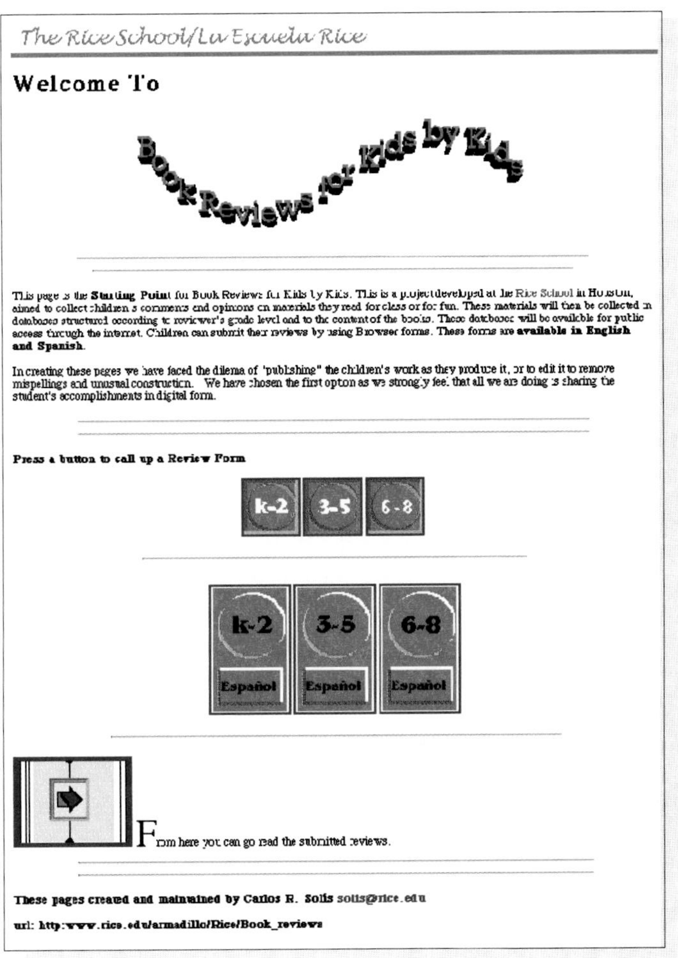

Reviews are categorized by book content as well as by grade level. Here's one in the K–2 Adventure category. Notice that consistent graphics in each section help viewers know where they are.

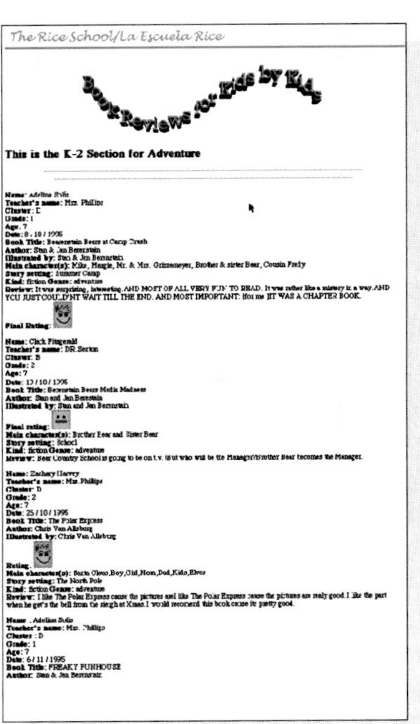

Special Features

Page 2

Rice School is unique in that it was created especially with the use of technology in mind. The building itself was built to encourage learning in small clusters. Its center core is the library, which is fully equipped with video disks, CD-ROM, and the latest in computerized on-line access to external databases and other resources.

The Rice School/La Escuela Rice: A New Way of Learning in HISD

In August 1994, the Houston Independent School District (HISD) opened the doors to a newly designed school that will offer students unique and challenging learning experiences, focusing on an integrated approach to curriculum. The Rice School/La Escuela Rice, the product of a collaboration with Rice University, will serve youngsters in kindergarten through eighth grade in an environment that will nurture lifelong learning, critical thinking, and responsible citizenship. (See the **philosophical vision** of the Rice School for the guiding principles of this collaboration.)

The photo above shows the classroom side of The Rice School/La Escuela Rice during construction - March 2, 1994.

Planning and Design

In designing The Rice School/La Escuela Rice, a planning committee of school and community representatives decided how best to create a school that would serve as a model for innovative, effective instruction and professional development for teachers throughout the area. After three years of careful planning, the result is an exciting new program that makes full use of available resources and challenges both students and teachers to reach their full academic potential.

The building itself is a model of architectural excellence, from its uniquely crafted structure to its highly functional interior. The two-story, 167,000-square-foot facility was custom-built with the school's mission in mind--to encourage learning in small clusters. The center core of the facility is the library, which will be fully equipped with video discs, CD-ROM, and the latest in computerized, on-line access to external **data bases** and other resources that stimulate research and problem-solving. The building also features project rooms and laboratories designed to engage students in science, art, computer-assisted learning, and music.

A Tour of The Rice School/La Escuela Rice:

- **Floor Plans and Photographs.**
- **Fiber Optic Cables for Computer Infrastructure.**

Program

The Rice School/La Escuela Rice offers students a unique educational program that fosters innovation and creativity. The school will feature:

- a challenging academic program that integrates the study of mathematics, science, social studies, language, the arts, technology, and physical development
- active learning projects and "mini courses" conducted by members of the Rice University faculty
- an opportunity for students in grades K-2 to develop skills in English and Spanish by participating in a dual-language program that will continue as they advance to each grade level
- a multi-age primary cluster program for grades K-2 that groups students by the interests and levels of development, rather than by age
- grade-specific and cross-age group settings for students in grades 3- 5
- independent house groupings, each representing K-2, 3-5, and 6-8 clusters, that allow students to learn from one another while developing a sense of community
- a community-developed honor code similar to that used by Rice University (see **Rice Honor Code**)
- a professional development center staffed by both HISD specialists and Rice University faculty members, focusing on innovative instructional practices for urban students

Web Filters for Illustrator and Photoshop

Adobe's GIF89a Export filter is fast and easy, and it's free to download on Adobe's Web site (www.adobe.com.). Here's how it works:

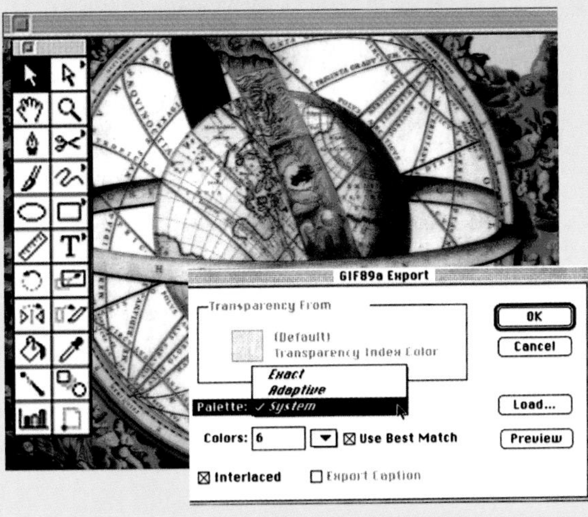

1 **Put the GIF89a Export filter** in either the Photoshop Plug-ins folder or the Illustrator 6 File format Plug-ins folder. Open the image in Illustrator or Photoshop. Make sure that it's in RGB mode and is 72 ppi.

2 **Choose File>Export>GIF89a Export.** For this anti-aliased, black-and-white image, six colors and an Adaptive palette or System palette and Use Best Match will give good results. (An Adaptive palette with as few colors as possible is usually the best choice for many images.)

3 **Click Preview** to see what your image will look like with the palette you choose. Try different numbers of colors and palettes to find the best results for your image.

http://199.117.83.90/

Wilma M. Scott Elementary

Weld County District 6
Greeley, Colorado

This site uses sophisticated techniques—interlaced images, tables, animated GIFs—but keeps its kid-friendly flavor by featuring the students and teachers all through its pages. Ripley Casdorph, 2nd/3rd grade teacher and creator of the site, says he didn't want just another high-tech site. He wanted a friendly place kids "could go" on the Internet.

"Our site has really taught students about the Internet, and given them a place to view their own pages. Now the teachers have to keep up!"

—Ripley Casdorph, 2nd/3rd grade teacher and computer teacher

To see an image right away, save GIFs as "interlaced" in Adobe Photoshop.

Scott School is in the small town of Greeley, on the Colorado plains. The Rocky Mountains rise into the sky nearby, just 25 minutes to the West.

Mr. Casdorph's class helps keeps the site going. His kids' pictures are set up as an animated GIF, and they rotate on the page.

Pictures from the trip to the Boulder Planetarium were scanned in as JPEG files and posted on the site.

Showcasing students' activities gets top priority here. Every class, K through 5th grade, has its own page. When work is posted, everybody gets excited. Classes are always trying to improve their pages. But the e-mail capability has been the most popular part of the site. Through the Web, Scott School has had contact with people from all over the world, with especially enthusiastic responses in the Guest Book from alumni who went to the school back in the 1970s!

1 2 3 4

Last Updated:Fri Jun 21 04:57:24 1996

Staff & Classroom Pages | Monthly Survey | Sign Guest Book
Software & the Web | Information

New! Do A Yahoo Search From Our Page!

Search

|Hotspot || Museums & Exhibits || |Search & Info Sites |Teacher Sites |Space Shots |
Schools & Districts || |Language Sites || Our Whole List
Our Learner Centered Page

This is the number of people that have visited our page as of Sept 1, 1995 when our counter was reset!

14208

For questions regarding this site e-mail:

ripleyc@www.scott.w6.k12.co.us

Text, layout, and Original graphics Copyright
Ripley Casdorph & Scott School 1996 ©

2b Tables organize the home page links. Open the "notebook" of staff and student pages to any one of the framed groups of classes to find out more about a teacher or class project. 1b

Scott School Staff & Classroom Pages

This page and the pages that follow will be under constuction during the remainder of the '95-'96 school year. It is our hope that every staff member we will have a page and will begin to include student work and information about activities taking place in classrooms.

Latitudes With Attitudes		
Mr. Bator's Class	Mr. Casdorph's Class	Mrs. Cummings' Class
Mrs. Thomas' Class	Mrs. Endres' Class	Mrs. Schauermann's Class
	Mr. Wass' Special Education Page	

Olympians		
Mrs. Bomgardner's Class	Mrs. Griffith's Class	Mrs. Life's Class
Mrs. Manuello's Class	Ms. Sanchez Class	Mrs. Strohauer's Class
Mrs. Roberts' Page	Mr. McClure's Page	

Penguins		
Mrs. Discoe	Mrs. Gorze's Class	Mrs. Houtchens' Class
Ms. Nadas' Class	Mrs. Nickell's Library	Ms. Streitz Class
Mrs. Wagner Class	Mrs. Smith's Page	

Soaring Eagles		
Mrs. Fern's Class	Mrs. Johnson's Class	Mrs. Haefeli's Class
Mrs. Harr & Mrs. Trautner's Class	Mrs. Messinger's Class	Mr. Osentoski's P.E. Class
	Mrs. Shaw's Class	

Administration	
Mr. Voelz	Mrs. Ramey
Scott TA page	Office Staff

Back to the Home Page!!

Text, layout, and Original graphics Copyright
Ripley Casdorph & Scott School 1996 ©
Last update 3/20/96

3c One link leads to teacher Mr. McClure and his portrait, done by the 4e students. Each staff member has a brief biography and linked e-mail address.

Meet Mr. McClure

Mr. McClure has been at Scott School for six years. He is our outstanding school community facilitator. This is his second year in the "Olympian Family." As a school Psychologist, he is a member of A.P.A., N.A.S.P., and P.D.K.

You can e-mail him at jeffmc@alpha.psd.k12.co.us

See more classroom pages.

Text, layout, and Original graphics Copyright
Ripley Casdorph & Scott School 1995 ©
Last update 3/9/96

Animated GIFs 1b highlight various links; Staff & Classroom Pages brings visitors to the kids pages. Small images (20k) keep the site moving.

(2b) *Clicking on Mr. Casdorph's class brings up combined pages from this year's 2nd grade and* (6b) *last year's 3rd grade. The pages about wind* (8a) *were created by last year's class. A digital camera recorded the class's windmill-building project; the kids wrote photo captions and poems.*

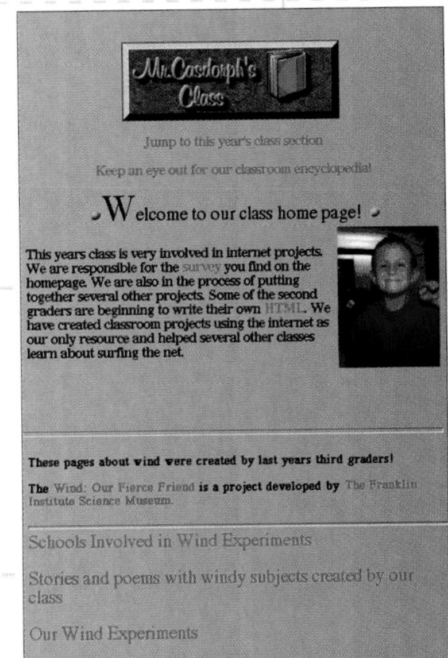
Mr.Casdorph's Class

Jump to this year's class section

Keep an eye out for our classroom encyclopedia!

Welcome to our class home page!

This years class is very involved in internet projects. We are responsible for the survey you find on the homepage. We are also in the process of putting together several other projects. Some of the second graders are beginning to write their own HTML. We have created classroom projects using the internet as our only resource and helped several other classes learn about surfing the net.

These pages about wind were created by last years third graders!

The Wind: Our Fierce Friend **is a project developed by** The Franklin Institute Science Museum.

Schools Involved in Wind Experiments

Stories and poems with windy subjects created by our class

Our Wind Experiments

Our First Experiments

We started our experiments by observing the wind and writing about what we saw and felt. Those writings can be found in the other wind file. After doing some research, we started working with the K-Nex and this proved to be very time consuming and challenging for both teacher and students.

The students first tried to construct blades out of the K-Nex and make a tower with only the original set of materials.

Then they made several attempts to make "good" towers.

After a couple of tries they even had a working windmill!

One group started trying new materials to see what would work and how the blade should be shaped.

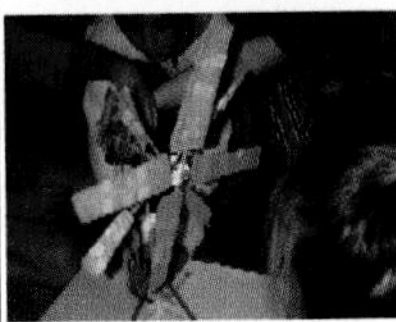

Another group brought in a broken light panel from home and cut it into the shapes that they wanted. This double blade setup proved to work well.

Special Features

Page 1

The Scott School site reaches out into the community and the world. The 2nd graders created the Scott School Survey. They developed seven surveys over the past year, asking questions like "What school do you attend?" and "Do you know how to swim?" Results from these surveys are always online. The survey builds very quickly and is simple to add in Adobe PageMill.

Scott School SummerSurvey

Please fill out our Summer survey. This will be our last survey of this school year. We are planning on compiling the data to share with those who take the survey. Next fall look for a new survey! If you have suggestions for a new survey e-mail us with the information.

- What school do you attend?
  1. ◉ Scott School
  2. ○ Another District 6 School
  3. ○ A different Colorado School
  4. ○ A School in the U.S.
  5. ○ A School Outside U.S.
  6. ○ I don't attend a school at all!
- If you attend school what grade level are you in?

  Not in School
- Do you know how to swim?
  1. ○ Yes, very well!
  2. ○ Sort of.
  3. ○ No!

  1. What do you like to do in the summer?
     - ☐ Sleep
     - ☐ Read
     - ☐ Go swimming
     - ☐ Get a Tan
     - ☐ Gardening
     - ☐ Cut the grass
- What kinds of summer sports do you like?
  1. ○ Soccer
  2. ○ Softball
  3. ○ Tennis
  4. ○ Volleyball
  5. ○ Golf
- What season do you like best?
  1. ○ Spring
  2. ○ Summer
  3. ○ Winter
  4. ○ Fall
- Would you rather wear sun screen or get a sun burn?
  1. ○ Wear sun screen!
  2. ○ Get a sun burn!

To send in your completed form :

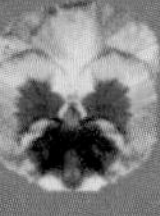

Send In My Summer Survey

Erase my information

It does take a few minutes to send in the information Please be patient!

Thank you for your time!

"The 4th graders were running their own site—two or three kids did all the layouts and backgrounds. They'd see something they liked that I had done on the school pages and they'd say, 'How did you do that? Show us how!' And they'd come in and we'd add to their pages." —**RIPLEY CASDORPH**

Welcome to the Scott School Guest Book

Please sign the guest book and leave a short note to our staff.

Your Name
Your Name

Your Email Address
Your E-mail

Your School Name
School Address

What were your favorite items from our home page?
Graphics

Where did you learn about Scott School's Page? (Check all that apply.)
☒ Web Search
☐ Web 66
☐ You knew of our school.
☐ Other

Feel Free to Leave Our Staff a Message!

Send Your Info to Scott School | Reset Defaults

See who has signed the guest book.

This will take you back to the home page!

Page 2

Ripley Casdorph reports that the Guest Book is a favorite page; alumni, as well as other people from far-flung places, log into the site here.

He's always looking for new ways to enhance the site. Next year, he wants to index all of the Web site to make it more reachable. Experimenting with setting up an Internet chat program on the site is also in the works.

GIF or JPEG?

An image file for the Web can be saved as GIF or JPEG. Which should you use? It really depends on your art.

1 Continuous-tone or full-color images look best saved as JPEG (medium or low is all you need) and also give you the smallest file size. If transparency is needed, save as GIF, using an Adaptive palette with the least number of colors.

2 Flat-color images (anti-aliased) do well without any dithering, so using Photoshop's Indexed Color mode (with an Adaptive palette and a Dither of None) and then saving as GIF will give you the best results with the smallest file size. The number

of colors you need will depend on the image —try using the least number possible to get the smallest file.

3 **Black-and-white images** need very few colors, so saving them as GIF with Photoshop's GIF89a Export filter lets you select a low number of colors (six colors works well on an anti-aliased image) and preview the image to quickly see how it will look.

4 **Gradations look best with** as many colors as possible, so JPEG Medium is the best option for gradations. (JPEG gives a much smaller file size than GIF with an Adaptive palette.)

http://www.asd.k12.ak.us/SchoolPages/West/West.html

"So much of education is doing the same old stuff year after year. The Internet and the ability to create Web pages is a totally new concept; it's fun to make that happen."

—Carol Goltz

West Anchorage High School

Anchorage School District
Anchorage, Alaska

The WAHS Web site began as a whim. A casual suggestion to Carol Goltz to start a site got her going, and in a short time it grew into a "full-service bank of ideas and images." Now the site showcases students' home pages and special projects, as well as a great list of links, including an interactive map of the school and a Korean version of the home page. There's even a section on creating Web pages!

Owen, Alison, and Rupa in the West Anchorage computer lab.

Located near downtown Anchorage, Alaska, WAHS is full of diverse students: 37 different languages are spoken at this school!

A dynamic mix of spirited students, dedicated staff, and highly involved parents contributes to the site. The site has a search engine attached to it, as well as parent networking pages, and links to numerous sites, including some well-designed school sites.

Peter creating links to new pages on the site.

(1a) *The home page is chock-full of links to the community and to Web resources. Education is our Business* (1c) *links to sites related to language arts, science, math, and others. Current school news appears under Timely Topics.* (1b)

Even alumni have come back to get involved. The Eagles' (1e) *Greatest Sites concept was created by alumnus Mike Groeneveld.*

(1c) *Clicking on the map takes you to Swedish exchange student Peter Henebeck's* (4d) *interactive plan of the school. Clicking on any yellow area takes you to a page with a photo and a brief description of that part of the school.*

Welcome to the Home of the Eagles.

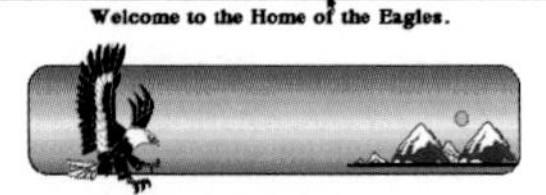

West Anchorage High School

West High School
1700 Hillcrest Drive
Anchorage, Alaska 99517
Principal: Dr. Laura Bowie (Bowie_Laura@msmail.asd.k12.ak.us)
Phone: (907)274-2502 Fax: (907)272-6176

West High is the oldest high school in the Anchorage School District. It has approximately 1500 students and is enriched by a very diverse cultural ethnicity in the student body. Located near downtown Anchorage, West enjoys the natural beauty of Westchester Lagoon and a panoramic view of the Alaska Mountain Range.

A spirited student body, dedicated staff, involved parent group and supportive community work together to provide a healthy learning environment where academic excellence and social well-being are highly valued. The West High Eagles -- past, present and future --are proud of our rich heritage and tradition, as well as of our current students, whose home pages we invite you to visit!

You may view the above text in Korean. And, you may now visit our school via an interactive map of West High.

Welcome to West Anchorage High School:

A Blue Ribbon School of Excellence!

Timely Topics **News about West, ASD, and a featured site**	Education is our Business **A collection of sites focusing on education and curriculum**	Research **Getting started with researching a topic of your choice**
The Internet **E-mail, Internet training, and creating Web pages**	Eagles' Greatest Sites **Personal home pages and popular subjects to explore**	Community and Partnerships **West's interactions with others in Anchorage and beyond**

Timely Topics

- Farewell and Enjoy Your Summer
- Anchored in Reading....Our New Grant!
- Important Information from the West Administration
- PTSA Information **Our Parent,Teacher, Student Association**
- Parent Network **Parents Networking to Help Students**
- West High Alumni Association **Send your Name, Graduating Year, and E-Mail Address**
- Recent Student Achievements **Congratulations!**
- ASD Special Dates '95-96 **Important Dates for This Year**
- ASD Calendar 96-97 **Important dates for Next Year**
- Owen Afrieth **and** Anne Kelly **Students Protesting Peacefully**
- The Eagles' Cache **Soon You Can E-Mail Order from our School Store!**
- Anchorage: My Kind of Town **A Project by Mrs. Frank's Period 2 Class** New!
- Featured Site of the Week: The Internet Tourbus

Education is our Business!

Alta Vista.....Excite.....InfoSeek Guide.....Lycos.....Open Text

Each search engine works differently. Read the search screen and be prepared to enter "key words" to help locate specific information. For a quick start, type your keyword(s) in the form below and hit the return key.

Enter search keyword(s):

Starting Point - MetaSearch

You may want searching tips for our school library. And, since you are doing electronic research, an MLA-style guide for citations of electronic sources may be helpful.

The Internet

- Staff E-Mail Addresses
- West Authorized Student User List and Student E-Mail Addresses, **and** Internet Application
- West High E-Mail and Internet Inservice
- West High Internet Class
- West High Home Page Class
- West High Internet Workshop
- Municipality of Anchorage Workshop

- HTML Quick Reference, The Basics to Writing HTML, A Beginner's Guide to HTML, HTML Tutorial, The Table Sampler, More Help With Tables, TableMaker, HTML Tables Tutorial, Help with Forms, The Transparent/Interlaced GIF Resource Page, Access to Images, Building Blocks, Source Art and Icons, Colored Text Help, Color Chart, ColorMaker
- The HTML Writers Guild Website
- The WebStar's Dictionary, Weblint

- Internet Resources on the Web New!
- Global Village's Internet Tour
- The Internet TourBus!
- Everything You Need to Surf the Net
- Patrick Crispen's Internet Roadmap
- Child Safety on the Information Highway

Eagles' Greatest Sites

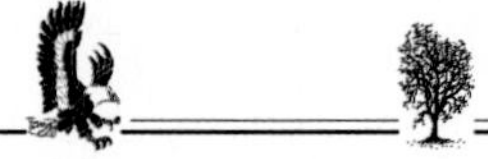

- New Kid In Town - **Personal Home Pages**
- Take It To The Limit - **Sports and Fitness**
- On The Border - **National and International News**
- Life In The Fast Lane - **Health and Social Issues**
- Peaceful Easy Feeling - **Mind, Body, and Soul**
- I Can't Tell You Why - **Reference Shelf**
- In The Long Run - **Careers and Higher Education**
- Wasted Time - **Exploration and Recreation**
- Sad Cafe - **Inquiry and Discussion**

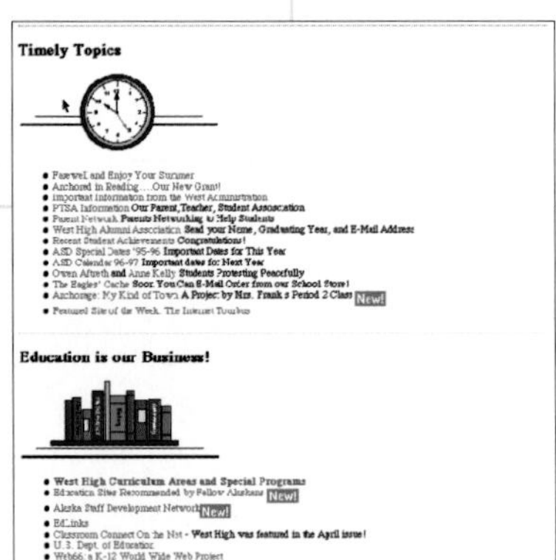

Timely Topics

- Farewell and Enjoy Your Summer
- Anchored in Reading....Our New Grant!
- Important Information from the West Administration
- PTSA Information **Our Parent,Teacher, Student Association**
- Parent Network **Parents Networking to Help Students**
- West High Alumni Association **Send your Name, Graduating Year, and E-Mail Address**
- Recent Student Achievements **Congratulations!**
- ASD Special Dates '95-96 **Important Dates for This Year**
- ASD Calendar 96-97 **Important dates for Next Year**
- Owen Afrieth **and** Anne Kelly **Students Protesting Peacefully**
- The Eagles' Cache **Soon You Can E-Mail Order from our School Store!**
- Anchorage: My Kind of Town **A Project by Mrs. Frank's Period 2 Class** New!
- Featured Site of the Week: The Internet Tourbus

Education is our Business!

- **West High Curriculum Areas and Special Programs**
- Education Sites Recommended by Fellow Alaskans New!
- Alaska Staff Development Network New!
- EdLinks
- Classroom Connect On the Net - **West High was featured in the April issue!**
- U.S. Dept. of Education
- Web66: a K-12 World Wide Web Project
- Education on Yahoo

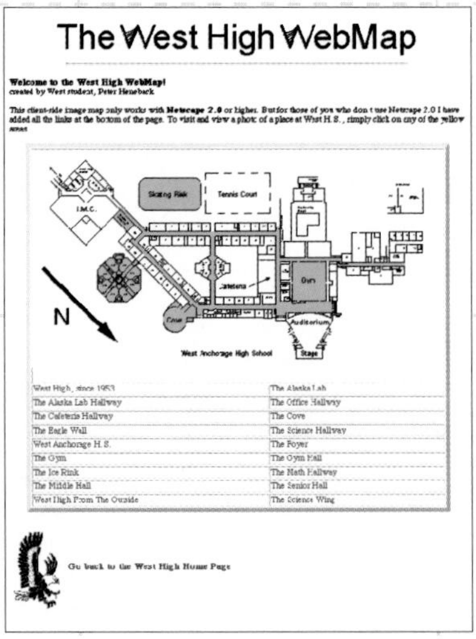

The West High WebMap

Welcome to the West High WebMap!
created by West student, Peter Heneback

This client-side image map only works with **Netscape 2.0** or higher. But for those of you who don't use Netscape 2.0 I have added all the links at the bottom of the page. To visit and view a photo of a place at West H.S., simply click on any of the yellow areas.

West High, since 1953	The Alaska Lab
The Alaska Lab Hallway	The Office Hallway
The Cafeteria Hallway	The Cove
The Eagle Wall	The Science Hallway
West Anchorage H.S.	The Foyer
The Gym	The Gym Hall
The Ice Rink	The Math Hallway
The Middle Hall	The Senior Hall
West High From The Outside	The Science Wing

Go back to the West High Home Page

(1d) *One link shows the kids' own home pages. Language Arts Teacher Diane Frank says they really understood how great the Web was when they* (5d) *created their own pages. She says, "They learned* (6b) (8a) *incredibly quickly!"*

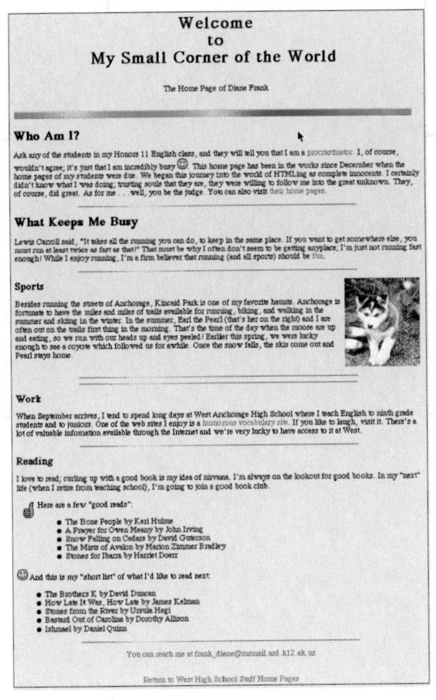

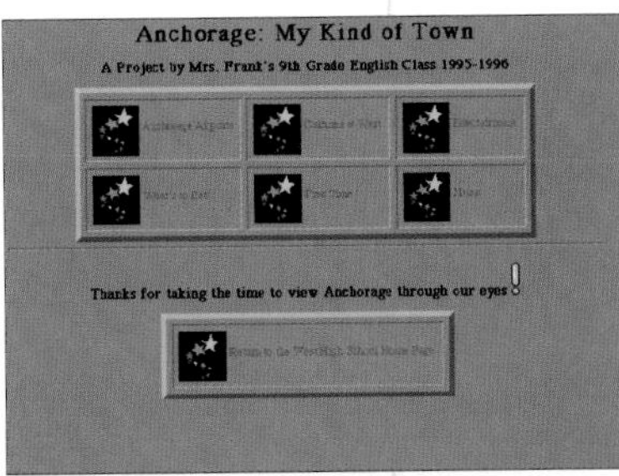

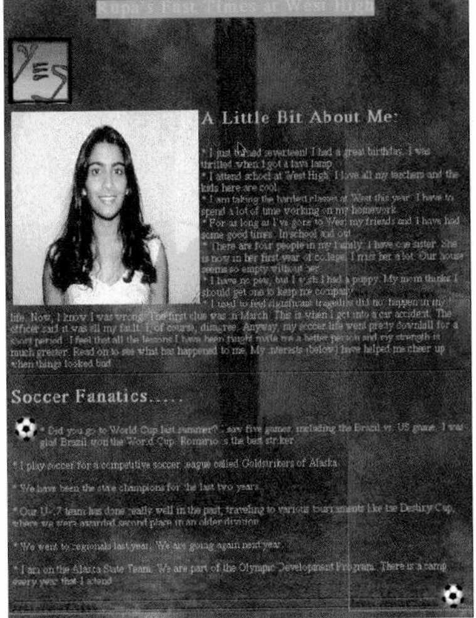

(1d) *The kids' link also leads to Owen's page, where he experimented with* (8d) *textured GIF backgrounds from Web archives. Rupa's used Claude Monet paintings to create* (6d) *backgrounds throughout her site.*

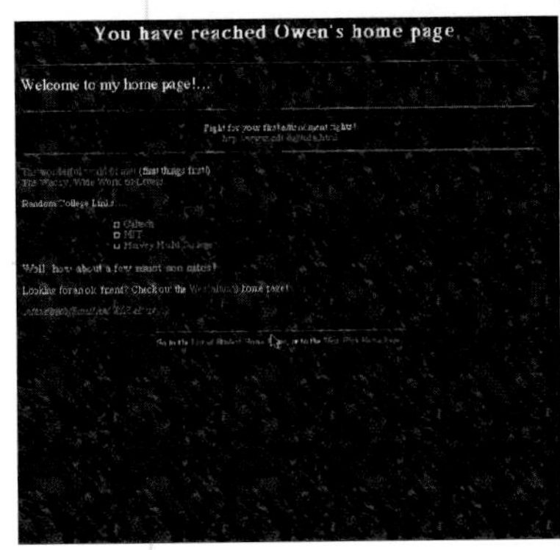

West Anchorage High School Site Map

Give your parents their own little area — and teach them how to use it.

Special Features

Page 1

Parents are especially involved in the Web site at WAHS. Malcolm Roberts, a WAHS parent who works in the mayor's office, has written this practical Parent Network page. This concept, originated by Mayor Rick Mystrom and his Crime Task Force, helps parents learn what they can do to keep their kids safe. It's based on communication among parents—through the Web and traditional avenues. Check it out!

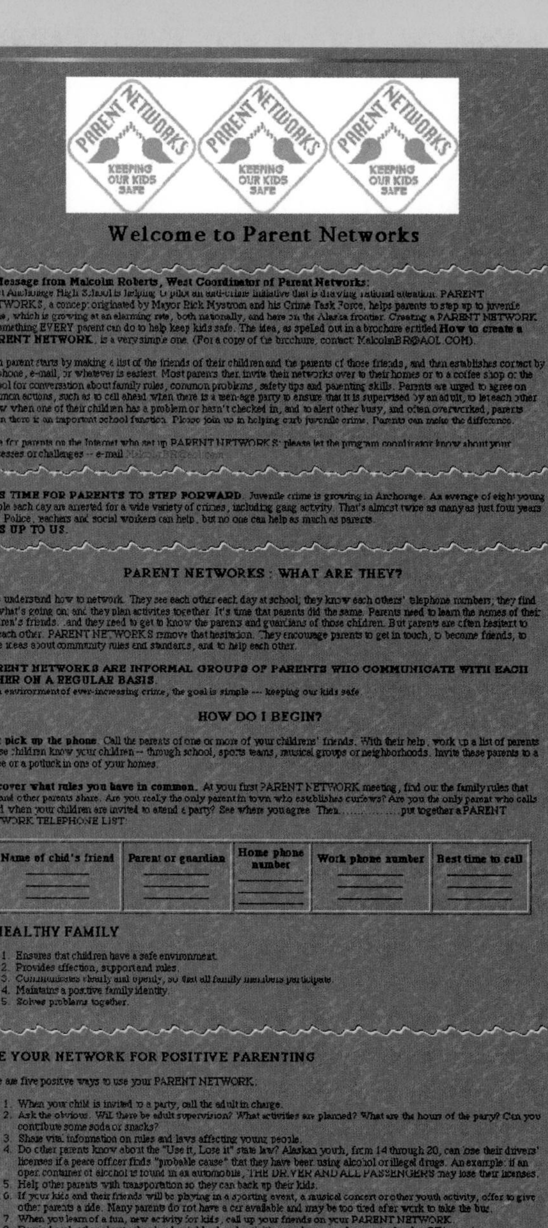

Welcome to Parent Networks

A Message from Malcolm Roberts, West Coordinator of Parent Networks:
West Anchorage High School is helping to pilot an anti-crime initiative that is drawing national attention. PARENT NETWORKS, a concept originated by Mayor Rick Mystrom and his Crime Task Force, helps parents to step up to juvenile crime, which is growing at an alarming rate, both nationally, and here on the Alaska frontier. Creating a PARENT NETWORK is something EVERY parent can do to help keep kids safe. The idea, as spelled out in a brochure entitled **How to create a PARENT NETWORK**, is a very simple one. (For a copy of the brochure, contact MalcolmBR@AOL.COM).

Each parent starts by making a list of the friends of their children and the parents of those friends, and then establishes contact by telephone, e-mail, or whatever is easiest. Most parents then invite their networks over to their homes or to a coffee shop or the school for conversation about family rules, common problems, safety tips and parenting skills. Parents are urged to agree on common actions, such as to call ahead when there is a teen-age party to ensure that it is supervised by an adult, to let each other know when one of their children has a problem or hasn't checked in, and to alert other busy, and often overworked, parents when there is an important school function. Please join us in helping curb juvenile crime. Parents can make the difference.

Note for parents on the Internet who set up PARENT NETWORKS: please let the program coordinator know about your successes or challenges -- e-mail MalcolmBR@aol.com

IT'S TIME FOR PARENTS TO STEP FORWARD. Juvenile crime is growing in Anchorage. An average of eight young people each day are arrested for a wide variety of crimes, including gang activity. That's almost twice as many as just four years ago. Police, teachers and social workers can help, but no one can help as much as parents.
IT'S UP TO US.

PARENT NETWORKS : WHAT ARE THEY?

Kids understand how to network. They see each other each day at school; they know each others' telephone numbers; they find out what's going on; and they plan activites together. It's time that parents did the same. Parents need to learn the names of their children's friends, and they need to get to know the parents and guardians of those children. But parents are often hesitant to call each other. PARENT NETWORKS remove that hesitation. They encourage parents to get in touch, to become friends, to share ideas about community rules and standards, and to help each other.

PARENT NETWORKS ARE INFORMAL GROUPS OF PARENTS WHO COMMUNICATE WITH EACH OTHER ON A REGULAR BASIS.
In an environment of ever-increasing crime, the goal is simple --- keeping our kids safe.

HOW DO I BEGIN?

Just pick up the phone. Call the parents of one or more of your childrens' friends. With their help, work up a list of parents whose children know your children -- through school, sports teams, musical groups or neighborhoods. Invite these parents to a coffee or a potluck in one of your homes.

Discover what rules you have in common. At your first PARENT NETWORK meeting, find out the family rules that you and other parents share. Are you really the only parent in town who establishes curfews? Are you the only parent who calls ahead when your children are invited to attend a party? See where you agree. Then................put together a PARENT NETWORK TELEPHONE LIST:

Name of chid's friend	Parent or guardian	Home phone number	Work phone number	Best time to call
________	________	________	________	________
________	________	________	________	________
________	________	________	________	________

A HEALTHY FAMILY

1. Ensures that children have a safe environment.
2. Provides affection, support and rules.
3. Communicates clearly and openly, so that all family members participate.
4. Maintains a positive family identity.
5. Solves problems together.

USE YOUR NETWORK FOR POSITIVE PARENTING

Here are five positive ways to use your PARENT NETWORK:

1. When your child is invited to a party, call the adult in charge.
2. Ask the obvious. Will there be adult supervision? What activities are planned? What are the hours of the party? Can you contribute some soda or snacks?
3. Share vital information on rules and laws affecting young people.
4. Do other parents know about the "Use it, Lose it" state law? Alaskan youth, from 14 through 20, can lose their drivers' licenses if a peace officer finds "probable cause" that they have been using alcohol or illegal drugs. An example: if an open container of alcohol is found in an automobile, THE DRIVER AND ALL PASSENGERS may lose their licenses.
5. Help other parents with transporation so they can back up their kids.
6. If your kids and their friends will be playing in a sporting event, a musical concert or other youth activity, offer to give other parents a ride. Many parents do not have a car available and may be too tired after work to take the bus.
7. When you learn of a fun, new activity for kids, call up your friends on your PARENT NETWORK.
8. Remind each other about school and neighborhood activities, such as open house at school, a PTA meeting, or parent conferences. Many kids forget or choose not to deliver notices that teachers send home.
9. If your children haven't checked in, get help locating them.

For their safety, you should know where your children are at all times. Have you visited the home where your child is spending a lot of time? You may make new friends, or you may find an unsafe environment. It's your job to check it out.

Note: If, at first, your kids don't like the idea of a Parent Network, don't worry about it. Their views will change once they discover that when parents lose some of their fears, they begin to trust their kids more.

SAFETY TIPS FOR KIDS IN A VIOLENT SOCIETY

"I enjoyed putting my Web page together! It was something new. I've been in school forever, and I haven't learned anything really different in a long time—and that's why this was so much fun for me!" — **ALISON, 11TH GRADE**

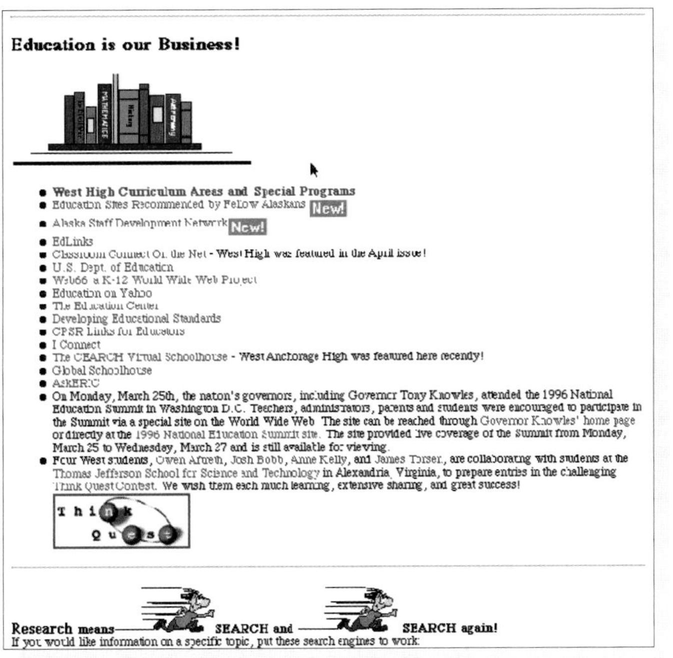

Page 2

The link between WAHS and the community is strong. Part of the mission of this site is to help educate the community about the Internet and the Web. Links on the home page lead to a short course in using search engines for finding information on the Web. A section on the Internet tells visitors everything they need to know, including how to make a home page.

http:/www.latin.pvt.k12.il.us

"In putting up the students' projects, we're trying to give back something to the Web. There's so much good will and so much great information out there that we want to be able to contribute in whatever way we can."

—Linda Gazzola, Computer Science Teacher

The Latin School of Chicago

Chicago, Illinois

The Latin School of Chicago first opened its doors almost a century ago—long before there was any such thing as a World Wide Web. Today, it's online with its own site. With academic standards that would surely make its founders proud, it now includes over 750 students from kindergarten to 12th grade.

Photoshop-tinted black-and-white images look great—and run fast!

The Latin School is set right in the middle of Chicago. It is a private school that draws a wide variety of students from all over the city.

Computer Science teacher Dennis Erickson in Latin's Internet Lab.

Academic excellence combined with imagination and creativity are the hallmarks of this site, which is being developed by Computer Science teachers Linda Gazzola, Kim Wendel, and Dennis Erickson. Although there are plans to develop the graphics side of the site and to add more "bells and whistles," the basic design is well executed with clean layout, clear links, and well-compressed, larger graphics.

The school's sports pages link to basketball, baseball, swimming, and tennis. Constant updating during the year has made these pages popular with students—and the community. Next year they hope to add photos to the latest scores.

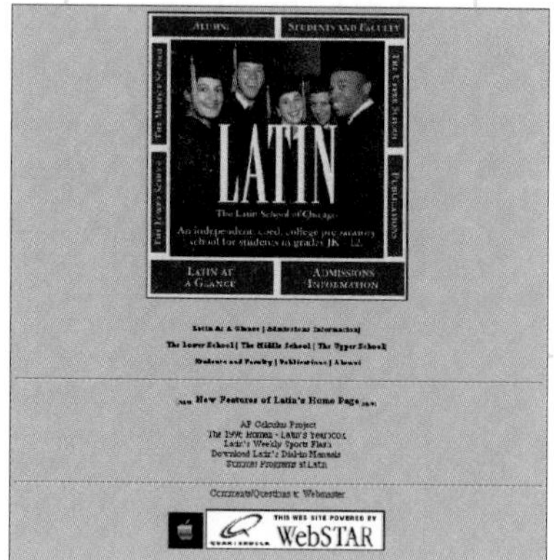

The home page (1a) is well designed and dominated by a large monochromatic graphic, compressed to load quickly (39k GIF). There are links to the pages for three divisions within the school—the Lower, Middle, and Upper Schools.

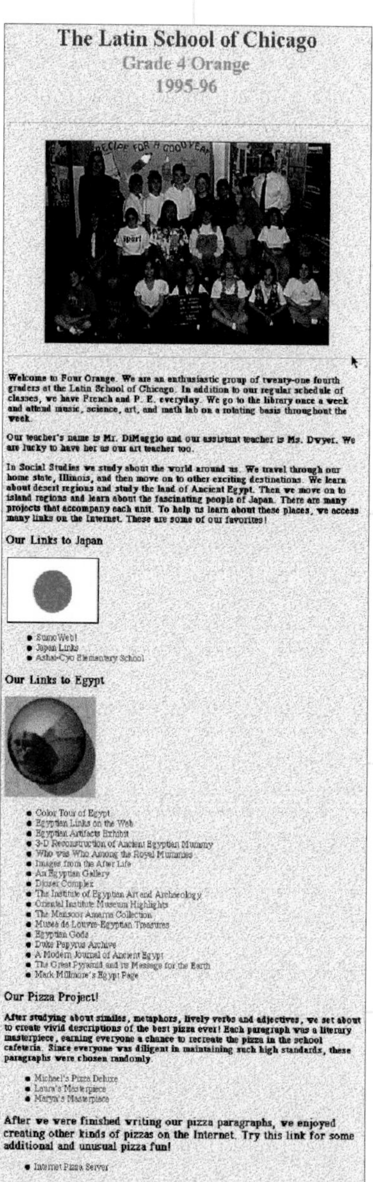

(1a) *Clicking on Lower School brings up the younger students' home page,* (4d) *with large artwork, compressed to only 39k. The 4th graders' home page* (2a) *points up its strong social studies emphasis with nice graphic links to Japan and to Egypt.*

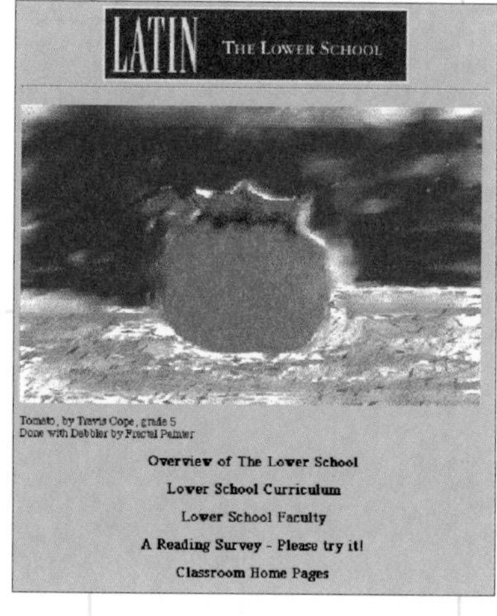

1a A link to the Upper School home page 8a again features student artwork—along with links to course descriptions, graduation requirements, and the home pages for various departments.

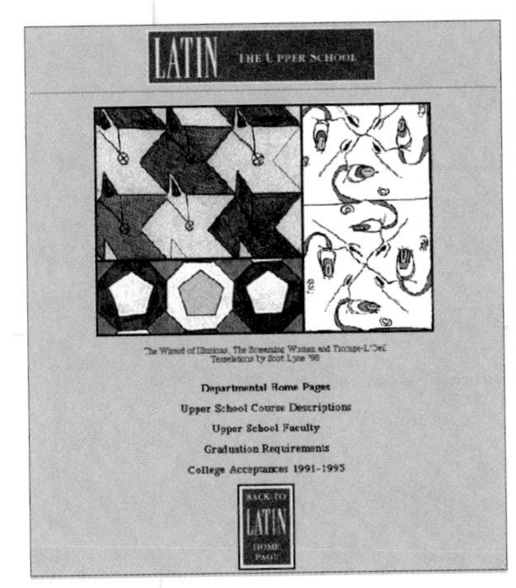

1a A link to the Middle School home page 6c features a topographical plot (GIF, compressed to 41k) created by students for an 8th grade science class. Links on the page lead to information on Middle School programs and departments.

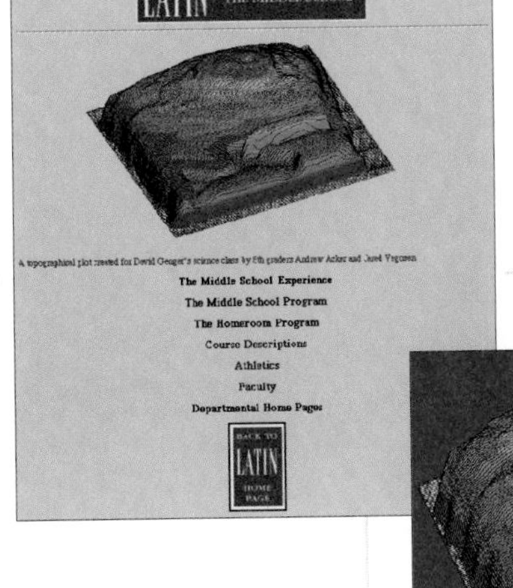

a b c d e

Special Features

Page 1

One of the main goals for this site, in the words of Linda Gazzola, was "to provide useful information to those in the Latin School community and the world at large."

This page from the Upper School's Mathematics Department is an in-depth study on "The History of Pi"—generated by the students at Latin. There are also many carefully selected links to other, far-flung information sites—links that explain the concept of Zen or that provide help in understanding calculus.

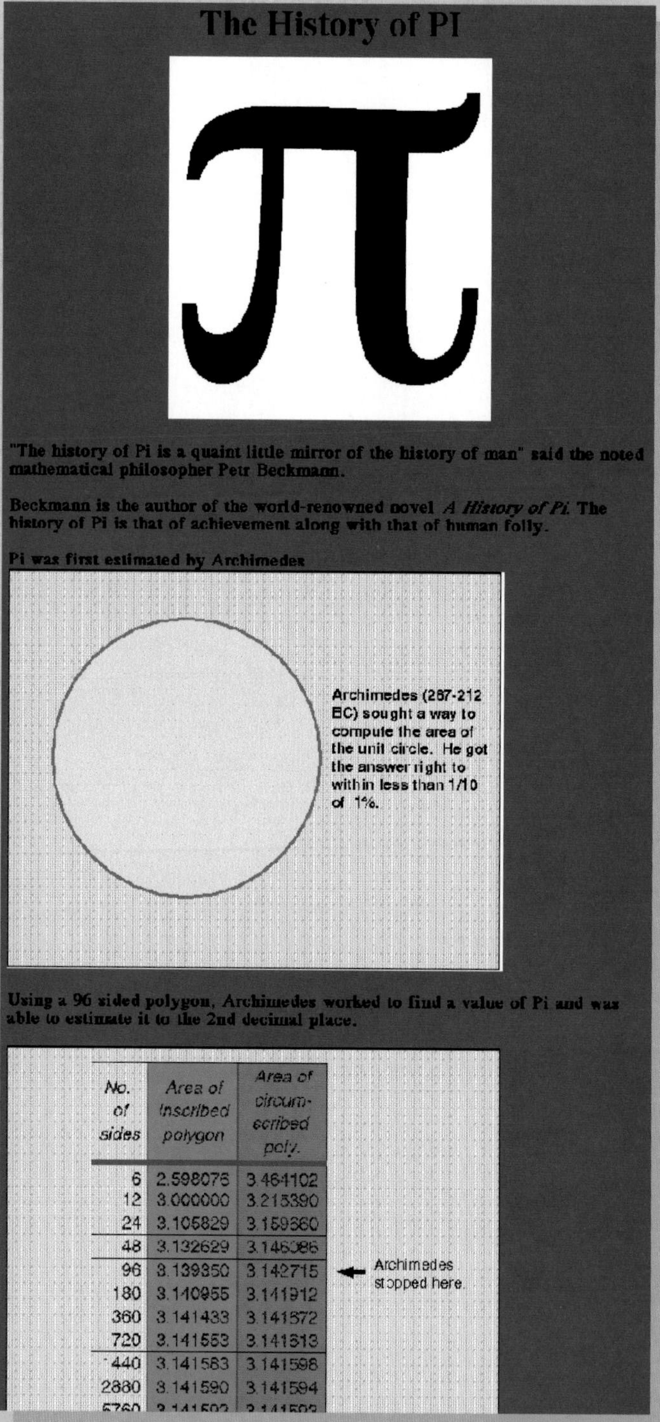

The History of PI

π

"The history of Pi is a quaint little mirror of the history of man" said the noted mathematical philosopher Petr Beckmann.

Beckmann is the author of the world-renowned novel *A History of Pi*. The history of Pi is that of achievement along with that of human folly.

Pi was first estimated by Archimedes

Archimedes (287-212 BC) sought a way to compute the area of the unit circle. He got the answer right to within less than 1/10 of 1%.

Using a 96 sided polygon, Archimedes worked to find a value of Pi and was able to estimate it to the 2nd decimal place.

No. of sides	Area of inscribed polygon	Area of circum-scribed poly.
6	2.598076	3.464102
12	3.000000	3.215390
24	3.105829	3.159660
48	3.132629	3.146086
96	3.139350	3.142715
180	3.140955	3.141912
360	3.141433	3.141572
720	3.141553	3.141613
·440	3.141583	3.141598
2880	3.141590	3.141594

← Archimedes stopped here.

"Home pages are an important part of a site because they personalize it. They show that behind the technology there are 'real' people."

—**CHRIS THOMAS, 10TH GRADE**

Zen and the Art of Calculus

(actually, only a little Zen)

Welcome to our (the Calculus AB AP class of the Latin School of Chicago, 1995-1996) Calculus homepage. Many of our over-achiever (and even some of our under-achiever) students have worked on creating these pages (as for me, well, I have been what one might call 'slacking off,' which is why our illustrious teacher, Dr Walid ElKhoury, has assigned me the inenviable task of creating this, a main page, for the class). Please, come into our world of Calculus (and a bit of Zen--if you're lucky and not looking for it, you might just find it), take a gander, point and click, stop, drop, and roll, and have a great time, all the while learning about Constructivism, the History of mathematical concepts, Resources and Graphics, and Lesson Plans for learning Mathematics and Calculus related sites. I would put them in a nice, easy directory below, but I have made the links already from the words above, and I don't like redundancy.

Dr ElKhoury, if you're out there and wondering why this page isn't finished, I'd like you to know it isn't my fault. The groups haven't all put their files in my folder, and I cannot access them to create links. Also, if you're a member of the Dr ElKhoury's class and wondering why your fancy background isn't showing up behind your beautiful page, it's because you haven't put the file for the background in my folder, and, as above, I have no way to access your background pattern. So, that's it. I'm leaving the country--no, that was last year. Uh, I'm just stopping work on this project, due to incompetency of supposed associates. Well, it was nice knowing you. Live long a due the prosperous thing. Then again, if the page is finished, I'll gladly take all the credit. Thank you, and have a pleasant tomorrow.

Love,

Lucas Klein

Hey, look, a bit of Zen:

Two monks were walking through the countryside in a rainstorm. As they approached a flooded river, they saw a woman unable to cross. "Dear Monks," she said, "will you help me cross this river?"

"Sure," said the older monk, and he picked her up and carried her across the river, letting her down at the other bank.

The two monks had again been walking for some time, when the younger monk turned to the older and said, "Uh, about that woman you carried across the stream, uh, you know, as monks we're never supposed to touch women, but you carried one across a river. What gives here?"

"Oh, that woman," the older monk responded. "I put her down long ago. Are you still carrying her?"

This page was devised and compiled by Lucas Klein, but is not maintained by same. It is maintained by his alter-ego, which is not to be confused with Ubermensch. The two are different, and linked only by a confusion of alter-ego and super-ego. I have both, or so I've been told. Personally, I think I have no ego, being the student of Zen that I am. But this is not true, for nothing is true, and all is nothing, except Mind, but, as a Zen master (I think it was Bankei, but I could be mistaken) said, "No mind, no Buddha."

Page 2

There's even a page for Latin's Library of Manuals for Dial-in Users. Here, students and staff can dial in to Latin's network from home; this gives them access to the Web, to printers at school, and to their personal files on the school's servers. Adobe SiteMill makes the dial-in option simple to plug in to any page.

The most requested dial-in page has been Lucas Klein's tongue-in-cheek essay, "Zen and the Art of Calculus."

The Latin School of Chicago

PhotoDeluxe Tricks for GIFs

GIF is used to display images on Web pages. With the GIF file format, you can define the parts of the image that you want to be transparent and select a transparency color for the Web browser. (When you leave an area transparent, it floats on the background.) GIF format also lets you reduce the total number of colors in the image to create a smaller file that is displayed and downloaded more quickly.

1 **You use Adobe PhotoDeluxe** layers to create the transparent areas. To prepare the photo, select the area you want to include, if you're not using the entire photo. Copy and paste that selection to a separate layer. Hide the original layer and any other layers that you don't want to include.

2 **To save the file in GIF format,** choose File>Export>GIF89a Export. The GIF dialog box appears. Select the option you want to use. For Windows users, click OK to save the file using the default values (adaptive palette, gray transparency color, and interlaced). To set your own options, click advanced and then set the options as described below.

3 **Selecting a transparency color:** Click the color box to select a color for the transparent areas. (To make the transparency the same color as the Web page background, leave it at the default gray setting.)

4 **Choosing a palette:** Choose Exact from the Palette menu if your photo contains 256 or fewer colors. This option displays the file in true-to-life colors. If your photo contains more than 256 colors, choose the Adaptive palette. The Adaptive option creates a palette from the most commonly used colors in the image. You can use the System palette to display the photo, but this option can produce unexpected results when the image is displayed on some monitors.

5 **Reducing the number of colors:** If you choose the Adaptive palette, type a number in the Colors text box or choose the number of colors from the Colors pop-up menu. Experiment until you have the smallest number of colors that still keeps the detail you want in the photo. To check how the photo will look in the Web browser with the selected number of colors, click the Preview button in the GIF dialog box. Click OK to return to the GIF dialog box.

6 **Choosing a download method:** Leave the Interlaced option selected if you want the image to be displayed gradually during downloading. Interlacing displays increasingly higher resolution detail as a photo is downloaded. Deselect the Interlaced option if you're using the photo as a background or texture, so that it's downloaded all at once.

7 **Click OK in the GIF dialog** box to save the file in GIF format. Adobe PhotoDeluxe automatically assigns a .gif extension to the file name. You're ready now to drag and drop it into a Web page builder like Adobe PageMill, or use HTML to physically tag the photo into its position.

http:oakview.fcps.edu/

Oak View Elementary School

Fairfax County School District
Fairfax, Virginia

Principal Greg Lock with Oak View's home page. Oak View's Web team has found that putting kids to work on the Web gives them a practical reason for doing assignments—it actually makes them better students.

Two things stand out in the Oak View site—first, it's got 100-percent commitment to making the Web part of its curriculum, and second, it's got both kids and parents involved in it every step of the way. As Principal Greg Lock puts it, the philosophy behind this site is that the Web is a great tool for research, a tool for publishing student work, and "a great way to get parents involved in the school."

Create GIF images for hot links. They're more eye-catching than lists of words.

Located in the city of Fairfax, Virginia, this public school serves students in grades K–6. The school is known for strong parental involvement.

Kelsey with her teacher, Joan Turner. Mrs. Turner's class developed the community pages.

Everybody gets into the act here. A team of parent volunteers, trained and coordinated by parent Alan Schultz, helps students browse the Web and get their work—done with the regular classroom teachers—up online. Along with student projects like a virtual exhibit of Greece, the site features an easy-to-use assortment of educational links—including a description of a new Oak View class: Designing a Web Page.

Fourth-grader Brandon also helped with the site's home page.

Oak View Elementary School

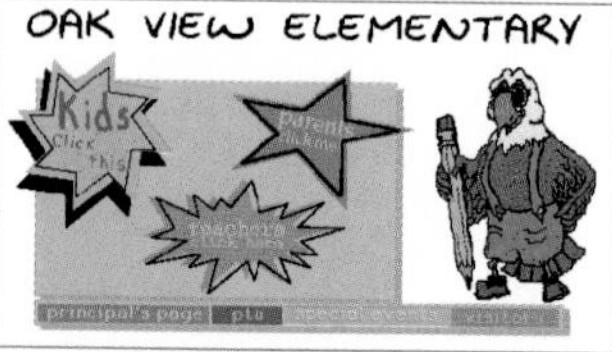

Oak View is on the Internet! Oak View is located in Fairfax, VA. and is a participant in George Mason University's Center for the New Engineer CNELink project. Join us as we explore the use of the Internet in K-6 education. Our pages are designed by the students, staff, and parents of Oak View.

Use your mouse to click on the image above, or select from the following list. (Try clicking on our name or the eagle!)

| Kids, click here | Parents, click here | Teachers, click here | Visitors |
| Principal's Page | The PTA | Special Events |

We want your feedback! Please send comments to Alan C. Schultz, schultz@osf.gmu.edu, Oak View Internet Project

Bright, fun, and easy to use, the Oak View home (1a) *page provides links for kids, parents, teachers, and visitors. The main GIF image is compressed and "mapped" so that clicking on different parts leads to different pages.*

Oak View Elementary
Kids' Page

On our kids' page, you will find links to all of the neat things produced for kids by Oak View students and teachers. You will also find a section of links to interesting things on the world wide web that are cool for kids. We have tried to find things that are appropriate for kindergarten through sixth grade. Have fun!

Here are things we have done here at Oak View Elementary

Our students and teachers are developing their own web pages. We would love to get feedback on what you find here!

Learn about different animals with Mr. Smith's fifth grade class as they write their Animal Research Projects. New!

Learn about some of the sixth grade electives from the Designing a Web Page elective. New!

A combination of fourth, fifth and sixth grade students describe our community, Fairfax County, in Oak View's entry to the Scholastic Inc. Global Community Project.

Follow along as Mrs. Cassella's fourth grade class learns about Virginia in Virginia Visions, a digital book being produced by the students.

In fifth grade, students are painting with words as they create poems in a variety of styles. See their work on Ms. Kennedy's Poetry Pages. New!

Mr. Smith's fifth grade class is learning about Greece. They are creating a virtual exhibit on Greece.

The ambassador from Papua, New Guinea visited Mrs. Burgess' third grade class. New!

Mrs. Klinge's second grade class is particularly fond of Winnie the Pooh. Come visit Pooh Corner!

Mrs. Jackson's third grade class would like to tell you about what they have learned with the internet, and give yo a tour of their classroom.

The Red Pod consists of five multi-age classes of first and second grader. Come see what we are learning froom the Web!

Mrs. Socci's home page contains links to science and the environment.

Mrs. Liggett's third grade class tells you about their year (94-95).

Take a look at some of the special email and messages people have sent to us.

We have many special events at Oak View. Take a look at our assemblies from the eyes of the students who write about them.

Please visit Oak View's library. Our librarian has some special things for you here.

Interesting links for kids to explore on the Web

Government

The White House
U.S. House Of Representatives - Home Page

Mathematics

MathMagic!

Art and Literature

Visit the Famous Artist exhibit from the Louvre, in Paris France. (If that link is slow, try this one.)
Kids Web - A World Wide Web Digital Library for Schoolkids
Book reports written by kids
Dead Sea Scrolls Exhibit
Soviet Archives Exhibit
Carlos' Coloring Book Home
Kaleidospace
Global Show-n-Tell - Home Page

Government and Politics

Inaugural speeches of the Presidents of the United States

Science

The Space Shuttle Page
Students for the Exploration and Development of Space (SEDS)
Preview The Heart
Helping Your Child Learn Science
B-EYE: The world through the eyes of a bee
Views Of The Solar System
nanohome html
Earth Viewer
Paleontology Exhibit
1492 Exhibit
Smithsonian Institute's Mineral and Gem Collection

Weather Information

Current Weather Maps/Movies
The Daily Planet

Reference Desk

Webster's Dictionary, Electronic version
The Virtual Reference Desk

Museums

The Smithsonian Institute
Tours, photos, resources, and much more.
The Franklin Institute Science Museum
An excellent science museum in Philadelphia.
Museum of Paleontology
Learn about dinosaurs.
The Louvre, an art exhibit
Visit the Famous Artist exhibit at the Louvre, in Paris France. (If that link is slow, try this one.)

Other places

Take a tour of Paris France
Virtually Hawaii
KidsCom Home Page

Indexes with kid's stuff

K-12 WWW Sites for Students & Educators
(Bob Allison's Home Page) Uncle Bob's Kids' Page
Children's Sites
Kids on Campus, 1995

(1a) *One part of the mapped image leads to the Kids Page, which has* (3a) *links to all the great stuff done by students in every grade. It also features carefully selected links to all kinds of information kids can find on the Web, from the Dead Sea Scrolls exhibit to a virtual tour of Hawaii.*

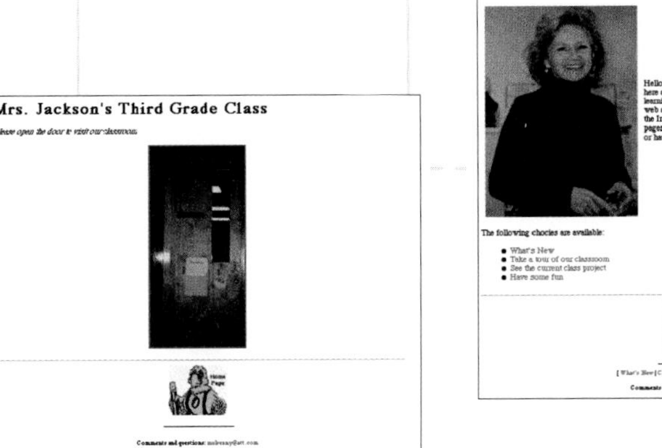
Mrs. Jackson's Third Grade Class
Please open the door to visit our classroom.

(2b) *One Kids' Page link leads to an open door.* (5b) *Clicking on the door takes you into Mrs. Jackson's Third Grade Class,* (6b) *where they meet the teacher and have a choice of looking at "What's New" or the current class project, taking a classroom tour, or "having some fun..."*

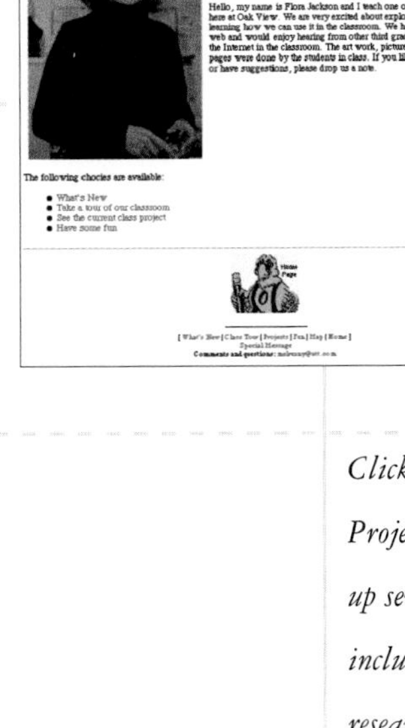
WELCOME
We are glad you stopped by!
The following choices are available:

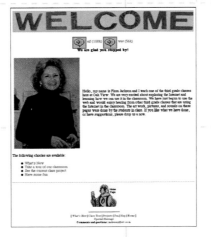

Clicking on Our Class Projects (6b) *might bring up several further choices, including a historical* (8a) *research project that led students to sound files of bagpipe music—which visitors can hear, too, using Mac AIF format or PC WAV format.*

Our Class Projects
Historical Research
Puppets that we made

(6c) *Clicking on another class project home page—one of the 6th grade's elective courses—leads to a description of the projects.*

a b c d e

Oak View Elementary School Site Map

In PageMill, images can be "mapped" so that clicking on different parts leads you to different pages.

Special Features

Page 1

One feature of this site is its remarkable degree of parent involvement. Webmaster Alan Schultz, himself a parent, organized training sessions for parents in two main areas: as tour guides to help students browse the Web, and as Web developers who actually help to create pages.

As tour guides, they help keep the kids focused on research goals and make sure they don't get sidetracked onto inappropriate areas of the Web. As developers, they help and advise the older students in creating their sites.

PTA information, and school announcements. You will also find links to information from around the world that are useful to parents. These links will include pointers to child development issues, LD information, and other helpful resources.

Oak View is on the internet as part of a George Mason University project to give...

- students and teachers access to the wealth of information available;
- parents, teachers, school staff, and students a means to share information;
- students and teachers the ability to interact with peers from around the world;
- students a chance to showcase their artwork, stories and other accomplishments.

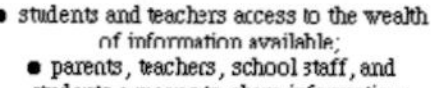

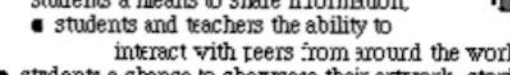

Help needed!

We are looking for parents to help with the **Internet Project** in several ways. We are hoping to have at least one parent in each class to help the teacher and students put the internet to work in the classroom. This includes assisting the children in browsing the resources of the internet, putting students' writing and art on the computer for others to see, and designing "pages" for the web. **Training will be supplied for those that volunteer!** If you have a little time to volunteer, please contact Alan Schultz at 323-6880 (evenings) or at schultz@aic.nrl.navy.mil

Links for parents

- See Oak View's **kids page** for interesting links for you to explore with your children. In particular, check out the pages designed by the students and teachers.
- The PTA has a page.
- Oak View Library
- If you are developing web pages for your child's class, here is a link to information on writing HTML.

Other education-related links

You can find many other education links on Oak View's **teachers page** .

- The National Parent Information Network provides information to parents. It is a service of ERIC (Educational Resources Information Center), a national information system supported by the Department of Education.
- Children's Literature Web Guide
- First Aid Online
- The U.S. Department of Education

Indexes and Search Engines

The indexes are easy to use to find just about any information, while the search engines can be used to perform searches for information. Read the instructions on the search pages to understand how to successfully find information.

- The WWW Virtual Library is an excellent index to Web resources.
- Yahoo is a large index arranged hierarchically. (From Stanford University)
- InfoSeek Net Search is fast and accurate.
- The Web Crawler is a search engine.
- WWWW: The World Wide Web Worm, another search engine.
- Galaxy maintains both an index, and a search engine to make it easier to find resources.

Return to Oak View Elementary's Home Page

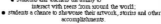

"Today we have so much information. The trick is how to focus on what you're looking for, and to pare down your thoughts."

— **ALAN C. SCHULTZ, PARENT VOLUNTEER AND WEBMASTER**

Oak View Elementary

Libraries and Book Stores

Oak View Library
Our own library gone virtual!
Book Stacks, Inc.
This site has links to an electronic library, links to publishers, book reviews, and informaton on authors; order books.
Children's Literature Web Guide
Information on kid's books, including reviews, and information on book awards (e.g. Caldecott) and authors.
University of Virginia's Electronic Library
Complete library services from University of Virginia.
The library of Congress
Information about the library of Congress, and complete services; access electonic publications.

Lesson Plans and Curriculum materials

ERIC Lesson Plans
Curriculum materials from the Educational Resources Information Center (ERIC), a federally funded national information system.
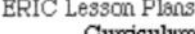
SpaceLink Instructional Materials
Instructional materials and lesson plans from SpaceLink, NASA's educational network.

Other Education Resources on the Web

Reference resources
Dictionaries, encyclopedia, maps, fact books, etc.
Webster's Dictionary
An electronic version that returns the definition, where each word in the definition is a link back into the dictionary.
The U.S. Department of Education
The Department of Education maintains a lot of information of interest to educators.
School Psychology Resources Online
Providing links to sites of interest to the school psychology community.
Space Link
Nasa's educational network, complete with instructional materials, educational services, NASA news, and special projects.
The Space Shuttle Page
These pages contain information about the current shuttle mission, including video footage, photos, the countdown and landing details, and information on tracking the shuttle. Find out when you can spot the shuttle flying overhead at night!

Links to other collections of educational links

- EINet's (Galaxy) Education Page
- Yahoo's K12 Education Index
- Houghton Mifflin/GNN Educaton Site

Collections of information for kids

Kids Web: A World Wide Web Digital Library for Schoolkids
This site contains many links of interest to kids arranged in categories -- very comprehensive.

Other schools on the Web

Comprehensive list of schools on the web
Click on this map to find schools on the internet almost anywhere in the world.

Newspapers, TV networks and other Media

- Corporation for Public Broadcasting
- Channel 4 (NBC)

Page 2

Oak View's Teachers Page is a treasure trove of educational resources that includes Libraries and Book Stores, Lesson Plans and Curriculum Materials, and every kind of resource from the Space Shuttle Page to the Corporation for Public Broadcasting. For links to research, this site's got it all.

Oak View Elementary School

http://www.azstarnet.com/~slmc/

Sahuaro High School

Tucson Unified School District
Tucson, Arizona

"My goal in creating the site was to help the other kids at my school feel more comfortable with the Web. I wanted them to have a starting place where they could look around and not feel lost."

—CINDY NORDAHL, STUDENT

What's remarkable about this site is that it was created and maintained largely by one person—and that one person was a student. Senior Cindy Nordahl began with creating her own page on her home computer.

To do this, she taught herself HTML by looking at what was "out there" on the Web. Then, she says, "I discovered that Sahuaro had Web access. Then the idea hit me—Sahuaro needs a home page!"

Solid color backgrounds look great and are simple to add in PageMill.

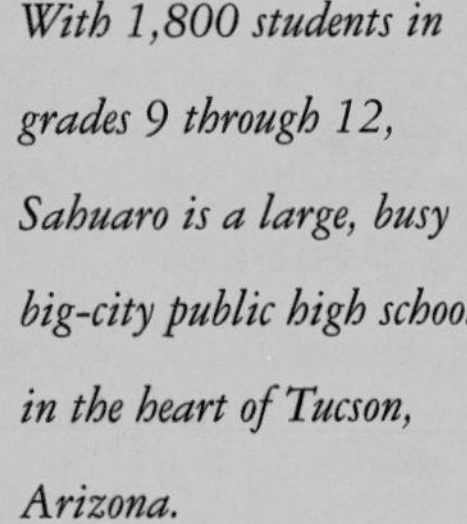

With 1,800 students in grades 9 through 12, Sahuaro is a large, busy big-city public high school in the heart of Tucson, Arizona.

Cindy with librarian Sharon Gaddis.

Cindy had another goal, too. A basketball player herself, she says, "It's a competitive thing. When I started the page, there was only one other high school in Tucson up on the Web. They were our basketball rivals. They had an article in the newspaper about their site, and I wanted to have an article about my school, too!"

The site, full of bright backgrounds and colorful GIF images, won first prize at Arizona's Young Publishers Competition.

The site can be accessed on the libraries' Macintoshes and PCs.

1 2 3 4

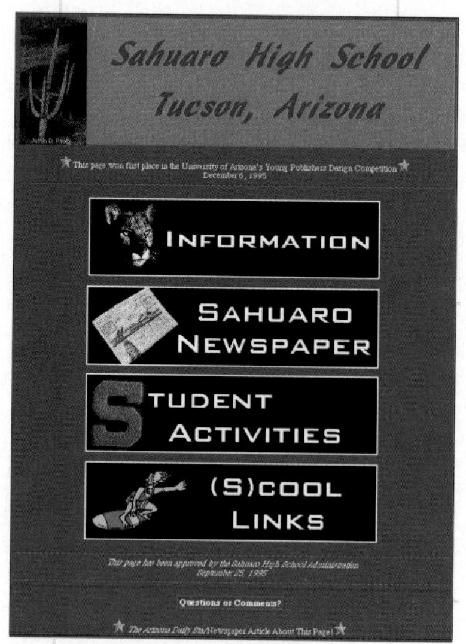

Nicely designed and simple to use, this home page (1a) *features a solid background and compressed GIF links (12k each.).*

School Song

Fight the team across the field
Show them Sahuaro's here
Set the earth reverberating
With a mighty cheer,
Rah--rah--rah
Hit them hard and see how they fall
Never let that team get the ball
Hail hail the gangs all here
so let's beat (the team) now!

MAIN INFORMATION NEWSPAPER STUDENT ACTIVITIES (S)COOL LINKS

Sahuaro's Epidemic of Color: The Miss Clairol Project

MAIN INFORMATION NEWSPAPER STUDENT ACTIVITIES (S)COOL LINKS

Clicking on Information (1a) *brings visitors to another attractive page with a bright background.* (2b) *The links are made of larger, custom type. These look better and are easily created in Adobe Photoshop.*

The Information page also links (2b) *lead to pages on the school and the city, including the school fight song.* (2c)

From the home page, (1b) *there's a button to Cool Links, a hip list of TV shows, newspapers, Web guides and the Rainforest Action Network.* (3c)

a

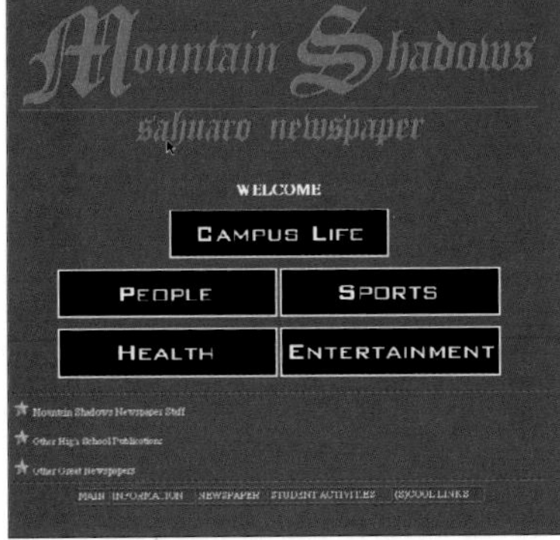

b

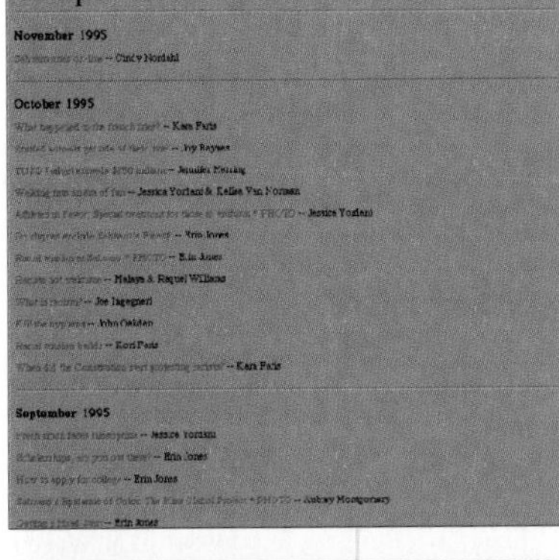

(5d) *This page proves that Cindy achieved one of her original goals—to get the school mentioned in the newspaper. A button on the home page* (1c) *leads to this article, which ran in* the Arizona Daily Star.

c

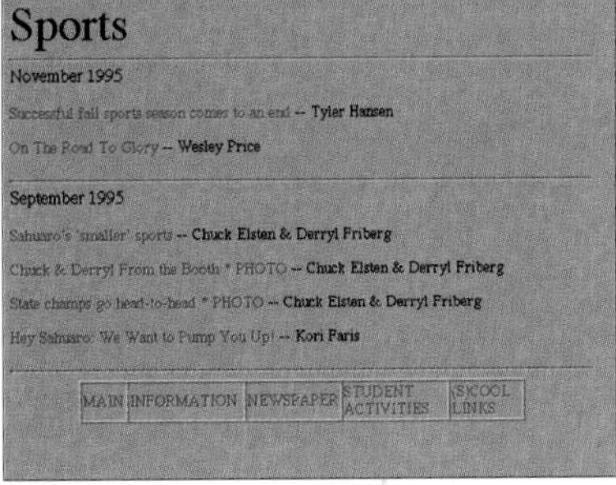

d

Sahuaro High's home page

November 12, 1995

Several Tucson schools have home pages on the Internet, and among the best is the Sahuaro High page put together by Cindy Nordahl, a senior at that school.

She began using the Net's World Wide Web in June when she got a new computer. In late September she decided Sahuaro needed a home page.

Her former English teacher, Bill Thompson, also is an adviser to the school newspaper, Mountain Shadows. He agreed to have Nordahl put the paper online and to give her independent study credit.

The paper is the cornerstone of the home page. Its ever-changing content offers a look into what's happening at the school and what's important to its students.

The current issue, for instance, has stories on race relations, student body president Nellie Cho and the bodybuilding club.

The home page also has an activities calendar and lists of the clubs, administrators and student government officers. There's a long list of links to other high school, college and university pages.

Nordahl says she spent about 80 hours putting the Sahuaro page together and continues to work about 10 hours a week maintaining it. Her next development is to add photos from the school paper. She does all the changes and improvements from home.

Nordahl, who also works, for credit, at the University of Arizona's Digital Image Analysis Lab, has this advice for other students who want to put together home pages: Learn all you can about Hypertext Markup Language (HTML), the computer code for building Web pages. Study other pages and make lists of features you want to include on your own page.

"It's a lot of hard work and dedication," Nordahl says, "but the results can be amazing."

Nordahl says she hopes to find another student or a teacher to take over the page when she graduates.

Over the next few weeks, we'll publish occasional stories about other Southern Arizona schools and students who have home pages. If you'd like us to take a look at your school page, please drop a note to [illegible]@azstarnet.com.

News Links

Meanwhile, look at the Sahuaro page at [illegible]

(1c) *Another home page link takes you to the school newspaper—*Mountain Shadows. (8b) *In addition to departments on* (6b) *Campus Life, People, Sports,* (6c) *and Entertainment, there are links to other high school publications and newspapers. The sections are laid out in tables for a clear, clean look.*

e

Sahuaro High School Site Map

Placing Text in PageMill

With Adobe PageMill, adding text to your Web page is simple—the same as adding text to any document. You just type it, cut and paste it, or drag it from another page or application. You can also add text styles, such as italic or bold, and change headings or text width. A special option is adding color to the text where you want to emphasize words or highlight links.

Assigning styles to text

1 **Select your text and open** the Attributes Inspector; the Text Attributes panel should appear. Assign styles by using the commands on the Style menu.

2 **Select a physical style** (Plain, Bold, Italic, or Teletype) to change the appearance of the selected text.

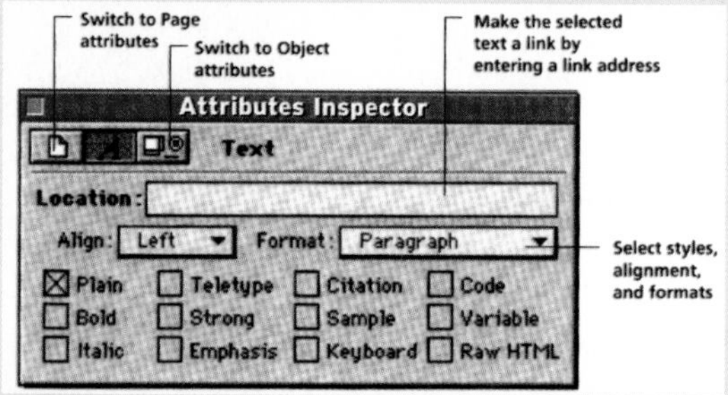

3 **Select a logical style** (Strong, Emphasis, Citation, Sample, Keyboard, Code, or Variable).

4 **To insert HTML tags** directly into your page, use the Raw HTML command. This is useful for entering tags that are specific to a particular browser or server, or for tags that PageMill does not yet understand.

Adding color to text

1 **Open the Attributes Inspector** and click on the Page icon to select Page Attributes.

2 **Select Custom on the pop-upText** menu and then choose a text color from the color picker dialog box.

3 **Set the pop-ups for Normal,** Active, and Visited links to Custom and choose a text color for each. As soon as you change the color in the pop-up, the new color is displayed on the current page.

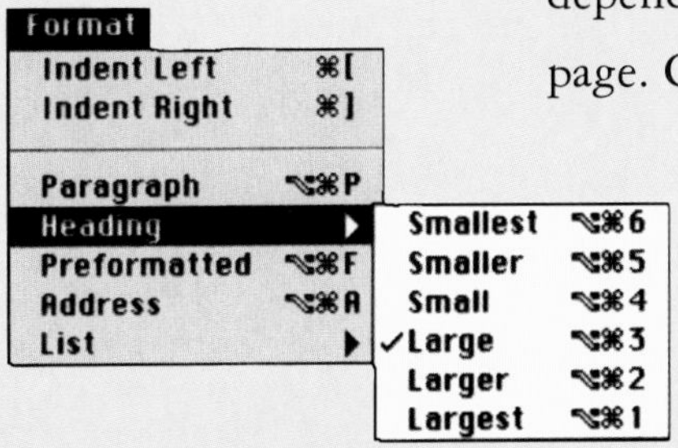

Format
Indent Left ⌘[
Indent Right ⌘]
Paragraph ⌥⌘P
Heading ▶
Preformatted ⌥⌘F
Address ⌥⌘A
List ▶
Smallest ⌥⌘6
Smaller ⌥⌘5
Small ⌥⌘4
✓Large ⌥⌘3
Larger ⌥⌘2
Largest ⌥⌘1

Assigning formats to text

1 **Open the Attributes Inspector** (the Text Attributes panel should be selected). Here, you can assign formats using the commands on the pop-up Format menu.

2 **To make the text wider** or narrower on the page, use the Indent Right and Indent Left commands.

3 **Use the Heading format** to add "punch" to your page and to separate your text into different sections. You can choose from six heading sizes. Actual display sizes depend on the browser used to view the page. Generally, it's good to use the largest size as the main heading and other sizes for subheads.

http://www.bhs.berkeley.k12.ca.us/index.html

"The Internet is a great solution to many of the age-old problems of education."

—LAWRENCE J. LEE, PRINCIPAL

Berkeley High School

Berkeley Unified School District
Berkeley, California

Alive with urban energy and a mix of cultures that embraces everything from Chinese dance to African-American poetry, Berkeley High is a diverse and complex place. Its 2,400 students, grades 9 to 12, come from all over the district and from many racial and ethnic groups. Their Web site, which is relatively new, reflects this diversity and energy.

In PageMill, set your pages up in two vertical columns for a unique look.

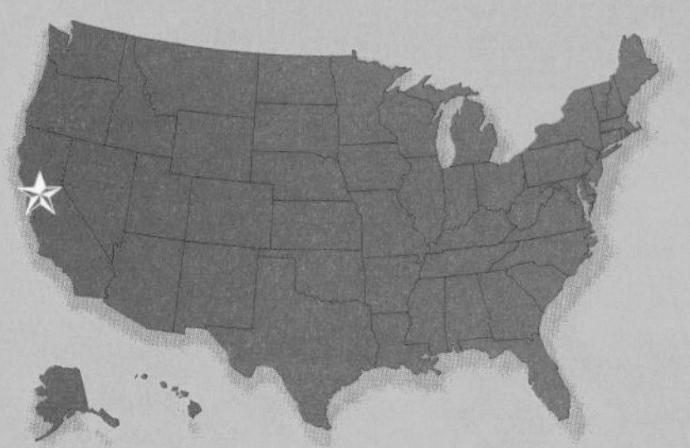

Located in Berkeley, California, a few blocks from the University of California, Berkeley High reflects the town's intellectual energy and ethnic and cultural diversity.

School clubs, like the International Ambassadors, have their own home pages on the site.

It all began with *The Jacket*, the student newspaper, going online. Under the direction of Computer Science teacher Paul Goessling, and with lots of work by computer-savvy student Webmaster Gabe Benveniste and others, the site has since expanded to include student projects, department news, school club profiles, and student home pages, all done with a clean layout and sophisticated graphics.

One day after the Million Man March, the school's Center for African-American Studies posted an informational page.

Berkeley High School

1 2 3 4

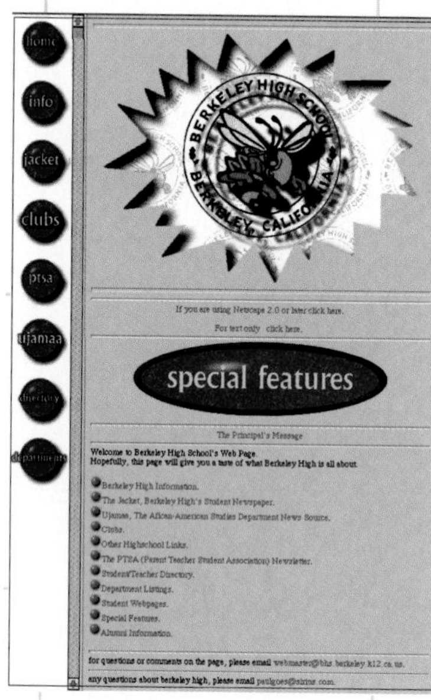

(1a) *The home page features top-of-the-line graphics, including a custom PageMill menu strip running down the left side of each page. Paul Goessling says, "To create these effects, we used Adobe PageMill and Adobe Photoshop—constantly!"*

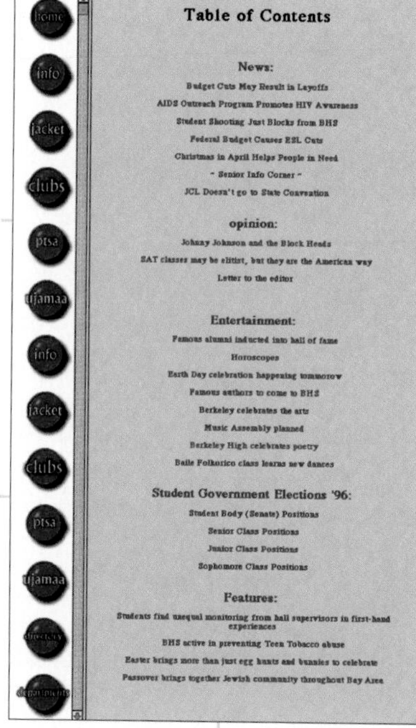

Clicking on the button for The Jacket *brings* (1a) *visitors to the student newspaper that started it.* (2a) *Click on the current date and get today's Table of Contents,* (2c) *articles on an AIDS outreach program, an opinion page, sports scores, and a feature on Passover. The page is designed in a straight forward way, so viewers can easily find what they're after.*

a

(2d) *The Contents also links to Entertainment pages of the paper.* (5c) *A Hall of Fame assembly featuring alumni, like jazz musician Benny Green, a Horoscope page, and reports on Earth Day celebrations all contribute to the mix.*

(1b) *A home page link takes you to a page* (6c) *for the African-American Studies Department, detailing the latest happenings, including reports on Black History month, "Food for the Soul," and Hip-Hop news.*

b

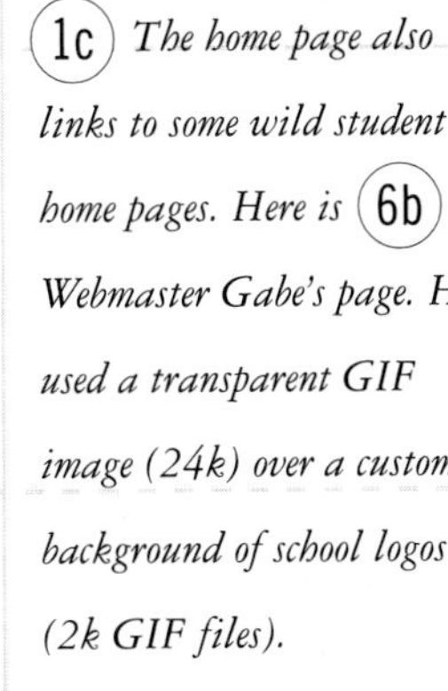

(1c) *The home page also links to some wild student home pages. Here is* (6b) *Webmaster Gabe's page. He used a transparent GIF image (24k) over a custom background of school logos (2k GIF files).*

c

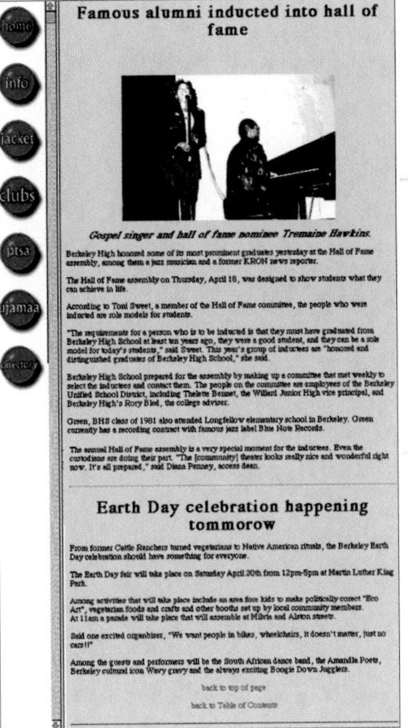

Famous alumni inducted into hall of fame

Gospel singer and hall of fame nominee Tremaine Hawkins.

Berkeley High honored some of its most prominent graduates yesterday at the Hall of Fame assembly, among them a jazz musician and a former KRON news reporter.

The Hall of Fame assembly on Thursday, April 18, was designed to show students what they can achieve in life.

According to Toni Sweet, a member of the Hall of Fame committee, the people who were inducted are role models for students.

"The requirements for a person who is to be inducted is that they must have graduated from Berkeley High School at least ten years ago, they were a good student, and they can be a role model for today's students," said Sweet. This year's group of inductees are "honored and distinguished graduates of Berkeley High School," she said.

Berkeley High School prepared for the assembly by making up a committee that met weekly to select the inductees and contact them. The people on the committee are employees of the Berkeley Unified School District, including Thelette Bennet, the Willard Junior High vice principal, and Berkeley High's Rory Bled, the college adviser.

Green, BHS class of 1981 also attended Longfellow elementary school in Berkeley. Green currently has a recording contract with famous jazz label Blue Note Records.

The annual Hall of Fame assembly is a very special moment for the inductees. Even the custodians are doing their part. "The [community] theater looks really nice and wonderful right now. It's all prepared," said Diana Penney, access dean.

Earth Day celebration happening tommorow

From former Cattle Ranchers turned vegetarians to Native American rituals, the Berkeley Earth Day celebration should have something for everyone.

The Earth Day fair will take place on Saturday April 20th from 12pm-5pm at Martin Luther King Park.

Among activities that will take place include an area fore kids to make politically corect "Eco Art", vegetarian foods and crafts and other booths set up by local community members. At 11am a parade will take place that will assemble at Milvia and Alston streets.

Said one excited organbizer, "We want people in bikes, wheelchairs, it doesn't matter, just no cars!!"

Among the guests and performers will be the South African dance band, the Amandla Poets, Berkeley cultural icon Wavy gravy and the always exciting Boogie Down Jugglers.

back to top of page

back to Table of Contents

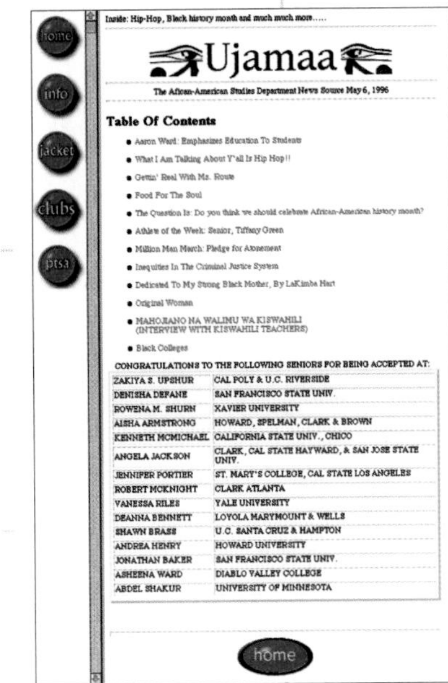

Inside: Hip-Hop, Black history month and much much more.....

Ujamaa

The African-American Studies Department News Source May 6, 1996

Table Of Contents

- Aaron Ward: Emphasizes Education To Students
- What I Am Talking About Y'all Is Hip Hop!!
- Gettin' Real With Ms. Route
- Food For The Soul
- The Question Is: Do you think we should celebrate African-American history month?
- Athlete of the Week: Senior, Tiffany Green
- Million Man March: Pledge for Atonement
- Inequities In The Criminal Justice System
- Dedicated To My Strong Black Mother, By LaKimba Hart
- Original Woman
- MAHOJIANO NA WALIMU WA KISWAHILI (INTERVIEW WITH KISWAHILI TEACHERS)
- Black Colleges

CONGRATULATIONS TO THE FOLLOWING SENIORS FOR BEING ACCEPTED AT:

ZAKIYA S. UPSHUR	CAL POLY & U.C. RIVERSIDE
DENISHA DEFANE	SAN FRANCISCO STATE UNIV.
ROWENA M. SHURN	XAVIER UNIVERSITY
AISHA ARMSTRONG	HOWARD, SPELMAN, CLARK & BROWN
KENNETH MCMICHAEL	CALIFORNIA STATE UNIV., CHICO
ANGELA JACKSON	CLARK, CAL STATE HAYWARD, & SAN JOSE STATE UNIV.
JENNIFER PORTIER	ST. MARY'S COLLEGE, CAL STATE LOS ANGELES
ROBERT MCKNIGHT	CLARK ATLANTA
VANESSA RILES	YALE UNIVERSITY
DEANNA BENNETT	LOYOLA MARYMOUNT & WELLS
SHAWN BRASS	U.C. SANTA CRUZ & HAMPTON
ANDREA HENRY	HOWARD UNIVERSITY
JONATHAN BAKER	SAN FRANCISCO STATE UNIV.
ASHEENA WARD	DIABLO VALLEY COLLEGE
ABDEL SHAKUR	UNIVERSITY OF MINNESOTA

home

d

e

With PageMill, it's a snap to add QuickTime video to your site.

Special Features

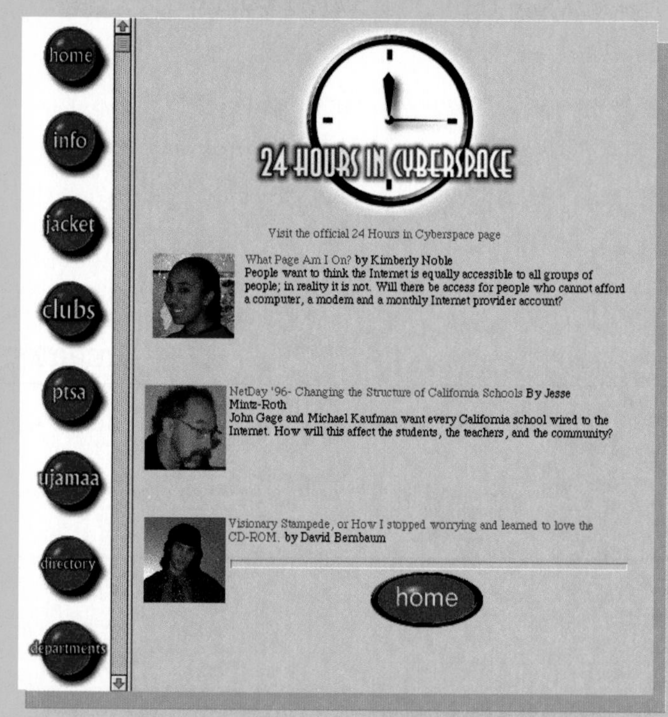

Page 1

Students at BHS have participated in some exciting special projects that gave their site a big boost. One was Rick Smolen's photojournalism project, 24 Hours in Cyberspace. *As its contribution to this Internet event, BHS posted its story on Berkeley High's Spring 1996 Poetry Class, with a live link to the 24 Hours home page.*

"The yearbook and the newspaper are laid out entirely by students, using Adobe Photoshop and Adobe Pagemaker. The newspaper has gone digital now; they send their layouts direct to the printer via modem."

—PAUL GOESSLING

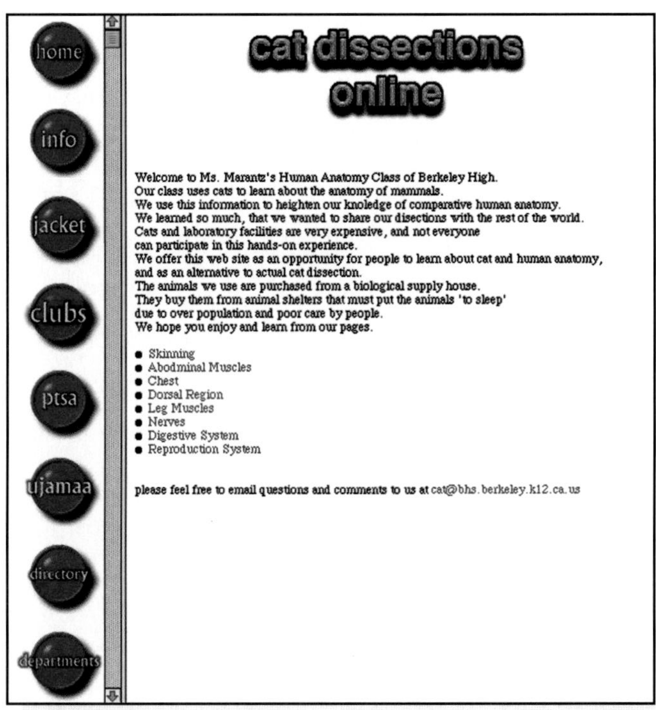

Page 2

One of the students' most ambitious projects to date is its entry in the Think Quest contest. For their entry, Gabe and the students created Cat Dissection Online in conjunction with the Human Anatomy Class. The dissection was filmed using a digital camera, processed in Adobe Photoshop on a Power Mac, and finally assembled in Adobe PageMill.

Advanced Web Content with Adobe Acrobat

The newest version of Adobe Acrobat 3.0 includes an easy way of getting paper documents, or documents designed like paper, up and onto the Web. Acrobat uses a compatible file format to HTML, called PDF. A free PDF viewer called, Acrobat Reader, works with Netscape Navigator or Microsoft Internet Explorer and allows Acrobat documents to be viewed within the Web browser window. Now, memos, tests, charts, papers, graphics and more can be created with your normal computer applications, converted into the PDF file format, and served up on your Web site. This can really take your Web site to a new level!

1 How Acrobat 3.0 Works

You use your normal computer applications like Microsoft Word, Adobe PageMaker, ClarisWorks, Microsoft PowerPoint, Home Publisher, and any other applications you already know how to use. After you've installed Acrobat 3.0, instead of printing to a printer, you print it as an Acrobat file. What you have is a electronic document that looks exactly like the one you might have printed to paper. File size has been compressed and all the text and graphics are identical.

There are lots of other features too long to list here, but you can assign a password to the digital document. You can put in links both within the document and to Web site URLs. You can make pages of any size, you can attach electronic sticky notes to the pages, and you can even take existing paper documents, and convert them into the PDF file format in a few quick steps.

One of the neatest things about Acrobat 3.0, just like Web pages, is that any computer can open and see the document exactly as it appeared in Microsoft Word. So a Mac file can be served onto your Web site and Windows users can open and use it! And anyone can print the Acrobat file and it will print just like the original, even though you might be half a world away from the Web site!

2 How to get the Free Acrobat Reader

Thousands of Web sites already use PDF files to augment their Web content. Almost all of them point to the Adobe Web site (www.adobe.com/acrobat) so users can download the free Acrobat Reader. When you purchase the full Adobe Acrobat 3.0, the Reader is included, as well as information for your Webmaster on how to post and "serve" PDF files onto your Web site.

3 How Does This Change your Web

Site? Adobe Acrobat 3.0 allows you to post anything you might create in paper onto your Web site. Your school newspaper, yearbook, or PTA newsletter are perfect examples. Instead of creating long HTML pages create a PDF file instead and post it. Viewers have the option of reading it within their Web browser or downloading the file and reading it off-line—in either mode you can always print it.

A Web page can have a simple list of dozens of PDF files, with each PDF file incorporating hundreds of pages. Acrobat can simplify your Web site while alleviating a lot of HTML programming, because PDF and HTML work together.

But most importantly, you use the desktop publishing tools you already own and use. You take your existing Word, or Excel, or PageMaker file and simply convert it to PDF. Post it to the Web or e-mail it as an attachment. You're done!

http://gcsc.k12.in.us/GCHSHome.html

Greenfield Central High

Hancock County School District
Greenfield, Indiana

"When students know they have a world-wide audience viewing their work, they produce much higher quality. I'm not saying the days of posting artwork on the refrigerator are extinct. It's just that the refrigerator is now the World Wide Web."

—DON GILROY, TECHNOLOGY COORDINATOR

Greenfield Central High has long understood the value of the Web. This shines through in its site, which is proudly called "Indiana's Oldest Secondary School home page." Tech Coordinator Don Gilroy started the site along with Science Department Chairperson John Rihm. Their goal was to make Greenfield's site a model of teachers and students working together.

Columns and tables mean less scrolling and make long lists easier to read.

Greenfield is located in central Indiana. It's a city that's self-described as having a "small town" atmosphere with "big city" resources.

The site approached Greenfield's home-grown Olympian, Jaycie Phelps, about setting up a page on their site.

"We don't believe in creating a list of lists," continues Don Gilroy. "Rather, we believe in providing a view into the educational lives of our students and community." This site does just that, with lots of links to resources on the Web (such as search engines) and pages for parents, information on the city of Greenfield, as well as the coolest new sites.

1 2 3 4

CONGRATULATIONS
To Greenfield native Jaycie Phelps and her placement on the 1996 Olympic Women's Gymnastics Team

Welcome to
Greenfield-Central High School

Greenfield, Indiana, USA

Indiana's Oldest Secondary School HomePage

The Home of Cougar Pride

Dear Friends,
I am proud to introduce you to Greenfield-Central High School, one of the best secondary schools in the state of Indiana. Within these walls our students and staff honestly care for one another, and they value and honor learning and achievement. Our students distinguish themselves at both the state and national levels in academic endeavors and artistic pursuits. We strive to educate the whole student, keeping traditional academic emphasis in the forefront.
This World Wide Web site illustrates and describes our truly wonderful school. It is an institution that brings pride and recognition to a great Hoosier community.
Philip M. Boley
Principal

(1a)(2a) *This broad and comprehensive home page is designed in two columns and uses small icons next to links to make it easier to understand and use.*

(1a) *The Areas to Explore section gives basic information about the school, as well as amazing Web resources.*

Areas to Explore:
CLICK HERE TO SEARCH THE ENTIRE CONTENTS OF OUR SERVER

Academics
GCHS is a school with an exceptional academic program. See what exciting things were doing to prepare our youth for the future.

Staff eMail Directory
Are you looking for a staff member at GCHS? Check here for all the details you need.

Corporation QuickGuide
School board, Superintendent, tax rates, and the school calendar are but a few of the tidbits of information you'll find in this area.

CougarNet SportsLink
Everything you ever wanted to know (and more, moRE, MORE) about our sports teams -- rosters, coaches, history, pictures, and updated scores from each event! This will also be our first "student published" area.

Internet SuperSearcher
This page was developed with you (the student) in mind. You will find a number of Internet World Wide Web search engines incorporated into an "easy-to-use" interface.

Greenfield, Indiana
Enjoy the "small town" atmosphere with "big city" resources. Were located within a 20 minute drive from Indianapolis. "Experience our Past...Share our Future!"

The G-C Journal Online
Find out whats happening in our school by visiting the G-C Journal Online: The GCHS Parent Newsletter. Current and archived editions are available.

Little Red School House
The May 6th, edition (and archived editions) of the Greenfield-Central Community School Corporation Parent Newsletter.

CougarNet
Information on the Internet can sometimes be a bit confusing. Let us help with a click in the right direction. Also visit other secondary schools and universities in Indiana.

G-C HEART Environmental
See what our students are doing to educate the school in the three R's; Reduce, Recycle, and Reuse. Also visit the Environmental Ed. Resource Web.

IABT HomePage
This Internet home of the Indiana Association of Biology Teachers provides membership information and upcoming events relevant to biology educators.

Alumni Center
Are there others like us out there? Reaching out to the final frontier for alumns -- stop in and drop us a note. Check out our snazzy new directory!-- *Updated 06/04/96*

What's New?
Whats cool? Whats the word? Whats happening? Whats New? A week-by-week account of high-points at GCHS. Details on the remodeling project are now online!-- *Updated 02/26/96*

Acceptable Use Policy
This is our Board approved policy for Acceptable Internet Resource Use in the Greenfield-Central Community Schools -- also includes the Student Account Application.

Our Favorite Links
The Links found on this page represent community ties, educational collaboration, and area information. Highly useful if you are visiting the Greenfield/Indianapolis area.

Partners in Education
A partnership between Eli Lilly and Company and GCHS was formed in 1984 with the objective to develop programs that would relate current class activities and projects with Lilly facilities and personnel. This homepage will display the excitement generated from this program.

Recognized as a "School of Excellence"
by the Indiana Department of Education

The best is the Internet (2b) *Super-Searcher, where you'll find the top nine search engines on one page! Here you can find anything.*

(1a) *A link at the top of the home page leads to Greenfield's Olympic Gymnast Jaycie's Olympic page.* (4c) *Webmaster used GIF images of parallel bars as a background for Jaycie's page. By clicking on the NBC icon, the browser can connect to NBC's Olympic Web site.* (4c)

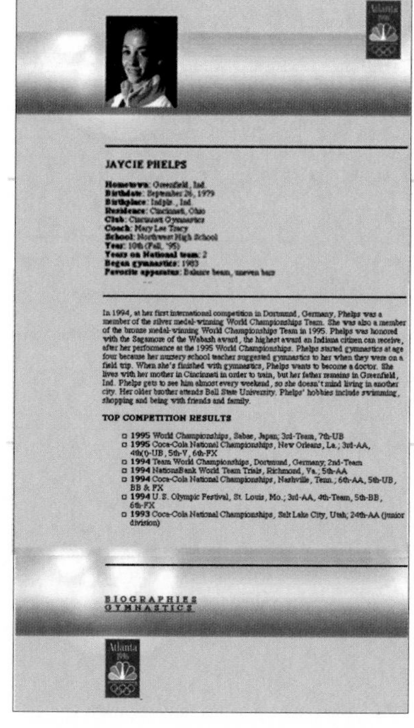

JAYCIE PHELPS

Hometown: Greenfield, Ind.
Birthdate: September 26, 1979
Birthplace: Indpls., Ind.
Residence: Cincinnati, Ohio
Club: Cincinnati Gymnastics
Coach: Mary Lee Tracy
School: Northwest High School
Year: 10th (Fall, '95)
Years on National team: 2
Began gymnastics: 1983
Favorite apparatus: Balance beam, uneven bars

In 1994, at her first international competition in Dortmund, Germany, Phelps was a member of the silver medal-winning World Championships Team. She was also a member of the bronze medal-winning World Championships Team in 1995. Phelps was honored with the Sagamore of the Wabash award, the highest award an Indiana citizen can receive, after her performance at the 1995 World Championships. Phelps started gymnastics at age four because her nursery school teacher suggested gymnastics to her when they were on a field trip. When she's finished with gymnastics, Phelps wants to become a doctor. She lives with her mother in Cincinnati in order to train, but her father remains in Greenfield, Ind. Phelps gets to see him almost every weekend, so she doesn't mind living in another city. Her older brother attends Ball State University. Phelps' hobbies include swimming, shopping and being with friends and family.

TOP COMPETITION RESULTS

- **1995** World Championships, Sabae, Japan; 3rd-Team, 7th-UB
- **1995** Coca-Cola National Championships, New Orleans, La.; 3rd-AA, 4th(t)-UB, 5th-V, 6th-FX
- **1994** Team World Championships, Dortmund, Germany; 2nd-Team
- **1994** NationsBank World Team Trials, Richmond, Va.; 5th-AA
- **1994** Coca-Cola National Championships, Nashville, Tenn.; 6th-AA, 5th-UB, BB & FX
- **1994** U.S. Olympic Festival, St. Louis, Mo.; 3rd-AA, 4th-Team, 5th-BB, 6th-FX
- **1993** Coca-Cola National Championships, Salt Lake City, Utah; 24th-AA (junior division)

BIOGRAPHIES
GYMNASTICS

(3b) *By clicking on the Greenfield, Indiana, button on the Areas to Explore page, the browser connects to the town page where they are invited to "Experience our past . . . share our future."* (5c) *The page includes a great informational graphic on the town (17k GIF image).*

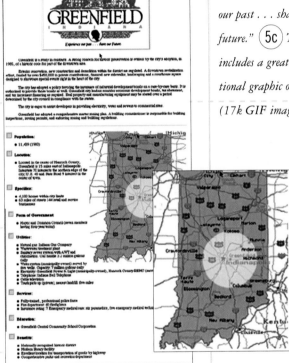

Greenfield Sister City Program

cougarnet
Greenfield-Central High School
Return to the GCHS HomePage

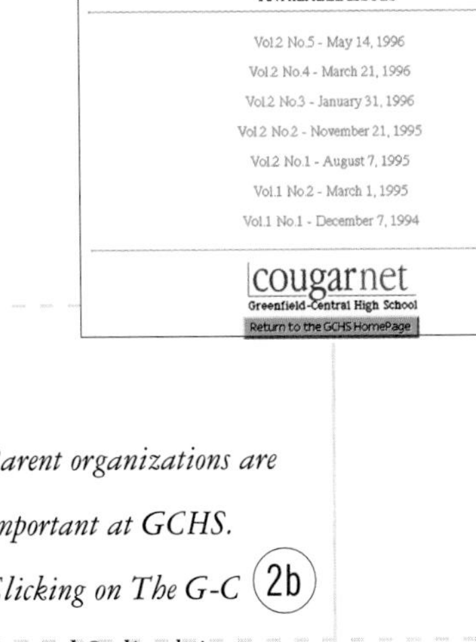

G-C JOURNAL Online

THE PARENT NEWSLETTER OF GREENFIELD- CENTRAL HIGH SCHOOL

The G-C Journal Online is a method for sharing information and good news about Greenfield-Central with parents and the Internet community. In the past, there have been newsletters from the guidance department, from the athletic department, and from the school administration, but this is the first attempt in a while to incorporate these three areas, and more, into one, innovative electronic newsletter.

By reading the G-C Journal Online, you'll learn about new programs, about classroom successes, about special events, and you will celebrate with us when someone or some group earns special recognition. You'll find out about the latest in curriculum innovations, get an updated schedule of happenings, and generally learn the latest scoop from GCHS.

We hope to publish a minimum of three issues of the G-C Journal Online each year. Let us know if you enjoy this area, especially if you have suggestions for making it better.

AVAILABLE ISSUES

Vol.2 No.5 - May 14, 1996
Vol.2 No.4 - March 21, 1996
Vol.2 No.3 - January 31, 1996
Vol.2 No.2 - November 21, 1995
Vol.2 No.1 - August 7, 1995
Vol.1 No.2 - March 1, 1995
Vol.1 No.1 - December 7, 1994

cougarnet
Greenfield-Central High School
Return to the GCHS HomePage

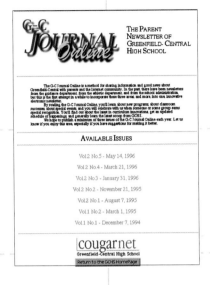

Parent organizations are important at GCHS. Clicking on The G-C (2b) *Journal Online brings up the school's newsletter for parents;* (7a) *complete current and archived editions are on-line.*

a b c d e

Special Features

Page 1

The students and staff at GCHS have worked hard to create the special feature of their site called CougarNet. This resourceful link features "Information Access for Students, Teachers, Administrators, and Parents." Included are buttons for Web links to such subjects as English, languages, business, technology, music, and special services, arranged with a combination of tables and standard lists.

cougarnet
Greenfield-Central High School

Information Access for Students, Teachers, Administrators, and Parents

Each of the buttons below will take you to World Wide Web links relating to the subject.

Looking for larger resources? Click here for our Internet SuperSearcher HomePage.

Administration	Art	Business
English	Languages	Guidance
HomeEc	PhysEd	Technology
Library	Math	Music
Science	Social Science	Special Services

Other Indiana Schools

Anderson Community Schools -- Anderson
Bartholomew Consolidated School Corp. -- Columbus
Bloomington High School North -- Bloomington
Bloomington High School South -- Bloomington
Brookview Elementary School -- Indianapolis
Emmerich Manual High School -- Indianapolis
City of Evansville Public Schools -- Evansville
Greenwood Middle School -- Indianapolis
Loogootee Community Schools -- Loogootee
Martinsville Schools -- Martinsville
Nobelesville Middle School -- Noblesville
North Knox High School -- Northern Knox County
Northwest High School -- Indianapolis
Riley High School -- South Bend
Scott Middle School -- Hammond
St. Joseph's High School -- South Bend
Swayzee Elementary School -- Swayzee
Tri-Central Elementary and Tri-Central Jr./Sr. High School -- Sharpsville
Valparaiso Community Schools -- Valparaiso

Return to the GCHS HomePage

"Our goal for the site was simple. We wanted it to be a model site for other schools in Indiana—with strong content."

— SCIENCE DEPARTMENT CHAIRPERSON JOHN RIHM

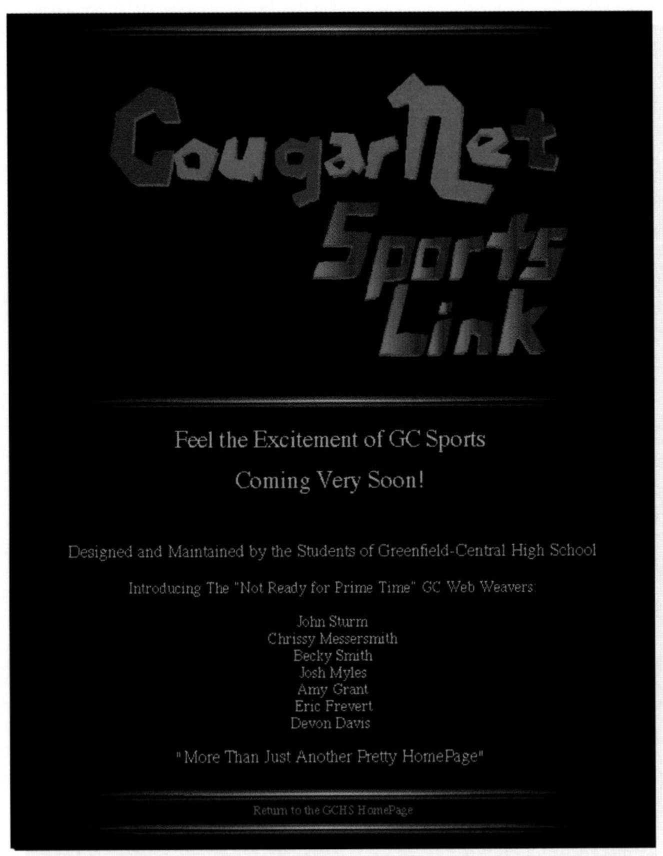

Page 2

There are big plans afoot for the future of the site. Following summer renovation work, there will be no fewer than seven computer labs. Don Gilroy says, "A group of students have been meeting 'virtually' over the Internet using e-mail and are ready to begin creating new pages for CougarNet." Student Webmaster Chrissy Messersmith is leading the group, organizing assignments for a new area called CougarNet SportsLink, which will be the first feature of the site.

Creating an Image Map in PageMill

You can add multiple links to an image by creating an image map. To create an image map, you draw hot spots on the image and then add links to the hot spots. When you save the image and change to Preview mode, you can click the hot spots to see the linked pages. Before you create your image map, you must let Adobe PageMill know which type of server you're using.

Specifying type and location of server

1 **Choose the Preferences** command from the Edit menu.

2 **Choose a server type**— either CERN or NCSA—from the Map Format pop-up.

3 **If you're editing your file** on one machine but will upload your site to a remote Web server machine, click the Remote Server check box. (If you're editing directly on the same machine that is serving the pages to the network, make sure this check box is not checked.)

4 **If you clicked the Remote Server** box, you must specify the Local Root folder by clicking the folder icon; use the standard file dialog box to select the topmost folder containing your site. Enter the Server Root Directory, specifying the path to the directory where your site resides on the server.

Drawing the hot spots

1 **Double-click the image** to open (or choose the Open command from the File menu to open an image on your hard drive.)

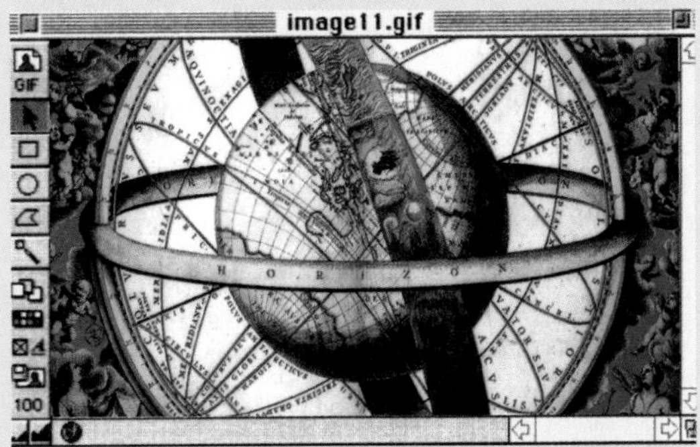

2 **Select a hot-spot shape tool** and draw a shape on the image. Drawing hot-spot shapes (rectangles, circles, polygons) in PageMill works the same as in any simple graphics program. After you draw a shape you can select it, move it, or reshape it by using the arrow tool. PageMill numbers each hot spot as you draw it, with lower-numbered hot spots in front.

Adding links to hot spots

1 **Drag a page icon,** an image icon, or an anchor onto a hot spot. Or

2 **Type the link address** into the Link Location Bar at the bottom of the image view. Click to the right of the globe icon and type a URL address; press the Return (or Enter) key.

When all your hot spots and links are in place, save the image and close the image view. Let PageMill know the image is a map. You will also need to tell the server the image-map location. Then upload the image map to test it.

http://www.louisville.edu/groups/camden-www/index.html

Camden Station Elementary School

Oldham County School District, Crestwood, Kentucky

"We take on projects that are new and exciting, that we don't know much about. We jump in and learn together; everybody helps out and participates."

— Sue McHargue, Library Media Specialist

There's plenty of excitement in the air surrounding the Web site at Camden Station School. Almost all of the kids participate, from writing text, to creating GIF and JPEG files, to helping add new pages. The students' art and literature takes center stage on this site, which features a magazine, a gallery, and special illustrated "book" projects. It's a site that's colorful and fun—one that has "kids" written (and drawn) all over it.

"My Dad likes me using the computer because he wants to get the Internet at home, and he doesn't know how to use it right now. So I'm going to teach him."
—JUSTIN, 5TH GRADE

Camden Station Elementary is a public school in Crestwood, Kentucky, right outside Louisville. It serves 494 students, in grades K–5.

Sue McHargue with students who helped set up the site.

This site was developed by parent Michele Petry, along with the school's Library Media Specialist, Sue McHargue. Although the adults initially programmed the site, the creative ideas and the materials all come from the students' classrooms. The kids are especially enchanted with e-mail and have used it to "talk" to people from all over the world.

Megan logs on the site to see the day's new pages.

1 2 3 4

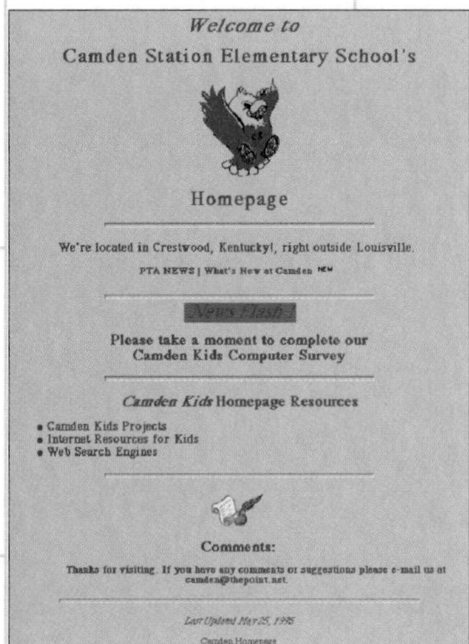

Welcome to
Camden Station Elementary School's
Homepage
We're located in Crestwood, Kentucky!, right outside Louisville.
PTA NEWS | What's New at Camden NEW
News Flash
Please take a moment to complete our Camden Kids Computer Survey
Camden Kids Homepage Resources
Camden Kids Projects
Internet Resources for Kids
Web Search Engines
Comments:
Thanks for visiting. If you have any comments or suggestions please e-mail us at camden@thepoint.net.
Camden Homepage

(1a) *Camden Station School's home page is simple and to the point. A solid background creates a colorful, clean design. It features links to Internet Resources for Kids and Web Search Engines. It also* (1b) *links to the variety of* (2a) *student projects.*

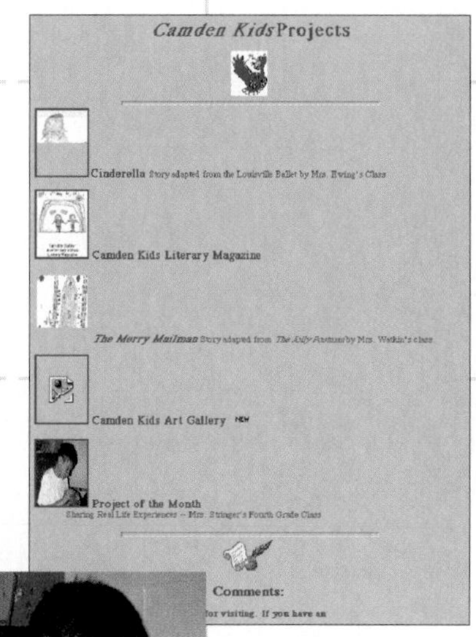

(2b) *The student Projects page features links to the Project of the Month and a new version of Cinderella.* (2c)

Camden Kids Literary Magazine

Camden Station Elementary School Literary Magazine

Meet the Staff of the Literary Magazine

Table of Contents

The Sea Animals *by Allison K., Lindsey P. and Maggie M.*	Silky Sue Bob *by Andrew N.*
Delicate Snowflake *by Bobby S.*(140k)	The Mystery of the Missing Dog *by Robbie M.*
The Tuxedo Bird *by Dustin M.*	The Big Snow *by Philip B.*
A Fairy Tale That I Made Up For You *by Jolene B.*	Keepers *by Mr. B., Camden Station Art Teacher*
Three Poems *by Alayna W.*	Snowman and Igloo *by Dave D.*
Under the Sea *by Lauren B.*	Olympics *by Jackie T.*
Snow Play *by Casey P.*	Right Before Dinner *by Shana B.*
Kids Rule Kids!! *by Lauren J.*	I Need a Hug *by Elizabeth G.*
My Brother Built A Robot *by Taylor M.*	Little Brother and Little Sister *by Mark L.*
Drivin' Miss Cassie *by Cassie and Betty S.*	Horses - a Fantasy *by Shannon P.*
The Magic Rabbit *by Jolene B.*	A Story About Fairies *by Katy and Robert F.*
The Lost Girl *by Jolene B.*	The Dog in The Box *by Allison K.*
The Frog Prince *by Mark L.*	Autumn *by Mary F.*
Autumn *by Allison B.*	Two Poems *by Andrew N.*
Poems *by Anne-Catherine H.*	Barney *by Garret W.*
Things That Make Me Smile *by Monique S.*	My Shoes *by Danielle B.*
How I'd Make A Gingerbread Cake *by Katy F.*	Remember November *by Mary F.*

(2a) *The Kids Projects list links to an ongoing Kids project the students are especially proud of, the Camden Kids Literary Magazine. The Table* (4b) *of Contents directs readers to individual stories and poems.*

5 6 7 8

a b c d e

(2a) *Clicking on one Kids Project brings up* The Merry Mailman, (5b) *a highly creative takeoff on the beloved children's book,* The Jolly Postman. *Buttons gives visitors two options—to read the story on Netscape 1.1 or to click on the map through "Fairy Tale Land."*

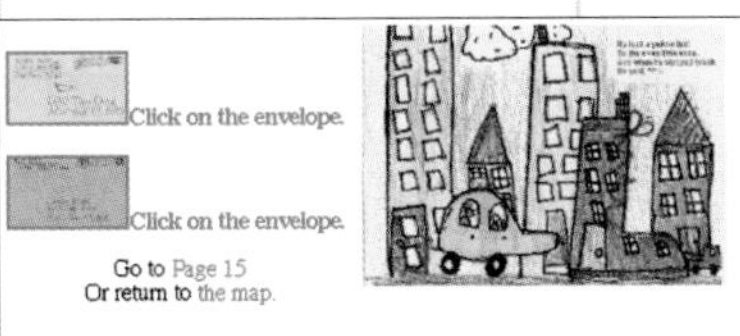

(5c) *Click on the map, and you're off on a cleverly designed trip to various mini-locations, such as this cityscape; click on the envelope and you open a "letter" from the Shoemaker to the Elves.* (6b)

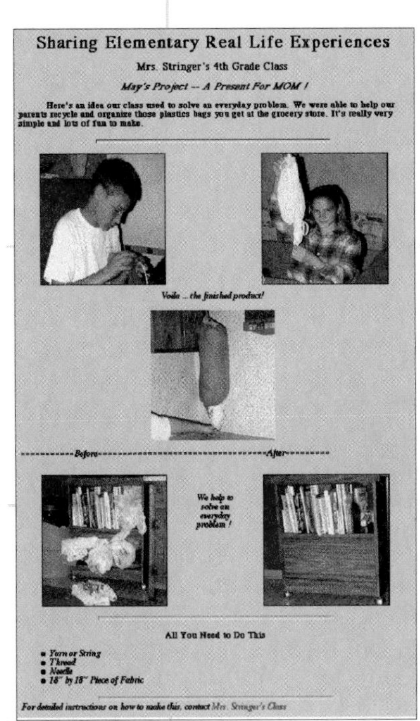

Another button on the Kids Projects page (2a) *links to Sharing Elementary Real Life Experiences.* (8a) *Mrs. Stringer's 4th grade class demonstrates a Mother's Day project, complete with GIF images. The class can be contacted through e-mail for how-to instructions.* (8c)

"With the Internet we communicate with people all over the world. Every time we talk to somebody new we get more information. It makes the world seem a little smaller." — DUSTIN, 5TH GRADE

Special Features

Using e-mail to send and receive messages is one of the kids' favorite parts of being on the Web. After they put up this page—Camden Kids Computer Survey—they they got responses from places as far-flung as South Africa, England, and Australia. Fifth-grader Tanner says, "We talked to people from Anchorage, Alaska—they wanted to know about Kentucky." And Justin, also in 5th grade, says, "It's fun because when you have e-mail, you don't have to wait to send stuff. We exchanged information with a guy in Oldham, England—he was a newspaper editor and he saw our school, in Oldham County, Kentucky, on the computer."

Camden Kids Computer Survey

Hi, we're students in Mr. McMannis's (Intermediate), Mrs. Stringer's (Intermediate) and Ms. Ewing's (Primary) class and we've teamed up to conduct a survey, using the internet. We'd like to know how many computers your school has and how many are connected to the internet. We will collect all the data and analyze the results. We will then write a report and make it available on our school page. We also plan on presenting the results of this survey to our PTA and Educational Foundation as part of a larger request for additional funding for more computers in our classrooms.

Thank you for taking the time to complete the survey.

Your Email Address:

1. Please fill out these fields:

Your School Name:

Number of Students in your school:

City:

State:

Country:

Type of school: Elementary School

Number of Computers at your school:

Number of Computers that are connected to the INTERNET:

Please tell us how computers have helped kids learn at your school:

Tell us a little about your class:

2. Click this button to erase all and start over if you want to.
   Erase All

3. Click this button to send your comments to Camden Kids' Computer Survey
   Camden Kids' Computer Survey

Back to Camden Station Elementary School Homepage

Setting up e-Mail

One of the easiest but most rewarding things you can set up as part of your Web site is a format for receiving e-mail. Netscape browser supports this mailto function; if you have another browser, check to see if it will support mailto. The mailto tag acts like an anchor, like standard links to other documents. To create a mailto link, follow these simple steps:

1 **Type in these words:** Send comments to <A HREF = mailto: "your address" TITLE = "Subject of message"< / A>

2 **When a mailto-capable browser** sees the mailto tag, it will create a separate e-mail form that the user can fill out. This will be sent automatically to the e-mail address specified in the link.

3 **Adding Title =** "Subject of message" will result in the Subject of message being inserted into the subject line of the e-mail editor.

http://www.halcyon.com/arborhts/arborhts.html

Arbor Heights Elementary

Seattle Public School District
Seattle, Washington

"Creating a Web site isn't so hard to do. It's something that doesn't take a lot of money—it just takes interest and time, and a good reason to do it. There couldn't be a better reason than education."

— MARK AHLNESS, 3RD GRADE TEACHER

The brainchild of one dedicated person—3rd grade teacher Mark Ahlness—this site proves that wishes do come true (if you work hard enough to help them along). Ahlness got the idea to put up a Web site after working on the Earth Day Groceries Project; he wanted to "be there" on the Web and use it to present worthwhile projects. He says, "We put it up as a long shot, realizing that we wouldn't have any funding. We didn't have a lot of money for technology at our school…but it worked."

This public school is in an urban neighborhood of West Seattle, Washington, where it serves 415 students in grades K–5.

The site features event reporting, such as the annual Young Authors Conference, where every student publishes their own book. Here author Arthur Dorros displays one book's artwork.

Sure enough, along came a fairy godmother in the form of corporate funding, given as a result of the appealing and creative site Ahlness had put together. Now the school has a computer lab, access to the Web—everything they want. "It was a miracle," says Ahlness.

The school logo was traditionally photographed, scanned in, and posted on the site.

(1a) *This home page is refreshingly different, with lots of icons and very little text. It's interesting and very easy to use, all arranged in tables. The page offers lots of choices, from the school newspaper to links for local city news and weather.* (1b)

(1b) *One unique link leads to the Room 12 Top Ten List. This lists the* (2b) *current favorite Web sites chosen by Mark Ahlness's 3rd graders, including movie and book sites, and other great picks.*

(1b) *One great link leads to the Cool Writers' Magazine.* (4c) *Supervised by teacher Gretchen Thompson, this online magazine has an open, friendly attitude. This page says, "If your school has pages with cool writing, let us know—we'll add a link."*

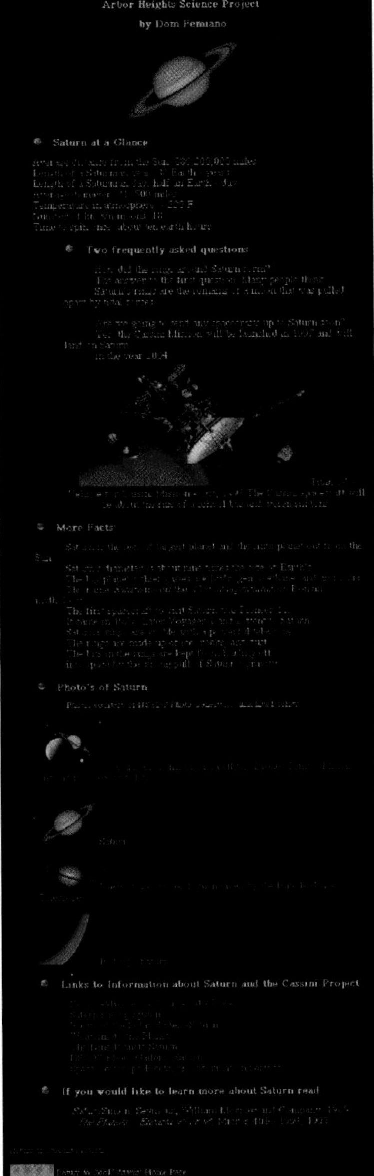

(1a) A home page link leads to this student science project, Uncover the Mystery of Saturn. It combines striking GIF files and a dramatic all-black (5a) background. The page offers useful links to more information, both in print and on the Web.

Another home page link (1b) goes to another student project, Maya's Sea Turtle Page. This is a 3rd grader's (8a) personal page; the appealing art (18k GIF) is done with Kid Pix.

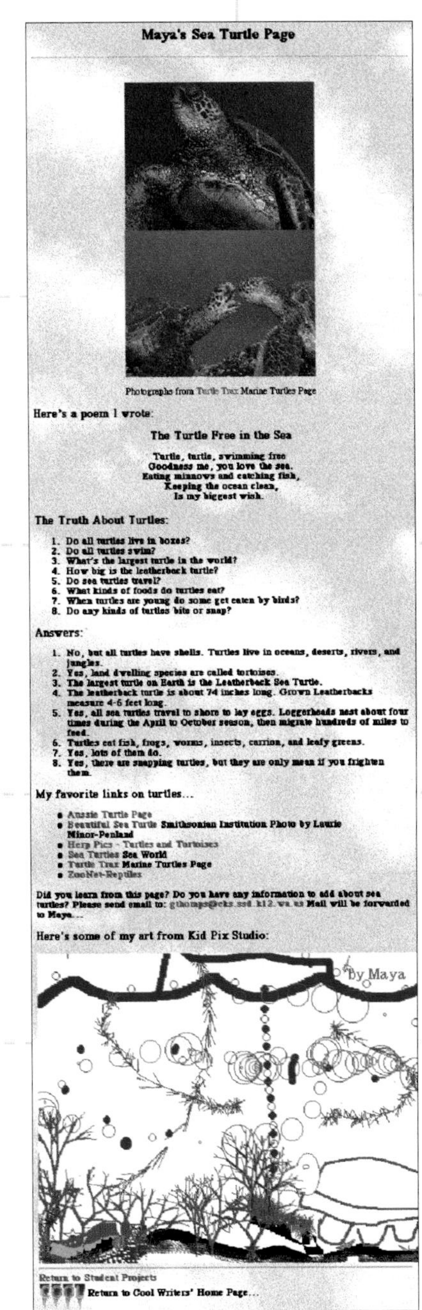

a

b

c

d

e

Arbor Heights Elementary Site Map

Be sure to save GIF files as transparent when placing on colored or textured backgrounds.

Special Features

The Earth Day Groceries Project Page is the one that started it all for this site. This project brings together many schools through the Web—students decorate paper grocery bags and pass them out at local supermarkets to promote environmental awareness on Earth Day. Everything gets reported on the site. This page features a clickable image map showing the locations of schools that have participated in the project.

Saving Adobe Illustrator Art for the Web

You can use Adobe Illustrator art on the Web when you save it as a GIF or JPEG. You'll need Adobe Illustrator 6 or later, and the free GIF plug-in mentioned on page 53. Here's how:

1 **Resize your artwork** to the actual size you want it to appear on the Web.

2 **For a GIF, Choose File>Save As.** Select the GIF89a option from the pop-up Format menu. Enter the file name and click Save.

For a JPEG, Choose File>Save As. Simply select the JPEG option. Enter the file name and click Save.

3 **If you saved as a GIF,** you'll be asked to select the GIF89a option. Specify your Row Order and Palette options. Choose Palette>Other to save your artwork with a custom RGB palette. Choose Transparent, to make all "paper" colored areas of the artwork transparent. Choose Anti-alias to smooth the edges of the artwork.

If you saved as a JPEG, you'll be asked to pick Image Quality. For most images, Good produces the best trade-off between quality and file size. However, sometimes Fair quality is all you need—be sure to experiment.

Kids do the Web

More than any other pages on the World Wide Web, school sites abroad show us a huge global community. Here we get a glimpse into countries and cultures that are a lot different from our own. Yet, as each site shows, kids in Italy or Japan aren't so different from you and your friends. Who knows—you may see something here that will inspire a new friendship or cooperative project with someone half a world away!

International Sites

http://hale.ssd.k12.wa.us/shinji.www/home.html

Akatsukayama High School

Kobe, Japan

Akatsukayama Guestbook

"As you read in our Guest Book, people from all over are enjoying what we do here. I am happy visitors can feel the atmosphere of a real Japanese high school."

— Shinji Masui, Webmaster

There's plenty of excitement on the AHS home page! As soon as the screen appears, the school logo flashes red, a ticker barks out highlights of the site, and a "What's New" button glows! The first two are animated GIFs, which are small enough (26k) to speed along; the third is a blink command. The page also contains 10 links to stories about the students, the school, and the earthquake of 1995.

Use Adobe PhotoDeluxe to create anti-alias text for banners, headlines, and any area that demands dramatic effect.

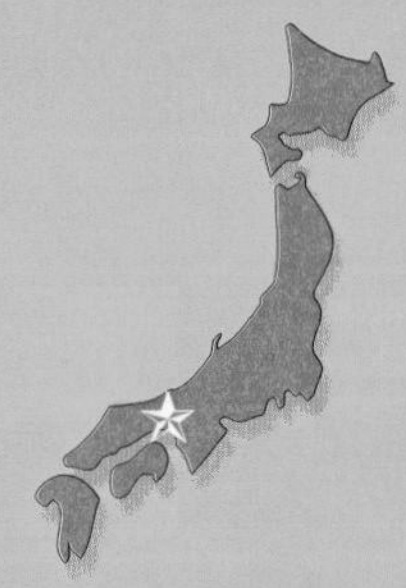

Kobe is a big, bustling port city located in the Kansai area of Japan. Since the devastating Hanshin-Awaji earthquake of 1995, the city has been furiously rebuilding.

The Akatsukayama campus in central Kobe.

This is a big, sophisticated Web site, with lots of "places" to go. Best of all, it accomplishes one of the goals set out by Webmaster Shinji Masui—"To tell people all over the world what Japan and Japanese life is really about." Many of the links lead to fascinating features that are uniquely Japanese: tours of the city, stories on what it's like to live in Japan, and lessons on reading Japanese calligraphy.

The devasting earthquake that hit the city of Kobe in January of 1995 has shaped much of the material and the way it's presented on this site. The students show how they have bounced back, with photos and stories on the rebuilding of the city and an archive of letters sent to the United Nations.

Students in the Akatsukayama Technology Class.

1 2 3 4

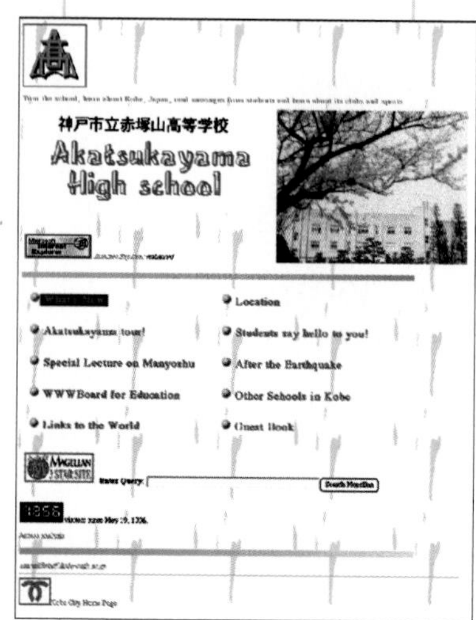

The home page incorporates great technology: animated GIFs, a running "barker" of text, and blinking text. While there's a lot going on, the design is simple and clear.

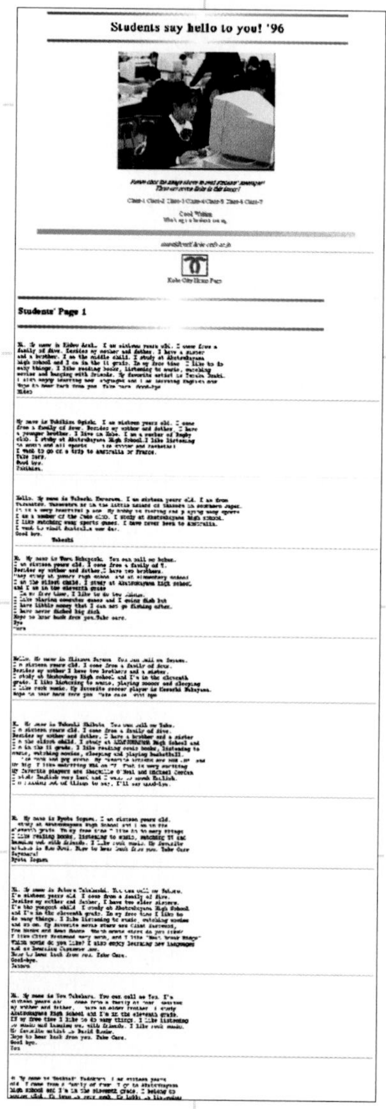

1a *Clicking on Students Say Hello to You! '96* 2b *really shows how everyone in the school got involved in the site. Clicking on the image takes you to these messages: each and every student has written a brief biography and friendly* 1a *greeting. The home page link for Akatsukayama Tour takes you to a page with a large photo that changes every* 4d *few seconds (animated GIF file). Rather than buttons for links, it shows four doors— each one opening onto a separate page.*

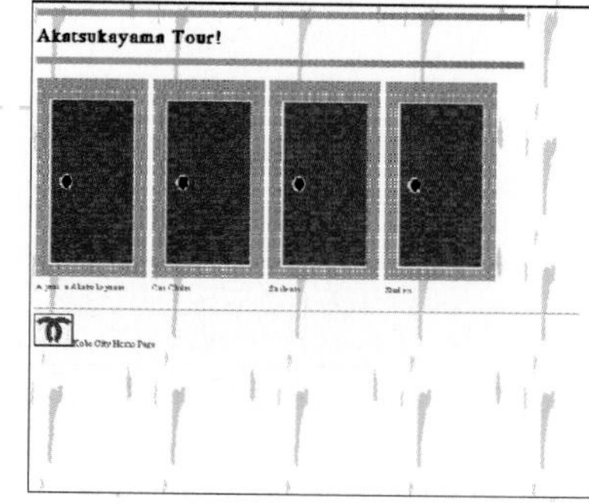

web tip **PageMill allows you to spec type to create attention-getting "blinking" type.**

1a *Another home page link that celebrates traditional culture is Special Lecture on Manyoshu. Manyoshu, the page explains, is the oldest collection of Japanese* 5d *poems— 4,500 in all— completed in A.D. 770 It also shows you how to read the Japanese characters.*

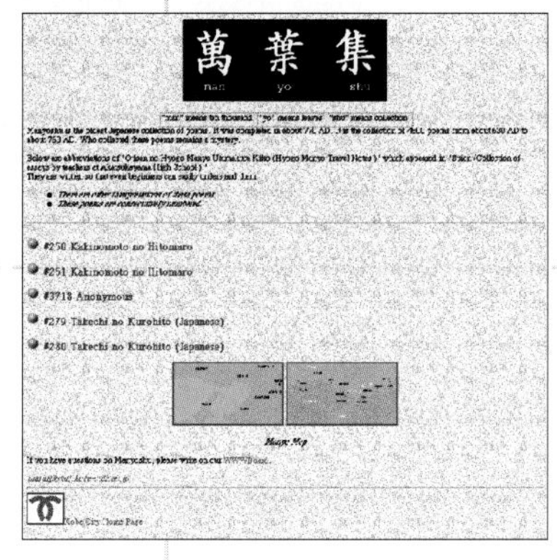

1a *The home page also links to the Akatsukayama* 7a *Guestbook. The book showcases a wealth of enthusiastic mail from all over the world— much of it from the United States. Visitors range from school children and teachers to adults who have visited Japan. And there's one letter from a student right in Kobe: "I enjoyed your page. I love it. I want to enter your school if I can..."*

Akatsukayama Guestbook

Thank you for visiting our pages. We would love it if you would Add to this guestbook we are keeping!

I'm just browsing through educational materials and resources to add to a world cultures curriculum. Scott Hall
Scott Hall <shall@wheat.mnsfld.edu>
pa usa - Wednesday, July 17, 1996 at 17:52:04 (EDT)

An excellent Home Page. Did the students do all of the developement? How long have you had your Home Page active?
Mike Nolan <mnolan4@dubuque.net>
Dubuque, IA USA - Tuesday, July 16, 1996 at 14:48:55 (EDT)

It looks like your school is a lot of fun to me, I'am 8 years old.
Jamee Ribelin <ribelinm@lps.k12.co.us>
Littleton, co USA - Tuesday, July 02, 1996 at 13:22:51 (EDT)

This was a fantastic home page, and I will point my students your direction. Congratulations on a job well done, and good luck learning English! You are doing well!
Heather Siler-Dobbs <steheadb@gate.net>
Okeechobee, FL USA - Friday, June 28, 1996 at 17:14:29 (EDT)

I was searching the net for information about Japanese education for a report for school. I think that it is neat to have a home page all about your school. I found a great deal of information for my report, plus it was interesting to see what your school is like. :>
Jennifer Spencer <ay457@yfn.ysu.edu>
Boardman, OH United States - Friday, June 28, 1996 at 11:53:41 (EDT)

I'm a senior at Babson College and just finished my second year studying Japanese. I was browsing the net and happened upon your school's homepage. I think the page is a great idea! I enjoyed reading the students' profiles and learning about Akatsukayama H.S.
Peter-Jon Kelley <Peter-Jon Kelley@StudentK@Babson>
Wellesley, MA US - Friday, June 21, 1996 at 15:13:13 (EDT)

I'm a student at the Massachusetts Institute of Technology and just happened to come across your web page while trying to avoid homework. Good work to all of you. I hope you are having fun working on the World Wide Web and improving your English at the same time.
Lee Yang <atlantis@mit.edu>
Cambridge, MA USA - Wednesday, June 12, 1996 at 01:36:42 (EDT)

Special Features

Page 1

Students at Akatsukayama High School were profoundly affected by the terrible 1995 Kobe earthquake. From the home page, this link to After the Earthquake features photos of volunteers supplying food to refugees, as well as shots taken after school resumed. Part of the process of dealing with the quake was communicating about it with others outside the area via e-mail. Pictures here show students having " a chat using the Web to talk with the students of Nathan Hale High School in Seattle, Washington, about the disaster."

Earthquake hit our city

January 17th 1995, a severe earthquake hit our city. Over 100 people were staying here. Now things are getting normal one year after the Earthquake. These pictures show volunteers supplying food to refugees.

Eyewitness of this earthquake

Messages sent to United Nations Voices of Youth

Voices of Youth World Summit for Social Development

Akatsukayama in News Paper --- Yomiuri Shinbun

Pictures taken just after club activities are allowed.

A year in Akatsukayama

School year begins in April. You can see beautiful sakura then.

We have a culture festival in June.

In October, we have a field day .

11th graders go on a skiing tour in January.

In Winter, we meet at the River Muko and run along the river about 10km.

School year ends in March. This picture is a scene of graduation ceremony.

This is Japanese traditional lunch called "Osekihan" we eat after such ceremonies.

Page 2

The students' hopefulness and resilience show in this page from the site tour called "A year in Akatsukayama." This page profiles the 1995 Culture Festival (a 27-year-old tradition), held just 5 months after the earthquake. The student organizers' aim for the festival was "to forget about the earthquake for just one day and enjoy ourselves." The site allowed the entire community to learn about the festival.

Akatsukayama High School

Designing Web Type

Standard HTML Web type defaults to the user's preferences, usually Times, Helvetica, or Geneva. But you have the ability to make your site look better by creating custom type for headlines, links, or special sections. It's best to create the type in Illustrator, Photoshop, or PhotoDeluxe; save as GIF or JPEG; and import into your document as image files.

1 To design custom type for the Web, you should follow some basic rules of typography. The most important thing is that your page be easy to read. Here's how to make sure it is.

2 There are two kinds of type: serif and sans serif. Serif type has small points at the tops and bottoms of the letters. San Serif is completely smooth.

Adobe Garamond (serif) and Franklin Gothic (sans serif).

3 Serif type, like Garamond or Times, is usually used in text sections, where you have a lot to read. For the Web, it should be used in at least 10 point, and it shouldn't be used in caps if there's a lot to read. When this type is used in headlines it gives the page a classic, literary look.

4 **Sans Serif type, like Helvetica** or Franklin Gothic, can be used in headlines for a bold, newsy look. Be careful using it smaller, though. Bold versions of these fonts are hard to read in small sizes. Some, like regular Helvetica or Futura, are fine for text, and give the page a more modern look than the serif typefaces. Again, make sure the type is large enough to be easy to read.

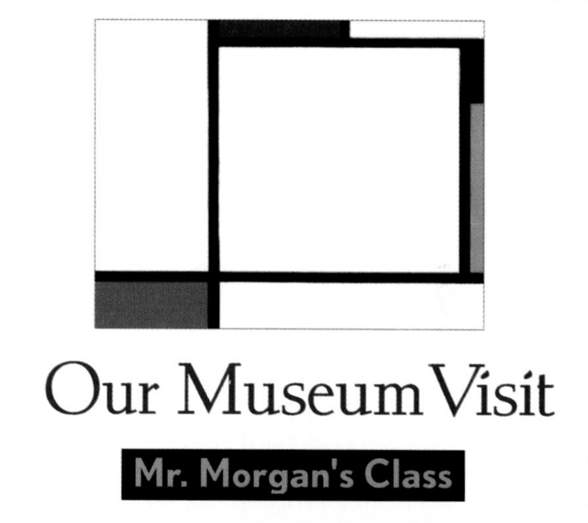

5 **You can mix serif** and sans serif faces; often it makes the page more exciting. Often a headline in serif is offset nicely by a subhead in sans serif—or vice versa. (See right.) Be wary of cluttering up a page with too many different typefaces, though—it's a sure sign of an amateur. One or two faces are usually enough for any page. Some samples of Adobe fonts that "mix" well: Baskerville, Garamond, Bodoni, Caslon, Goudy, Minion (serifs); Myriad, Franklin Gothic, Futura, Gill Sans, Giddyup (sans serifs).

6 **Finally, it is important** to maintain typographic consistency throughout your site. If there are certain areas you want to highlight, use a different type—but keep the majority of the pages looking similar. This helps viewers know where they are.

http://www.goldnet.it/scuola2giugno/eindex.htm

Primary School "2 Giugno"

Vicenza, Italy

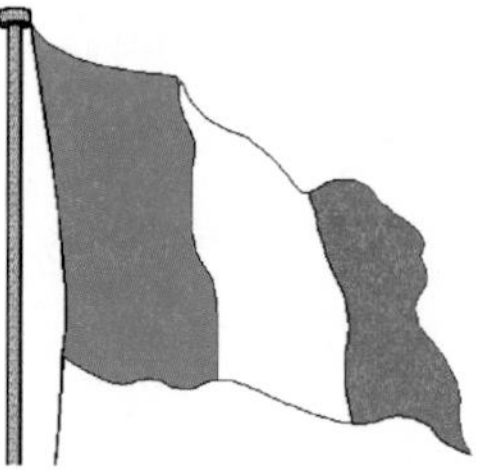

The e-mail page has become the most popular part of the 2 Giugno site. Alumni and students from around the world write regularly.

This small elementary-level school has 100 students, ages 6 to 11. Currently their small but charming site focuses on the childrens' art work from a recent exhibition. The site's interactive aspect—an invitation to visitors to chat, via e-mail, with the young artists—has been extremely popular. Especially since all the pages are published in both English and Italian versions.

Include clickable, thumbnail versions of large graphics for quick browsing.

Students from the Second Class: Damiano Calabro, Lucrezia Carlassara, Giorgio Catania, Martin Citarella, Sharon Di Carlo, Melania Disfatti, Elisa Maiorana, Cristian Nastas, Guilia Ongaro, Amedeo Polazzo, Anna Chiara Rigotto, Isabella Therani, and Maria Zanini.

"The City of Gold" is located in the Vicenza province of Italy, west of the city of Venice. It is home to 15th-century Palladio palaces as well as a sprouting of new, modern businesses.

An illustrated history of Vicenza is part of the site.

Primary School "2 Guigno"

1 2 3 4

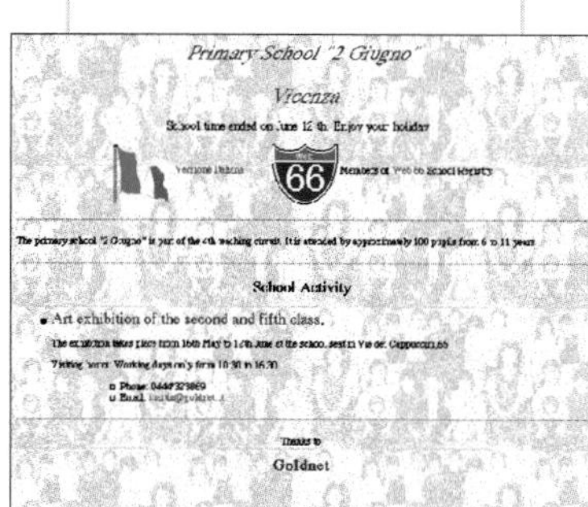

1a *A simple home page offers a link to both Italian and English-language versions of the site. The background is composed of speedy 2k GIF files. The home page announces the summertime offering: an art exhibition of works by the second and fifth classes.*

La storia di Vicenza.

Importante città capoluogo di provincia del Veneto, ricca di bellezze naturali e artistiche, sorta alle pendici settentrionali dei monti Berici sulle sponde del fiume Bacchiglione. La fondazione di Vicenza risale all'età preistorica, quando a stabilirsi in questo territorio, tra l'XI e il VII secolo a.C., furono gli Euganei. Nulla si conosce sulla provenienza di questo popolo, sopraffatto poi dall'immigrazione dei Veneti, venuti dall'Illiria. I Veneti furono i promi ad accettare l'alleanza con Romani. Nel 49 a.C. Giulio Cesare con la "Lex Julia" concedeva a Vicenza, l'allora Vicetia, la cittadinanza romana e la costituzione municipale, aggregandola alla Tribù Menenia. Il fastoso tetro di Bergia, l'acquedotto di Lobia, i mosaici, il cripto-portico scoperto durante gli scavi nella canonica del Duomo, costituiscono, assieme ad altri resti archeologici, la testimonianza della floridezza della Vicenza romana e del suo "territorium". Nel Medioevo Vicenza subì saccheggi e distruzioni a opera dei barbari di Alarico e di Attila e, dopo un perido abbastanza florido con i Goti, passò sotto la dominazione dei Longobardi (568-774) estendendo, dopo la distruzione di Padova, il territorio della sua influenza fino alle porte di quest'ultima. La città dopo la disgregazione dell'impero carolingio, passò, come molte altre città dell'Italia settentrionale, sotto gli Ottoni di Sassonia che la concessero in feudo ai vescovi-conti, per lo più ghibellini. Essa però, appena potè raggiungere una certa Barbarossa a Legnano (1176) divamparono le contese con i Comuni vicini e fra le varie fazioni. Prevalsero i ghibellini e, in particolare, gli Ezzelini che, con l'aiuto di Federico II che nel 1236 aveva devastato la città, se ne impadronirono tenendola soggiogata fino al 1259. Nel 1266 Vicenza strinse un "patto di custodia" con Padova, alla quale, in pratica, si sottomise. Conquistata da Cangrande della Scala nel 1311, rimase agli Scaligeri fino al 1387, passando poi con Verona ai Visconti, cui seguì il dominio veneziano (1404-1797) sotto il quale godette di quattro secoli di pace e di relativa prosperità. La vita rinascimentale vicentina conobbe nei secoli XV e XVI un periodo di grande splendore artistico ed economico con artisti del calibro del Palladio e di Giangiorgio Trissino. L'Accademia Olimpica con il famoso teatro Olimpico é ancora oggi il punto di incontro di grandiose manifestazioni culturali ed artistiche. Ad interrompere il lungo periodo di pace spravvennero i noti fatti di Francia che sconvolsero tutta l'Europa tra la fine del XVIII e l'inizio del XIX secolo. Il 12 aprile 1797, decaduto il dominio veneziano e proclamata la municipalità provvisoria, Vicenza, che dopo la caduta di Napoleone (1814) era passata agli Austriaci, entrò a far parte del regno Lombardo-Veneto. La città prese poi parte attiva al Risorgimento, opponendosi alle repressioni austriache. Le gloriose giornate del 1848 le meritarono la medaglia d'oro ma non furono coronate dal successo. Solamente il 18 novembre 1866 Vicenza si riuniva al Regno d'Italia, momentoi focale che vide un gran fermento culturale anche tra i vicentini: basti ricordare i nomi di Giacomo Zanella, Fedele Lampertico, Antonio Fogazzaro, Alessandro Rossi e Paolo Lioy.

Ritorna alla Goldnet Home Page

1a *Clicking on Vicenza leads to a description of the city peppered with colorful, small images of the* 2b *city. The images add a lot to the page, but are small enough (2k each) that they don't slow the reader down.*

1a *Another home page link leads to an Art Exhibition Page. The paintings are neatly organized by category:*

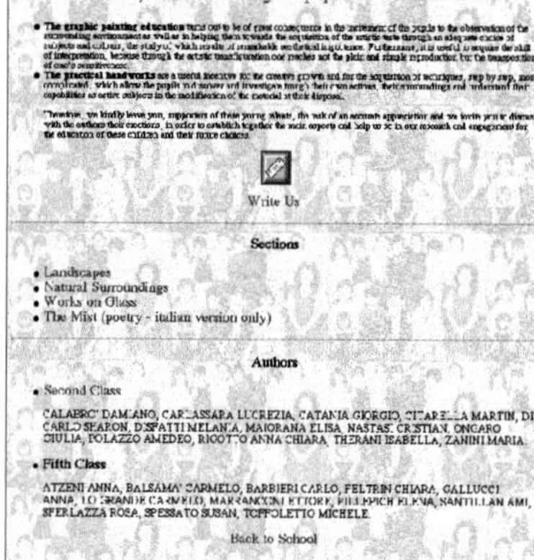

Landscapes, Natural Surroundings, Works on Glass, or The Mist (Italian poetry). 4d

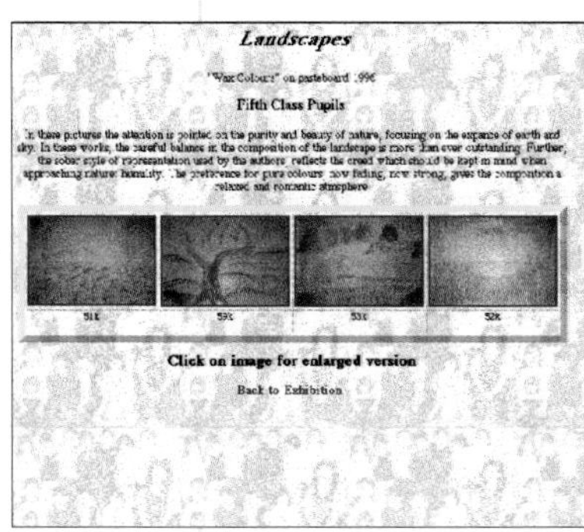

1a *The link to the Landscapes page takes you to pictures by the fifth class. The clever design shows small (8k) "thumbnails,"* 5b *which can be clicked on to reveal beautiful, large (55k) images. This allows the browser to preview the images and not be slowed down by rebuilding.*

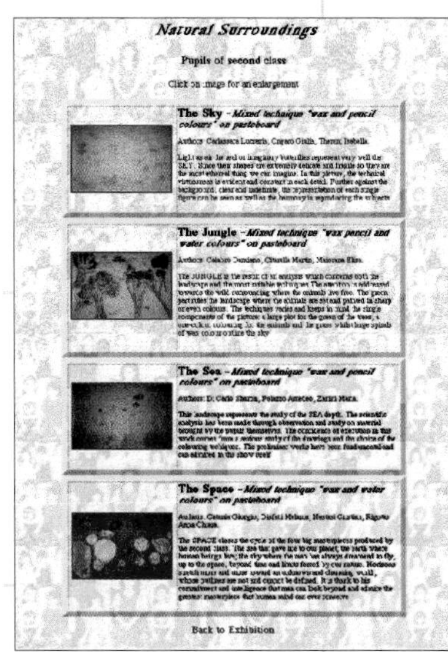

1a *There's also a link to the students of the second grade, who did the pictures in this gallery, called* 6a *Natural Surroundings. Each picture—The Sky, The Jungle, The Sea, and The Space—was done as a collaborative effort in "wax colors on pasteboard," then scanned directly into Adobe Photoshop.*

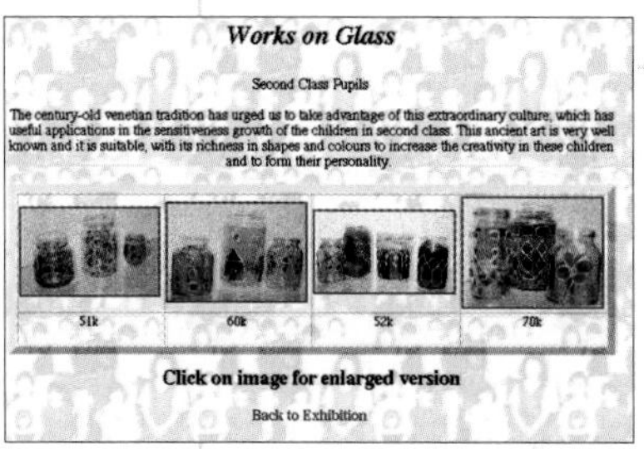

1a *Another link takes you to a centuries-old Venetian tradition.* 8b *The children of the second class have created works on glass as part of the exhibition. These are also displayed in the "thumbnail" style. The art was traditionally photographed; the prints were scanned in digitally.*

a b c d e

Primary School "2 Guigno" Site Map

Special Feature

Page 1

The entire Giugno site is presented both in English and Italian, including a special section on the history of Vicenza. The section includes this beautifully drawn map, created in Adobe Photoshop, saved and compressed as a 30k GIF file.

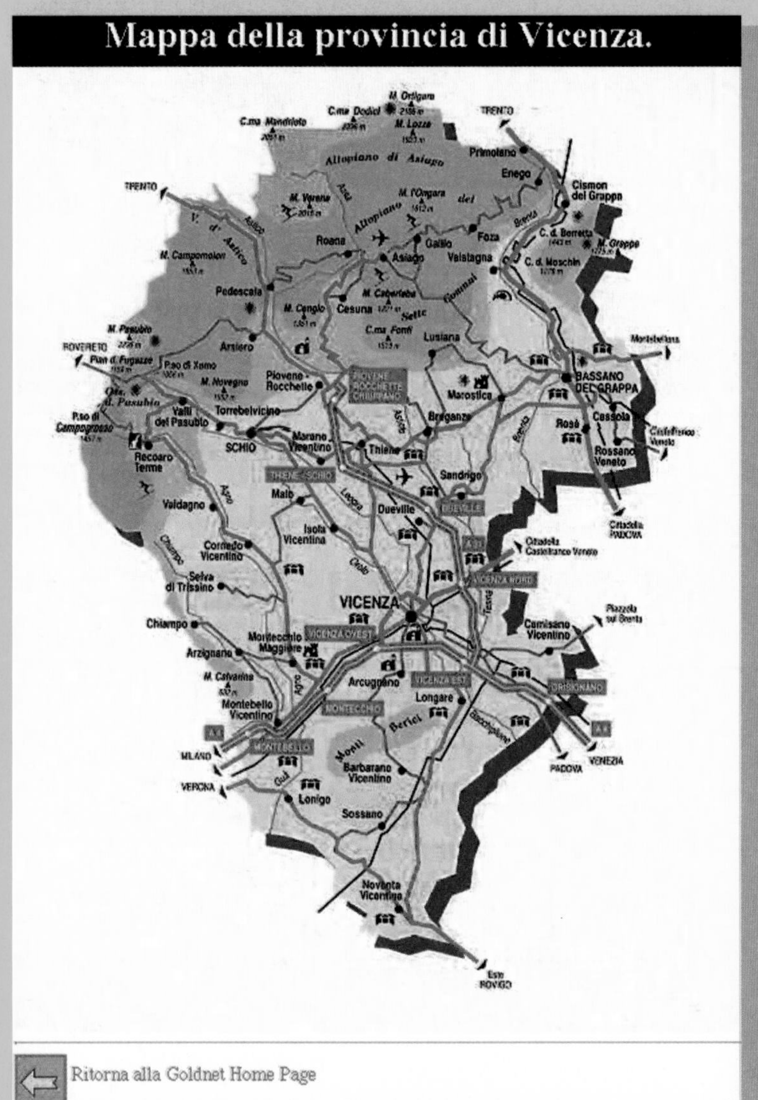

Creating JPEGs in Photoshop

Many Web browsers display images in Joint Photographics Expert Group (JPEG) format. It's the appropriate format for art and photographs that contain a wide range of color, such as a 24-bit photo. If you want to export a photo from an Adobe Photoshop or PhotoDeluxe file format to a JPEG format for use on your Web site, you'll need to follow the steps below. The JPEG format compresses your file by identifying and discarding the extra data that's not absolutely necessary for displaying the photo. In most cases, you can't tell the difference between the original photo and the compressed version.

1 **Open your image in Photoshop.** Make sure it's in either Grayscale or RGB mode and is 72 ppi.

2 **Choose File>Save As,** name the file with a .jpg extension, and choose JPEG from the Format pop-up menu.

3 **After you click Save,** you'll be asked to select from four Image Quality options. For most images, Medium produces the best trade-off between quality and file sizes. However, sometimes Low is all you need, so experiment.

http://www.ftech.net/~brit

"In the hands of good creative authors Interactive Multimedia is one of the most powerful tools for communication of information yet devised"

—CLARE VENABLES, BRIT SCHOOL PRESIDENT

BRIT School

Croydon, London

This is a state-of-the-art Web site from a new school that specializes in teaching media technology and performing arts. The BRIT School serves students aged 14 to 19 years old. It's represented as being the first of its kind in England, combining a general education with specialized vocational training. The lucky students have access to dance and music studios, a theater, and fully equipped TV, radio, sound recording, and video studios.

The British Record Industry Trust Performing Arts & Technology School is in Croydon, London, an area of wild social and cultural diversity. The site is maintained by a small core of devoted Webmasters, including Gary Hayes.

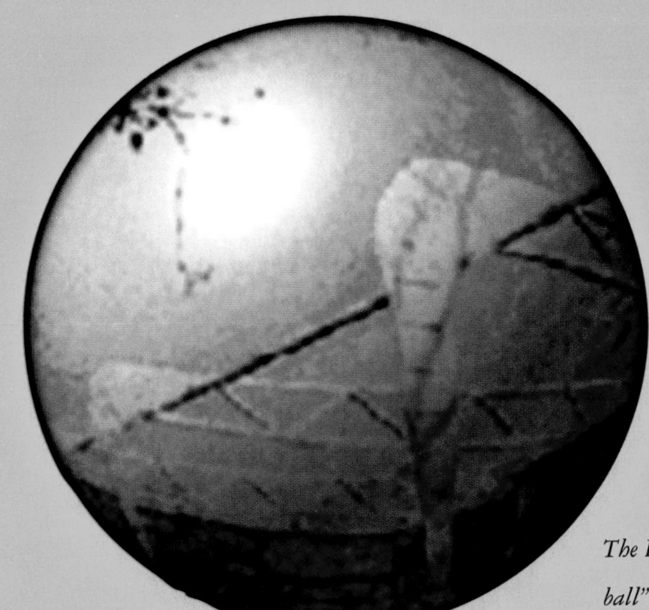

The BRIT School's "blue ball" site logo.

Well-designed pages, great backgrounds, and exciting graphics show up not only on the home page but throughout the site. There's a strong feeling of consistency and "pushing the limits." As the site creators suggest, "Our students' creativity now regularly uses electronic art and multimedia authoring."

BRIT School

1 2 3 4

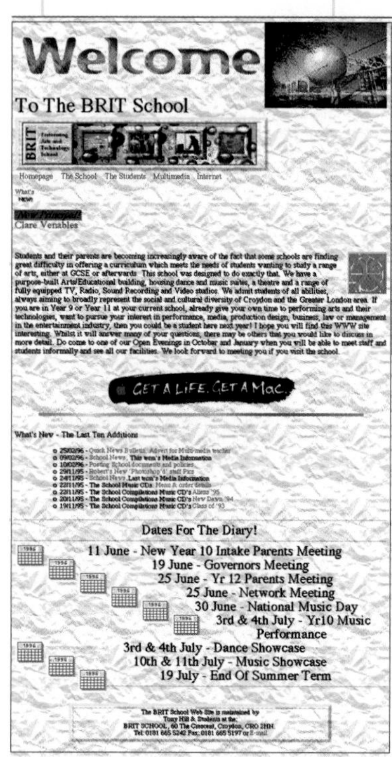

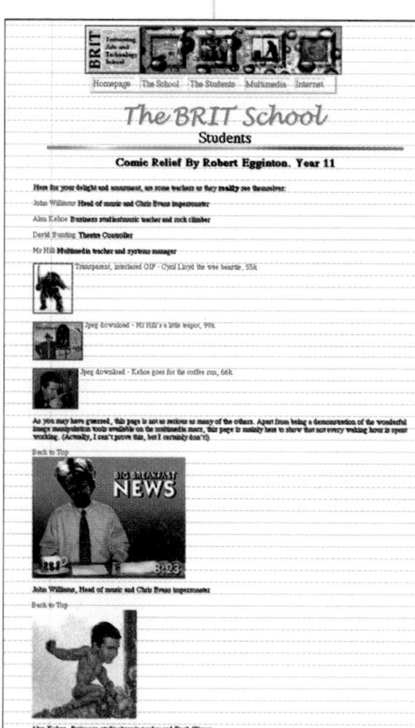

(1a) *One look at the BRIT School's home page shows visitors what they can expect from this site—bold, clean design; wild use of GIF images as backgrounds; and plenty of high-tech razzle-dazzle, like animated GIFs and blinking links. The Menu Bar lists four main areas of interest—The School, The Students, Multimedia, and Internet.*

(1a) *The home page links to the Student Page, an amusing page by Robert Egginton, Year 11.* (2b) *As its creator says, "This page is not as serious as many of the others." But he says it's "a demonstration of the wonderful image manipulation tools available on the multimedia Macs." Here, he has created joke images of some school instructors using transparent, interlaced GIF and JPEG files.*

5 6 7 8

a b c d e

1a *Clicking on the home page link to the Student Page brings up listings for selected student work,* 5e *including a gallery of digital artwork. It also links to the BRIT school magazine online. The page is laid out on a ruled paper background.*

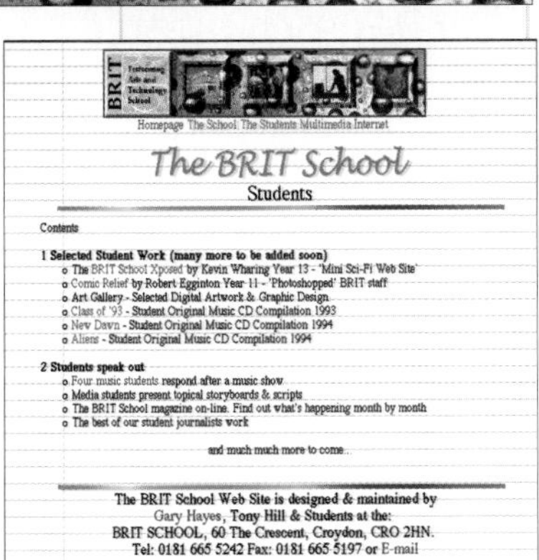

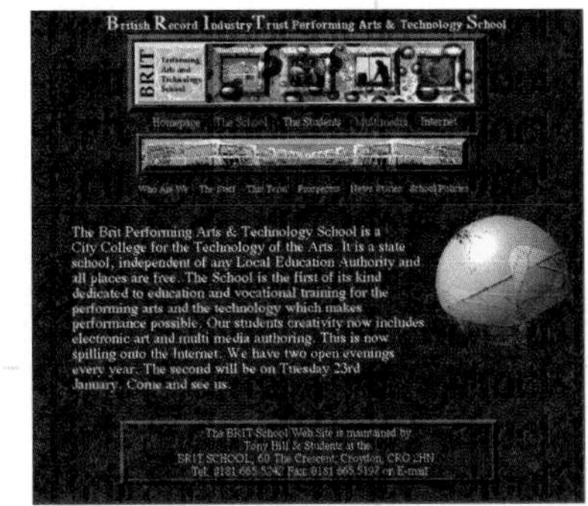

6b *This index of BRIT WEB Hotsites features links in the categories of Media, Performing Arts, Languages & Humanities, Music, Teaching & Education, and Internet & Multimedia, as well as Personal Sites. These cover everything from the BBC (British Broadcasting Corporation) Home Page to Music Week (a music industry newsletter) to UK Schools Internet.*

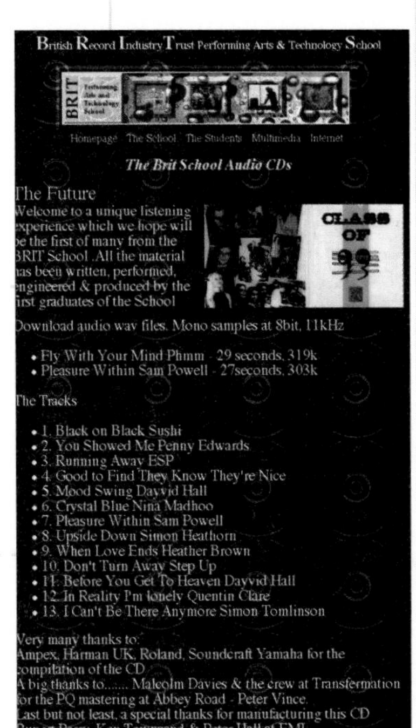

2b *Another link off the student page, Class of '93 Audio CDs, features a sampling of music CDs written, performed,* 8a *engineered, and produced by the first graduates of the school, using the school's music and recording facilities. For these, visitors download audio wav files.*

BRIT School Site Map

Special Features

Page 1

The BRIT School is pioneering not only in its Web design but in CD-ROM production, Web site creation, and creative digital arts. The site creators explain their interest in multimedia: "Multimedia is the combination of text, graphic arts, sound, animation and video elements, and when you allow an end user to have access control to these elements we call it Interactive Multimedia."

Homepage | The School | The Students | Multimedia | Internet

BRIT Multimedia

An active & developing area of the School - pioneering all aspects of CDROM production, WW creation & Creative Digital Arts

Multi Media Extravaganza

When The World Conference on Computers in Education (WCCE) came to England in July this year the organisers wanted to open the prestigious, week long proceedings with an example of the use of computers in arts and performance. So what did they do? They asked the BRIT School to open the show in the famous International Festival Hall in the centre of Birmingham. Two thousand international delegates poured into the large complex on the first Sunday of our summer holidays to an event sponsored by the big names in the industry like Intel and Apple.

In the weeks leading up to the opening ceremony a cross curriculum team of staff and students prepared a performance piece involving school musicians, dancers and the choir. A solo singing performance by Adelaide McKenzie of a song she wrote specifically for the event called 'Technology' provided a spectacular finale. The fifteen minute multi-media event was produced by Music Technology teacher Gary Hayes who, with student help, used new digital video editing facilities in the school to provide a video projected backdrop to live performance. A video of students working in multi media authoring was interwoven with action of the musicians, the choir, and dancers performing works recorded in Laban Notation on computers. This was projected on a massive fifty foot screen behind the stage by state of the art facilities in the same hall that Simon Rattle used to record live concerts. The video used computer generated menu systems run by a ghostly mouse cursor to move the piece through sections from each of the arts and performance areas to the next.

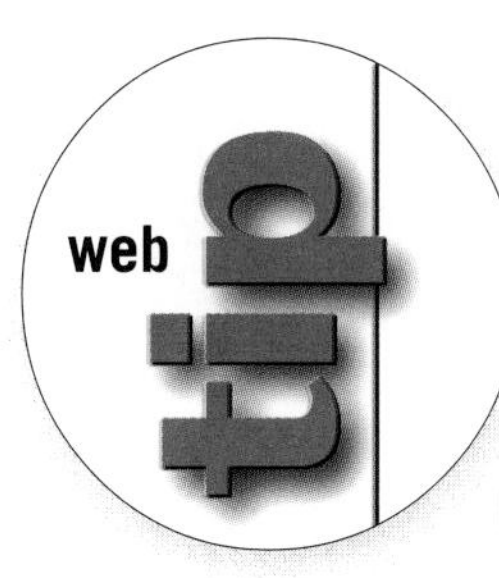

For speed and interesting effects, GIF files can be interlaced and made transparent in PageMill.

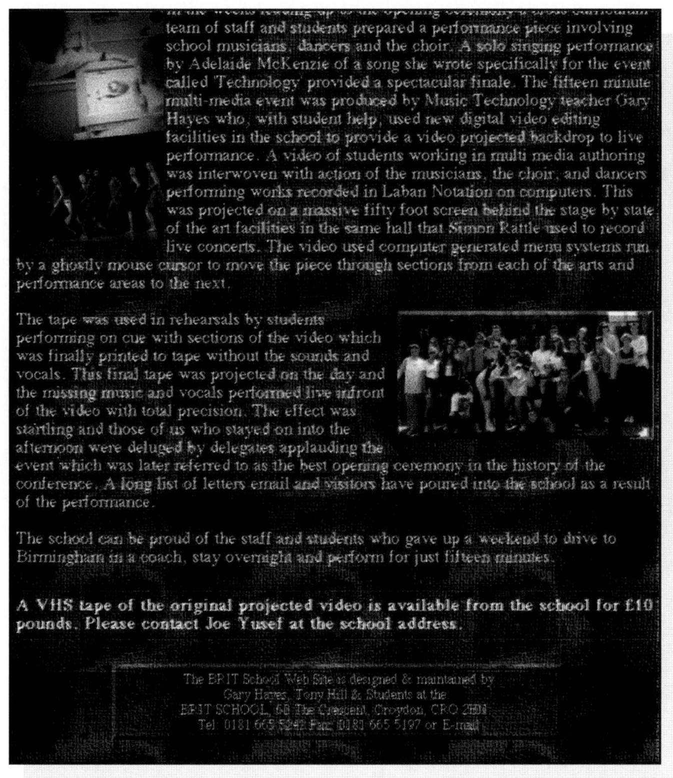

team of staff and students prepared a performance piece involving school musicians, dancers and the choir. A solo singing performance by Adelaide McKenzie of a song she wrote specifically for the event called 'Technology' provided a spectacular finale. The fifteen minute multi-media event was produced by Music Technology teacher Gary Hayes who, with student help, used new digital video editing facilities in the school to provide a video projected backdrop to live performance. A video of students working in multi media authoring was interwoven with action of the musicians, the choir, and dancers performing works recorded in Laban Notation on computers. This was projected on a massive fifty foot screen behind the stage by state of the art facilities in the same hall that Simon Rattle used to record live concerts. The video used computer generated menu systems run by a ghostly mouse cursor to move the piece through sections from each of the arts and performance areas to the next.

The tape was used in rehearsals by students performing on cue with sections of the video which was finally printed to tape without the sounds and vocals. This final tape was projected on the day and the missing music and vocals performed live infront of the video with total precision. The effect was startling and those of us who stayed on into the afternoon were deluged by delegates applauding the event which was later referred to as the best opening ceremony in the history of the conference. A long list of letters email and visitors have poured into the school as a result of the performance.

The school can be proud of the staff and students who gave up a weekend to drive to Birmingham in a coach, stay overnight and perform for just fifteen minutes.

A VHS tape of the original projected video is available from the school for £10 pounds. Please contact Joe Yusef at the school address.

The BRIT School Web Site is designed & maintained by
Gary Hayes, Tony Hill & Students at the
BRIT SCHOOL, 60 The Crescent, Croydon, CR0 2HN
Tel: 0181 665 5242 Fax: 0181 665 5197 or E-mail

Page 2

Also on this page, the school offers "Creative Reality"—the BRIT School Interactive CD-ROM Presentation, which includes 134 Quicktime movies, 270 full color screen resolution images, 30 audio sound tracks, animation, and the full text of the written prospectus. The prospectus was authored on Hyperstudio 2.0.

Creating Images with a Soft Edge

You can create irregularly shaped, soft-edge graphics in Adobe Photoshop 3 or greater. Here's how:

1 **Install GIF89 Export** into your Photoshop Plug-ins folder. (see page 53.)

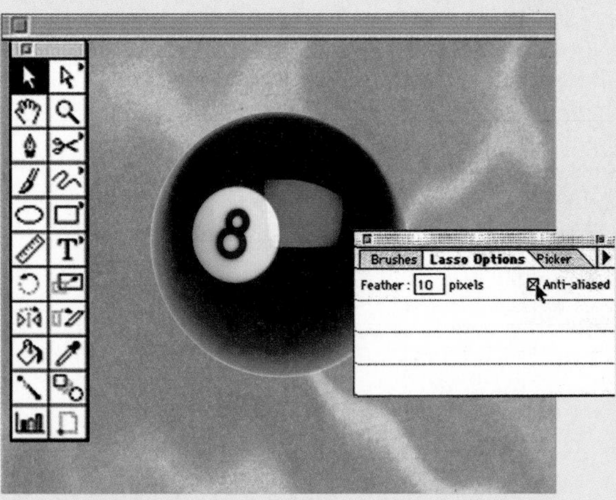

2 **Open the image;** make sure it is in RGB color mode and is 72 ppi. Check that the magnification is set to 1:1. Double-click the lasso tool and increase the feather value (10 is a good setting). Make sure that Anti-aliased is checked.

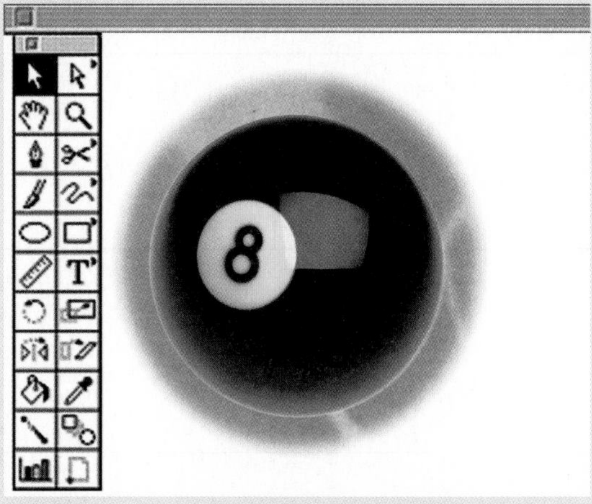

3 **Make a selection around** the image or area that you want on your Web page. You can hold down the Option key to constrain the lasso tool to straight lines. (The pen tool is a great way to make a more complex selection, since you can edit your pen tool path before you convert it to a selection.)

4 **Double-click the Background** layer in the Layers palette and give the layer a new name. Redefining the Background layer as a non-background layer lets you delete to transparent instead of white.

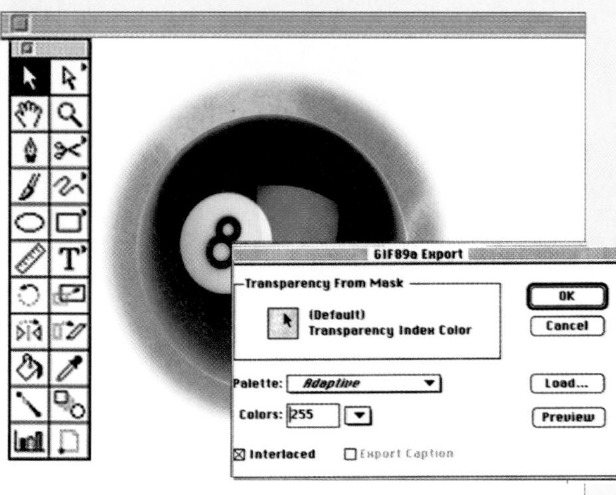

5 **Choose File>Export>GIF89.** Click the Transparency Color box and select your transparency color if it is something other than the standard Netscape gray.

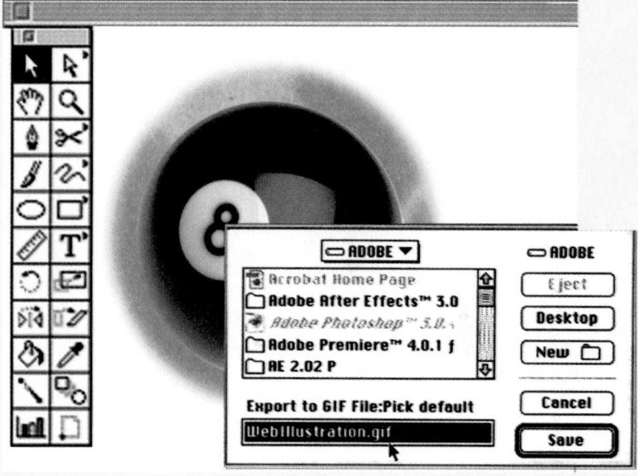

6 **To finish, click OK** in the GIF89a dialog box to export the file. Notice that the file name is now appended with .gif.

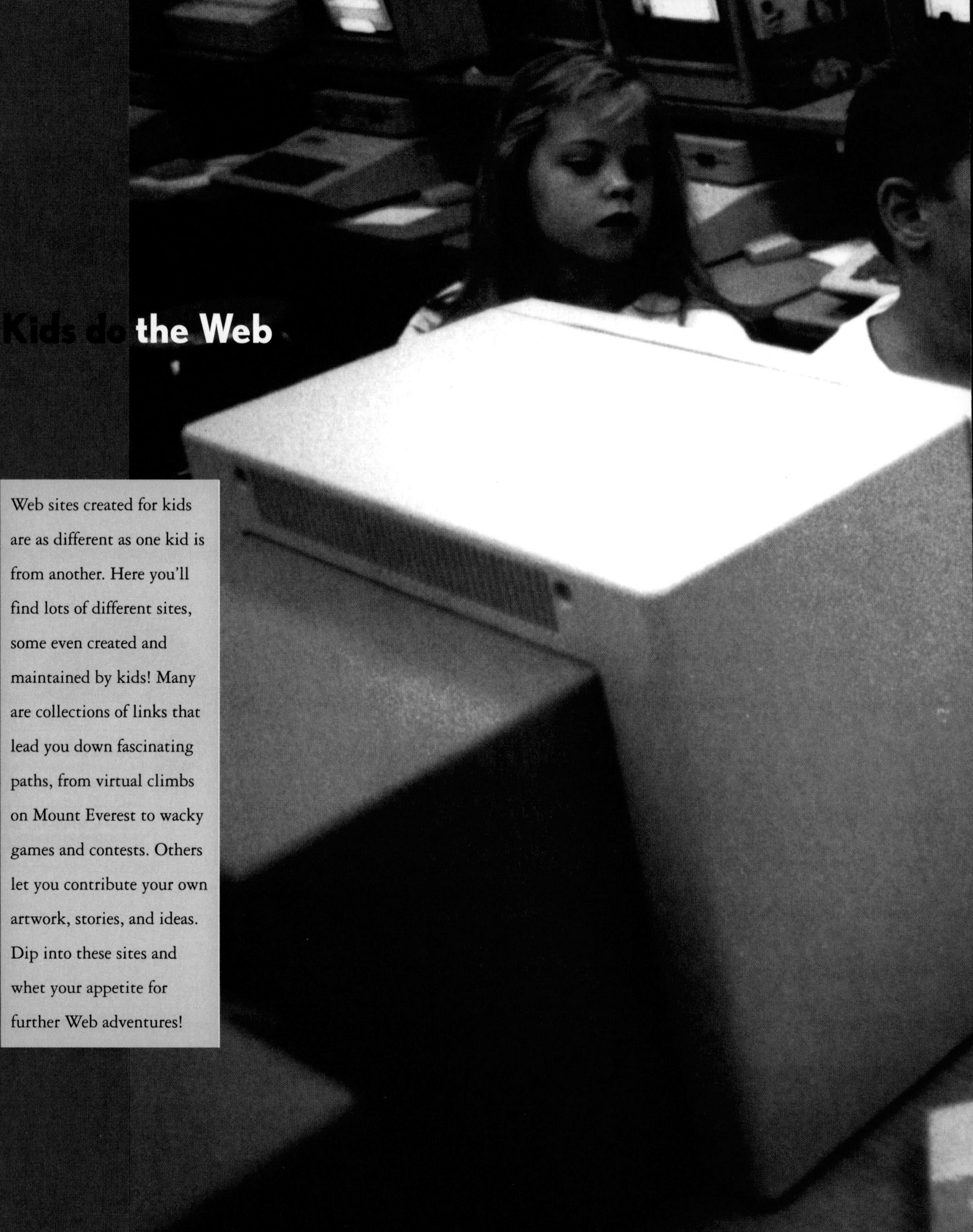

Kids do the Web

Web sites created for kids are as different as one kid is from another. Here you'll find lots of different sites, some even created and maintained by kids! Many are collections of links that lead you down fascinating paths, from virtual climbs on Mount Everest to wacky games and contests. Others let you contribute your own artwork, stories, and ideas. Dip into these sites and whet your appetite for further Web adventures!

Sites for Kids

http://cres1.lancs.ac.uk/~esarie/kate.htm

Kate's Page

Low Bentham, near Lancaster, England

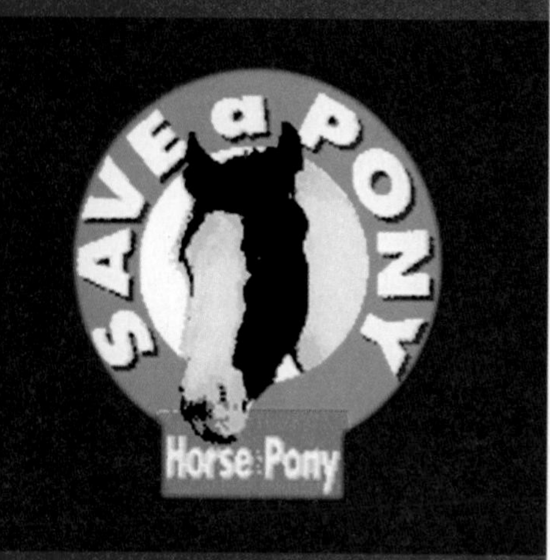

Eight-year-old Kate Edmondson-Noble's site is remarkable, to say the least. From a village in England's Yorkshire countryside, Kate and her father, I. Edmondson-Noble, have put up a site that's full of wit, fun, and individuality. With interesting links and built-in e-mail, they've managed to make contact with people from all over the world. It's a perfect example of what the Web is all about—people sending out "feelers" and getting back responses as varied as the people and places they come from.

Low Bentham, a tiny village, is located near the city of Lancaster, in northwestern England.

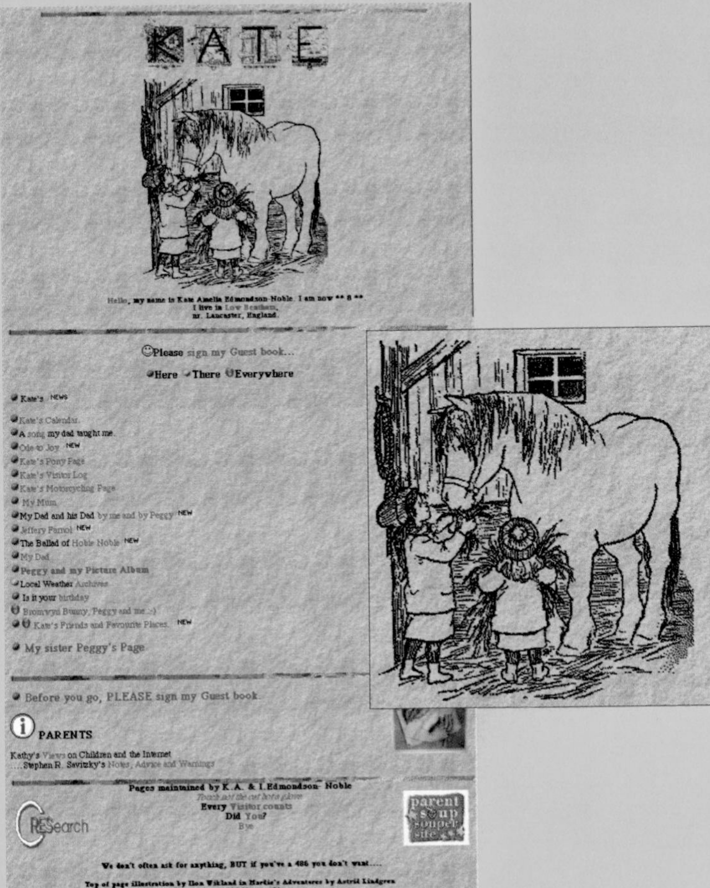

The home page sets the tone with its charming lettering and an illustration by artist Ilon Widland. Clicking on features brings visitors to new territory.

For a site created by an individual rather than an organization or school, this one has an impressive array of features. Songs and stories, poems and information about local sights and weather are mixed with pages about Kate's personal interests and pursuits.

Kate's Page

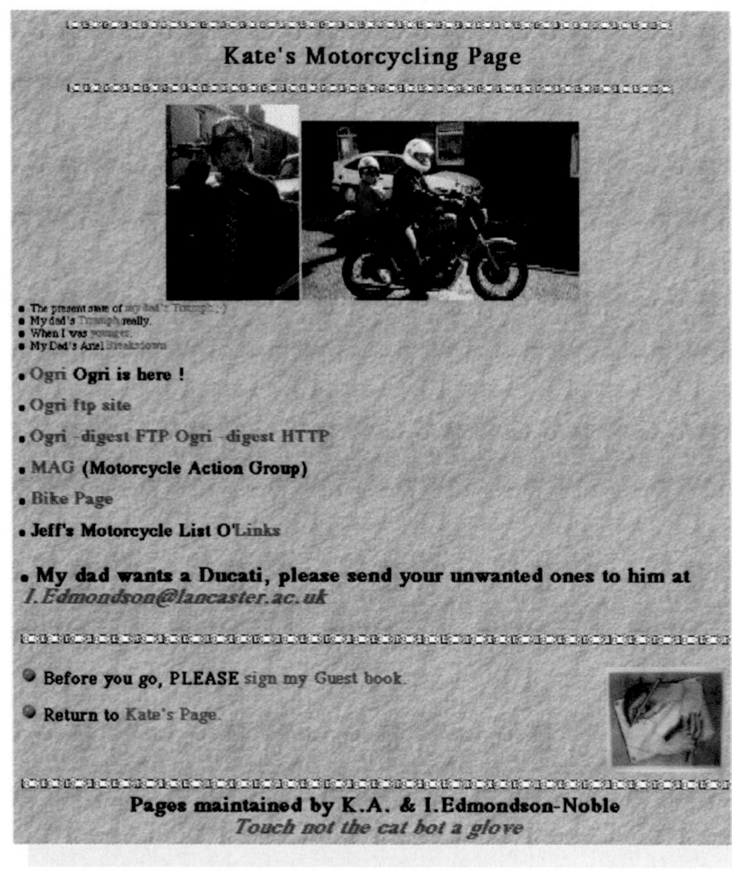

Kate's Motorcycling Page
Ogri Ogri is here !
Ogri ftp site
Ogri -digest FTP Ogri -digest HTTP
MAG (Motorcycle Action Group)
Bike Page
Jeff's Motorcycle List O'Links
My dad wants a Ducati, please send your unwanted ones to him at I.Edmondson@lancaster.ac.uk
Before you go, PLEASE sign my Guest book.
Return to Kate's Page.
Pages maintained by K.A. & I.Edmondson-Noble
Touch not the cat bot a glove

On another note, there's Kate's Motorcycling Page. This is obviously an interest (along with computers and the Web) that she shares with her father. Again, a short list of related links compiled by the busy duo is available here.

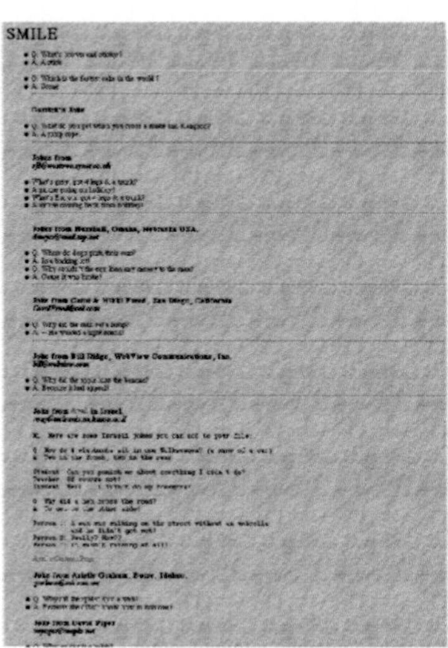

Clicking on "If you look in my file I'll give you a smile" brings visitors to Kate's Smile Page. This is where the interactive nature of the site really shows. From Ayal in Israel and Arielle in Idaho, to kids and corporate "surfers" taking a work break, come knock-knock jokes and riddles—all easily e-mailed in response to Kate's invitation, "More jokes welcome."

E-mail is often the most fun and popular page in a site. It's simple to build it right in to your site. **See page 109.**

Special Features

Clearly, Kate's first love is horses. On Kate's Pony Page photographs show Kate riding her pony, William. The links on this page lead not only to other pages in the site but also to other people's "horsey" home pages.

Kate's Page

http://www.cccnet.com

CCCNet
Computer Curriculum Corporation

Sunnyvale, California

Here's a bright, friendly site for students and teachers who want to learn about the Web. CCCNet is a provider of educational software geared toward students in grades K–12. The colorful and appealing home page, features an animated GIF (16k) of a whirling globe, embedded in nicely designed image map. The image map, with bright graphics and sophisticated typography, is large but builds very quickly and takes you to numerous interesting links.

COMPUTER CURRICULUM CORPORATION

You're plugged into CCCnet

COMPUTER CURRICULUM CORPORATION

A VIACOM COMPANY

A Leading Multimedia Publisher for Education

Welcome to **CCCnet!** CCC is a leading publisher of comprehensive curriculum-based educational software that uses the power of technology to deliver individualized instruction with appropriate assessment.

Teachers and educators, CCCnet brings you new content, ideas, and information regularly so bookmark your hotlist and make CCCnet your new home on the Web! Students and Teachers! This is the place for you to get wired on the Web while having fun - connect to what's new!

CCC Info Center contains company news, services and support, product information, and employment opportunities, as well as contact information.

Gallery is home to CCC projects past and present: a place to be inspired.

SuccessMaker Online brings you innovative, collaborative projects. Take a digital field trip, visit a virtual museum, or join in a cyberspace scavenger hunt here.

Teacher Link connects teachers around the world: keep up to date on news and features of special interest to teachers. Exchange ideas with educators, learn about conferences and upcoming online projects, and more.

Travel Ship is your launching pad on the Web. Find new pointers each week to imaginative, information-rich places, along with just-for-fun quizzes that encourage students to explore and learn.

Help is available from all levels of our site, so you're never more than a click away from answers to your questions.

Executive Produced and Directed by

COMPUTER CURRICULUM CORPORATION

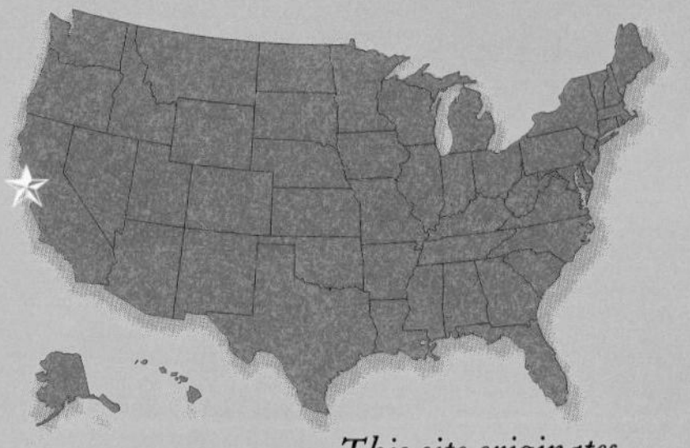

This site originates from Sunnyvale, California—a town in famed Silicon Valley—the center of computer technology.

Clicking on SuccessMaker Online brings up a page of special projects like Energy Flow in Amazonia and Shapes Around the World. Students and their teachers can preview a project, then register. All projects have a Lesson Plan and National Objectives Standards, which can be accessed in the Teacher Link—another button on the home page.

CCCNet

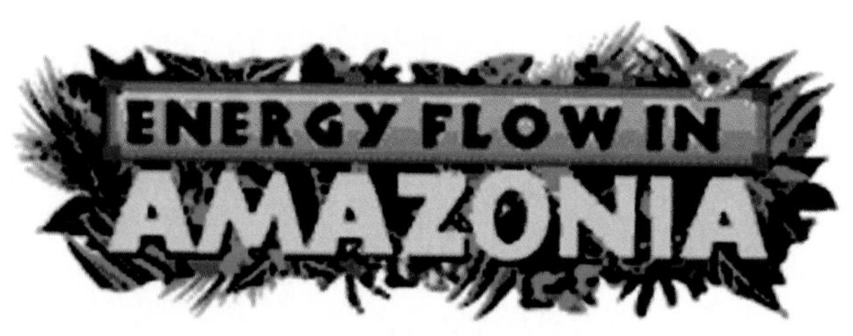

The Project Preview for Energy Flow in Amazonia, for 6th to 9th graders, asks the question, "How do plants, animals and other organisms obtain the energy they need to live?" Students discover the answers to these questions as they go on an Electronic Safari, explore the Energy Pyramid, and participate in other aspects of the project.

SuccessMaker Online

Welcome to SuccessMaker Online, where you participate in exciting new projects from CCC. We are currently offering two projects. You can preview the projects, learn how to register for them, check out extension activities and then enter the projects.

Energy Flow in Amazonia

- Preview
- Registration Instructions
- Register for Energy Flow
- Enter Energy Flow

Shapes Around the World

- Preview
- Registration Instructions
- Register for Shapes
- Enter Shapes
- Interdisciplinary Extensions

Important to note:

The Lesson Plan and National Objectives Standards for all projects can be accessed in Teacher Link.

SuccessMaker Online was designed to take advantage of Netscape technology.
Other browsers may not support all the interactive features of SuccessMaker Online.

Navigation:

Preview- takes you to preview page
Registration Instructions- takes you to instruction page
Register for Energy Flow- takes you to Registration for Energy Flow
Enter Energy Flow- takes you to the actual project for Energy Flow
Register for Shapes- takes you to the Registration for Shapes
Enter Shapes- takes you to the actual project for Shapes

Homepage | CCC Info Center | Gallery
SuccessMaker Online | Teacher Link | Travel Ship | Help

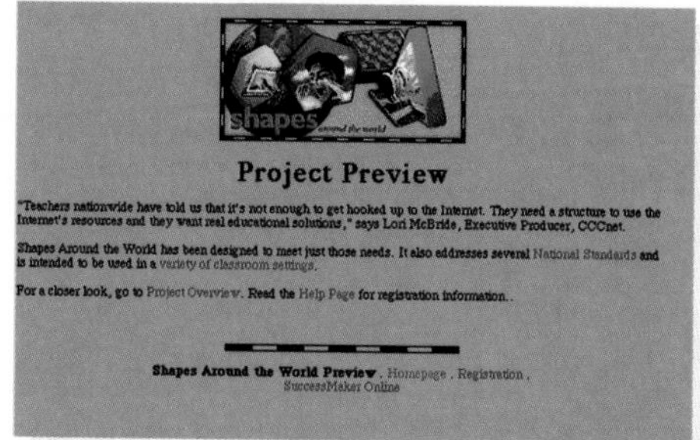

Project Preview

"Teachers nationwide have told us that it's not enough to get hooked up to the Internet. They need a structure to use the Internet's resources and they want real educational solutions," says Lori McBride, Executive Producer, CCCnet.

Shapes Around the World has been designed to meet just those needs. It also addresses several National Standards and is intended to be used in a variety of classroom settings.

For a closer look, go to Project Overview. Read the Help Page for registration information..

Shapes Around the World Preview . Homepage . Registration . SuccessMaker Online

Make toolbars and accessible links from anywhere on your site. Visitors need to be able to quickly jump from page to page.

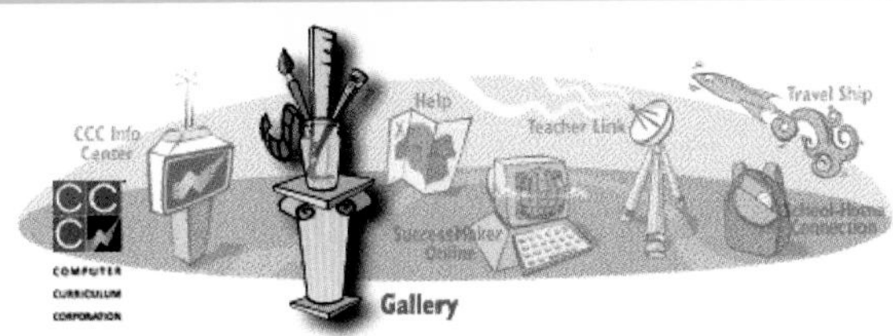

Gallery

Step inside the Gallery! Here you'll find student projects that feature the use of communication tools and electronic resources found on the Internet and World Wide Web.

This month we're featuring student work from the Energy Flow in Amazonia. In this project, students create a web page about an organism living in the Amazon rainforest and add it to the Energy Flow food pyramid.

Check what the following students did on Amazonia:

- Anaconda
  Charles of Rock Hall Middle School, Rock Hall, MD USA
- Brazilian Manatee
  Joe and Noah of St. Agnes School, Fort Wright, KY USA
- Panther
  Jeff and Ryan of St. Agnes School, Fort Wright, KY USA

A Call for Student Work . . .

We at Computer Curriculum Corporation would like to invite you to send us student creations for posting on CCCnet. All K-12 classes are eligible to participate, so long as the projects focus is related to the use of technology in the classroom. The most outstanding student projects will be selected and displayed on our gallery page. Find out how to submit student projects.

Homepage | CCC Info Center | **Gallery** | SuccessMaker Online | Teacher Link | Travel Ship | Help

Clicking on another button—Gallery—brings up student projects that feature the use of tools and electronic resources found on the Web. The page shown here features student Web pages from the Amazonia project.

Summer School

The Web is a year-round information resource. Following are some ideas for fun summertime Web activities.

1 Summer School. It doesn't have to be conducted in a classroom setting. Try conducting *virtual* classrooms over the Web and via e-mail. Reading lists, tests, presentations, and research assignments can be posted in special areas of a school's Web site. For summer school programs that have been affected by local budgets, *virtual* summer programs can offer those students who need the additional work a chance to self-pace themselves.

2 Summer Reading Lists. Post the reading list for student's summertime usage on your "Summer Web Site." Each grade level can have lists and even a synopsis of the books. Direct links to community libraries and even bookstores are a simple task.

3 Summer Crafts Projects. Summer isn't always fun and games. Many kids are lonely, bored, and just plain antsy. Crafts, arts, and fun things to make and do while at home alone are a real boon to many kids. It's important to get away from the computer, so try creating Web pages that get people out, doing stuff and making real, physical things.

4 My Summer Vacation. This perennial favorite can be done the day you get home! Fresh with photos and text, create your own HTML files with Adobe PageMill and Adobe PhotoDeluxe and then download them to Web administrator. You'd be surprised to learn what everybody is doing, especially those you tend not to see during the summer.

5 TV and Movies. Let's have real fun now—lists of upcoming movies and TV shows are great for summertime relaxing. Movies can have their own pages complete with the most honest of critics—kids. TV shows can be discussed and talked about, and just about every movie and TV show and channel has its own Web site! Entertainment Web pages are a fun way to get the real gossip on what's cool!

Sports

I Could Be Centerfield

by Scott Rader

CHSN's softball team is a perennial contender for the championship crown. Playing in a league stacked with competition, including the always strong North Rockland and the very competitive Clarkstown South, the Rams are heading into this season with confidence.

After a 1995 season in which the losses of three one-run games to Suffern, North Rockland, and archrival South was the difference between the fine season they had and the championship year they wanted, this year's team has high hopes. The Rams return nine out of twelve players, including six starters and their junior star, pitcher Danielle Beer. It's no surprise that Coach John Sullivan believes, "If the team is willing to work hard and be committed to softball like the previous Ram championship teams were, then we should do very well."

Go back to the article list

Return to the main menu

6 Sports. While there are plenty of professional sports Web sites, and sites devoted to professional sports, there is virtually nothing on the local level. Baseball leagues, soccer, biking, hiking, basketball, and football are just a smattering of some local reporting that informs and reflects the community.

7 Variations. Summertime bulletin boards and local chat lists. Money: where to make it, where to save on spending it. How to conduct a neighborhood theater performing your own plays, how to shoot a movie with a video cam, and how to write a book using your computer's programs.

http://www.ucalgary.ca/~dkbrown/index.html

Children's Literature Web Guide

Calgary, Alberta, Canada

The Children's Literature Web Guide

The Guide specializes in educational links, including a gallery of children's books (like Pinocchio*) made into film.*

For lovers of children's books, this site is a find. David K. Brown, Director of the Doucette Library of Teaching Resources at the University of Calgary, has compiled an amazing, award-winning list of links to young adult books. This site lists everything from children's book awards to times and dates of special book events. There's information for and about children's book publishers and authors, guidance for doing research, and even a selection of online children's stories, complete with illustrations.

The University of Calgary, is in Calgary, Alberta, one of Canada's largest cities.

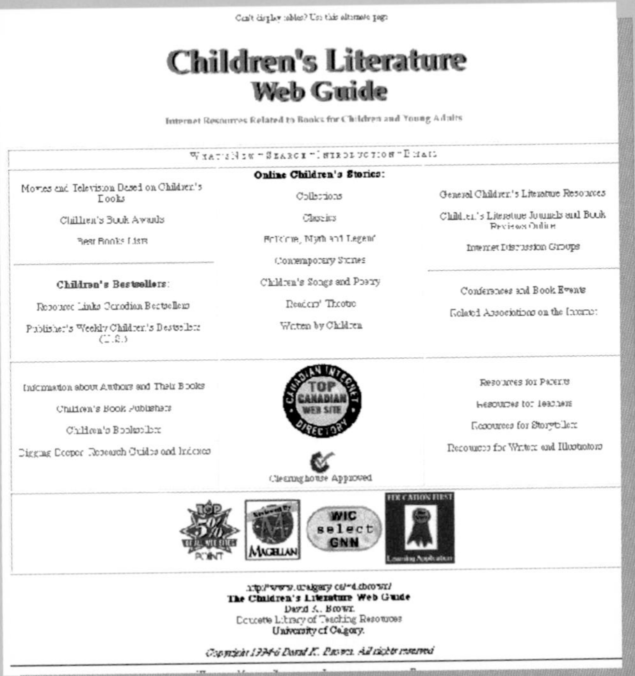

This site is a great take-off point for exploring children's literature, as well as all the awards, publishing ventures, movies, and reviews that surround it. And don't forget the many links to resources for parents and educators. A true librarian's careful, thorough methods and simple site navigation make these pages fast and easy to use.

"In Cyberspace," says Web librarian Brown, "no one can hear you shush." One cool feature he points us to is Movies and Television Based on Children's Books, which Mr. Brown has included because, in his words, "I love movies and movie reviews." And to make everything extra-easy to find, there's a great built-in Index Search.

Children's Literature Web Guide

Each of the hundreds of links provided are carefully annotated to give visitors a brief idea of what to expect. Clicking on Information About Authors and Their Books, for example, brings up a satisfyingly long page called Tell Me More! (Throughout, a colorful flower motif indicates resources that are especially valuable.) Scrolling down to one entry—Laura Ingalls Wilder—finds the My Little House on the Prairie Home Page, listed as having "good information on the real-life characters and locations that inspired the books, as well as information on more recent spin-off book series."

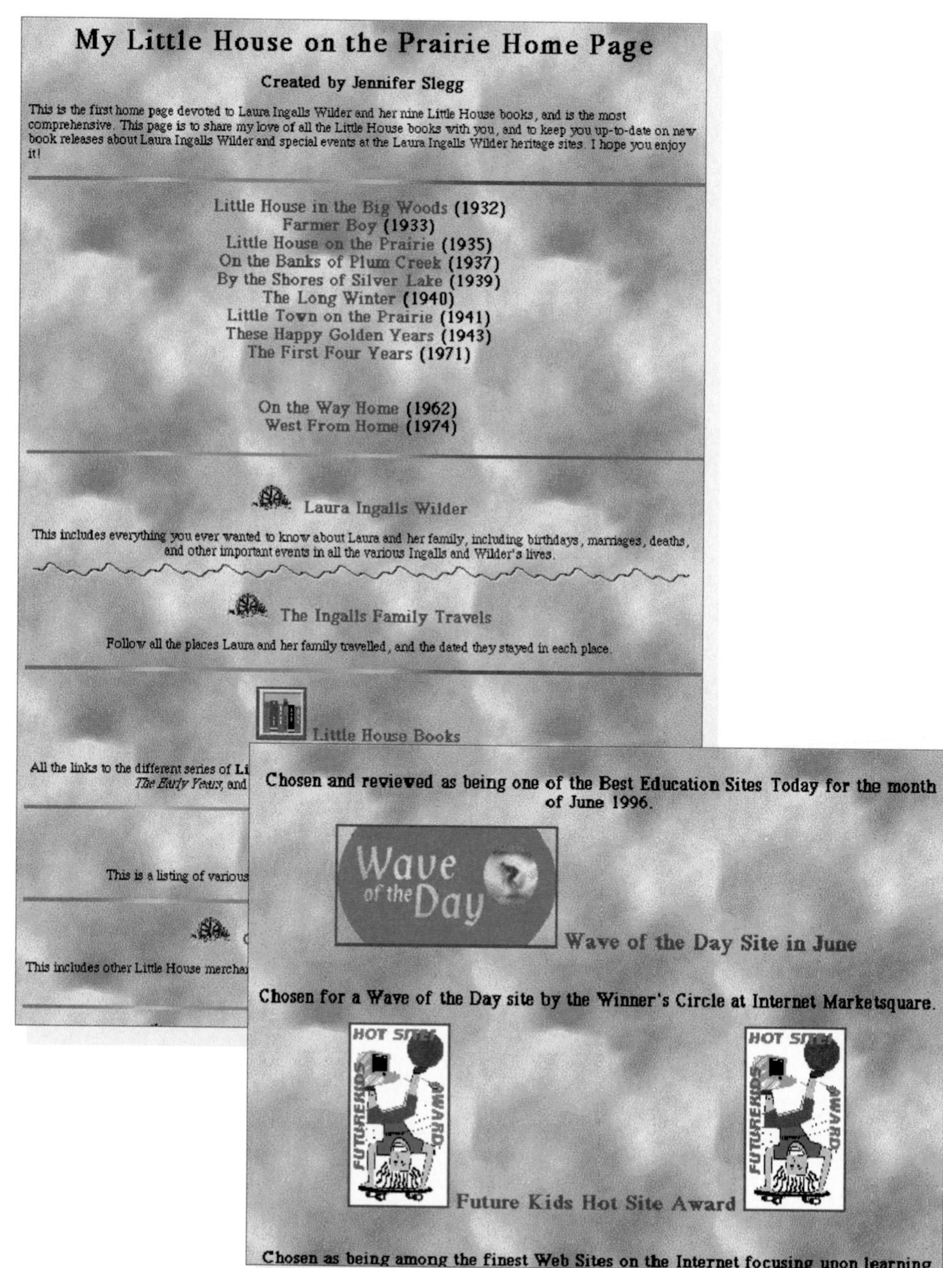
My Little House on the Prairie Home Page
Created by Jennifer Slegg
This is the first home page devoted to Laura Ingalls Wilder and her nine Little House books, and is the most comprehensive. This page is to share my love of all the Little House books with you, and to keep you up-to-date on new book releases about Laura Ingalls Wilder and special events at the Laura Ingalls Wilder heritage sites. I hope you enjoy it!
Little House in the Big Woods (1932)
Farmer Boy (1933)
Little House on the Prairie (1935)
On the Banks of Plum Creek (1937)
By the Shores of Silver Lake (1939)
The Long Winter (1940)
Little Town on the Prairie (1941)
These Happy Golden Years (1943)
The First Four Years (1971)
On the Way Home (1962)
West From Home (1974)
Laura Ingalls Wilder
This includes everything you ever wanted to know about Laura and her family, including birthdays, marriages, deaths, and other important events in all the various Ingalls and Wilder's lives.
The Ingalls Family Travels
Follow all the places Laura and her family travelled, and the dated they stayed in each place.
Little House Books
Chosen and reviewed as being one of the Best Education Sites Today for the month of June 1996.
Wave of the Day
Wave of the Day Site in June
Chosen for a Wave of the Day site by the Winner's Circle at Internet Marketsquare.
Future Kids Hot Site Award
Chosen as being among the finest Web Sites on the Internet focusing upon learning

Home pages with lots of information or hot links should be set up as tables in PageMill. This eliminates endless scrolling and makes the design cleaner and easier to read.

Special Features

For a little more contemporary reading material, visitors can scroll down to R. L. Stine "A World Wide Web page created by Stine's publisher, Scholastic Books." Up comes a simple, well-designed home page, followed by plenty of material on the popular author of creepy tales for kids. Clicking on another section of the site's home page—Online Children's Stories—on the subhead Folklore, Myth and Legend, brings up a wide selection of stories online, from Red Riding Hood to Folktales from around the World. One example is Anansi-—the spider folk hero of the Caribbean Islands. Here, there's yet another list of stories to click on and read.

Folktales From Around the World

People told folktales long before there were books, newspapers or televisions. Folktales were a way to bring news from one village to the next. Parents used folktales to teach lessons to their children. For instance, instead of telling their kids not to lie, they would tell a story about lying and the kids would figure it out for themselves. Pretty neat, huh!

Folktales were also a way for people to learn and understand the customs of their community. Folktales also helped people understand the wonders of nature, like thunderstorms and the moon growing bigger and smaller. In one of my favorite folktales, a bear hangs the sun out to dry in the morning and puts the sun to bed at night.

Folktales tell a lot about the peoples who invent them. For instance, the early American settlers believed in hard work and making it on their own. A lot of their stories are about rugged individuals like Paul Bunyan and Johnny Appleseed, who were strong and brave and accomplished a great deal. Many cultures have one character who is always getting into trouble. Native American Indians have Trickster, Cape Verdians have Los Nobos the wolf, and Africans have Anansi the spider.

Folktales are told over and over and they change with each retelling. I made up some of the folktales here. But most of them are hundreds of years old, maybe more. I just rewrote them to suit my own personality and sense of humor.

Each storyteller breathes a different life into a story. The storyteller is always making choices; where to begin, where to end, where to add a dash of humor or a sprinkling of suspense. It's like a big story stew.

When you read these folktales, you can click on words highlighted in blue. When you click, you will find a new path, a picture, an explanation or maybe all three!

Learn how to write your own, then write one and send it in!

Or choose a folktale below

Anansi Folktales.

Anansi is a clever spider from the Carribean Islands.

Cape Verdian Folktales.

http://obelix.helix.net/polar7.com/tnt/

Tristan & Tiffany's Cool Stuff for Kids

Coquitlam, British Columbia, Canada

This site is a real family affair, put together by seven-year-old Tiffany, her nine-year-old brother Tristan, and their father, Greg Tjosvold. Even their black poodle dog—Candy, the "spokesmodel"—gets into the act with her own Welcome page.

Coquitlam, British Columbia, is a small community in Canada's westernmost province.

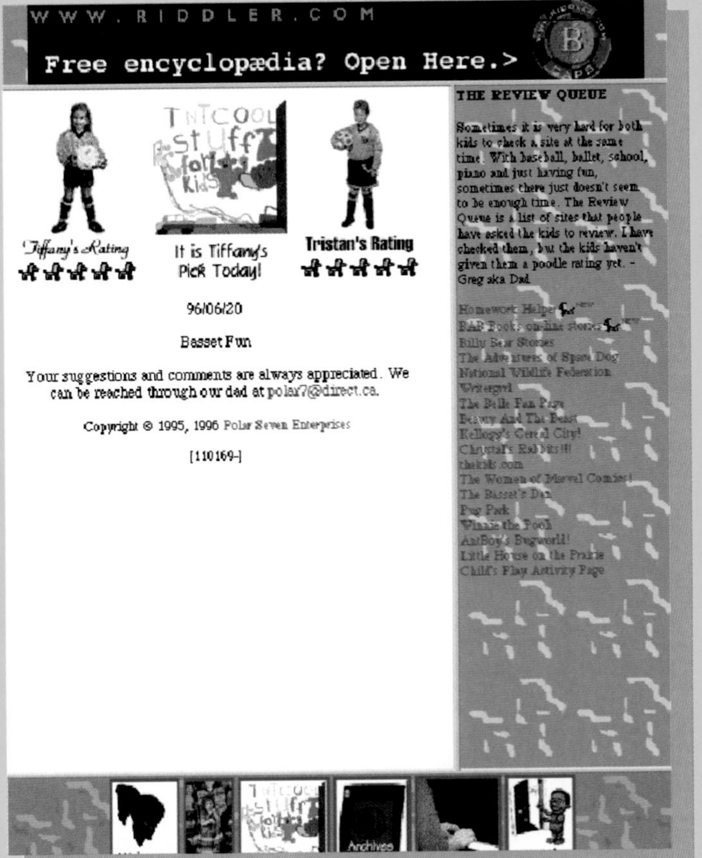

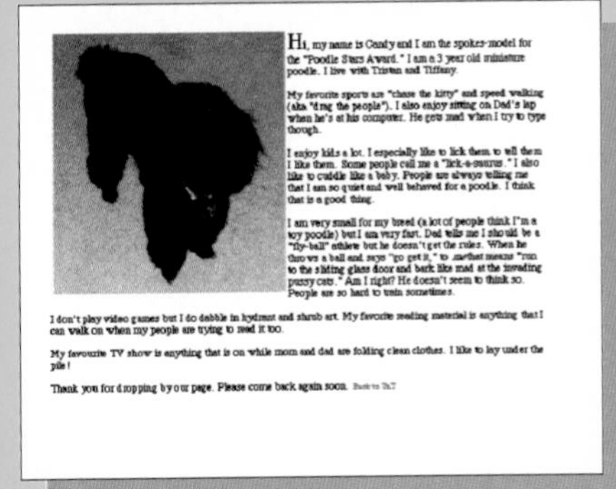

Greg, who runs a design studio in British Columbia, put the site together on his Mac. But Tristan and Tiffany are the stars: they were involved in the writing, editing, and programming!

Notice the clever "poodle rating system." Tristan and Tiffany review kid-friendly sites and give them one-, two-, three-, four-, or five-poodle ratings.

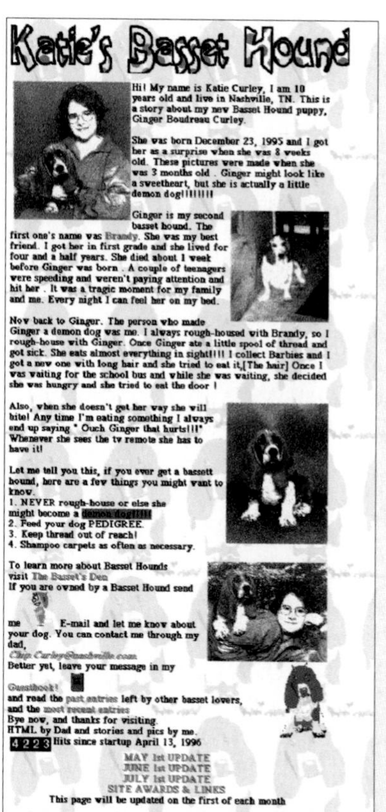

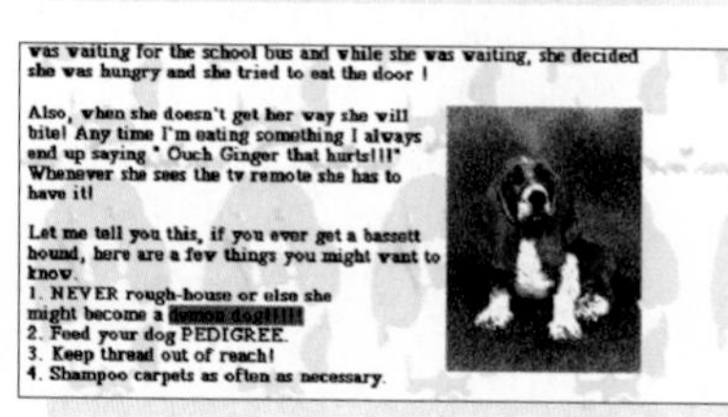

They also feature the "Pick of the Day." In this case, it's Tiffany's turn; she chose Katie's Bassett Hound, a delightful home page about a girl and her dog, complete with animated GIFs, a guest book that opens and closes, and an expressive little-girl figure that holds up a sign, "send me e-mail." These kids really do know what other kids like, and their picks are good ones to try!

web tip

To create these simple-looking, sophisticated effects, Greg Tjosvold used a Mac 660AV. To create the images, he used Photoshop (with a scanner plug-in), Adobe Premiere, GIFBuilder, and Fetch to transfer the graphics to the Web.

Special Features

One thing that really stands out on this site is the fun and creative use of graphics. The images are tiny (about 5k each) but are wildly colorful. The layout is clear and uncluttered; all the bright colors make it look fun.

To top it off, there are two animated GIFs (15k each): one of Tiffany dancing (one of her favorite pastimes) and another of Tristan playing baseball. Visitors can click on either the still photo or the moving one to bring up a biography page for each child.

http://www.advanced.org/ThinkQuest/

ThinkQuest

Armonk, New York

This site is the home of an exciting contest for students, grades 7–12. The site encourages kids (and their teachers) to participate in "an entirely new way of learning—the Internet style." Student teams, with their faculty coaches, use the latest tools to create Web pages of text, audio, image, and video.

Based in Armonk, New York, ThinkQuest is part of Advanced Network and Services, Inc.

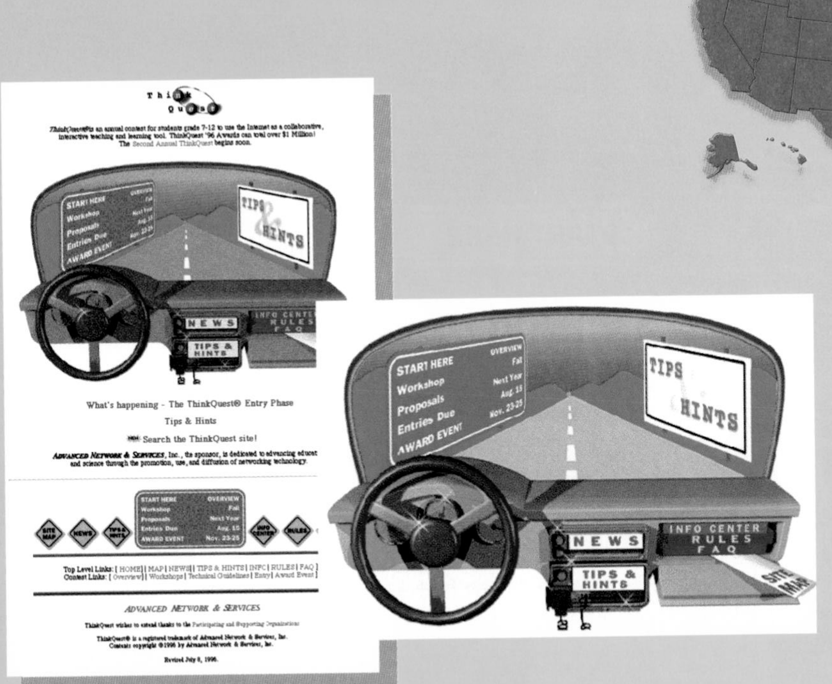

The ThinkQuest site provides lots of technical and content support, as well as links to helpful sites. A well-designed Site Map uses cool driving motifs—driver's seats, highway signs, etc.—to steer interested kids around the site. Links to rules, tips, schedules, and a search engine are all on the home page. Even the entry forms are available on the site.

In addition to being fun and challenging, the winner's prizes are substantial. Students can win up to $25,000.00 in scholarships. Teachers and coaches can win up to $5,000.00, with another $5,000.00 going to their school or institution.

Two of the schools in this book have participated by putting together entries in the ThinkQuest contest for 1996. Students from West Anchorage High in Alaska collaborated with students at the Thomas Jefferson School in Alexandria, Virginia, to prepare entries in the contest. And students at Berkeley High in California also prepared an entry—a project called Cat Dissection Online—in conjunction with a Human Anatomy Class.

START HERE OVERVIEW

Overview

The " *ThinkQuest*" Contest has *three* major ***Objectives***. They are to:

- Create **Collaboration** among Students, including those from Dissimilar Schools, using the Internet for Education
- Create a Structure in which Students can help other Students to Learn by:
  - **Building Exciting and Innovative Educational Tools and Materials** that Exploit and Enrich in the "Internet Style"
  - Enabling the **Broad Use of those Tools and Materials** by other Students and Schools
- Improve the **Quality** of Educational Tools and Materials available on the Internet

Students can win up to $25,000 in scholarships; teachers and coaches can win up to $5,000 with another $5,000 going to their school or Institution.

The Quest

The aim of *ThinkQuest* is to encourage students, guided by teachers or coaches from approved institutions, to build "Educational Tools for The Internet" that will make their favorite subjects more exciting, both for themselves and for other students. Using information age tools, students will help reshape how the world will communicate, learn, and work together tomorrow.

The Internet is changing the world, just as television and radio did in previous generations. But, unlike other forms of communication, this new medium is participatory and fosters collaborative work and learning.

ThinkQuest will help students prepare for a future dramatically different from today. And the quality of Web pages inspired by the contest will show how this new and exciting medium can help teach millions of students for years to come.

The Internet Style of Learning

Equally important, students will be experiencing an entirely new way of learning. It's called the "Internet style" because it takes advantage of the Net's unique capabilities. It emphasizes exploration, collaboration, and exploitation of the vast amount of information on the Internet and the World Wide Web.

Home Room to Home Page

ThinkQuest is structured to motivate students and teachers to take the leap from home room to home page by challenging students to build Web pages that take advantage of this learning style. The *ThinkQuest* team will provide tips and guidelines to get teams started, and from there what they create is limited only by their imagination.

For some examples, click here.

All About Learning

To help students continue their education beyond high school, we are sponsoring scholarship awards for students and cash awards for the coaches and their schools or approved institutions. Each of the five categories and the best entry will receive awards.

What next?

The *ThinkQuest* Contest, step-by-step.

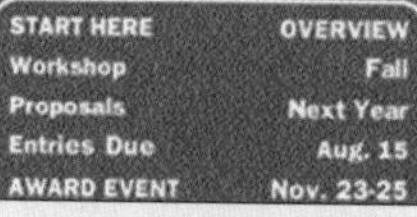

START HERE
OVERVIEW
Workshop
Fall
Proposals
Next Year
Entries Due
Aug. 15
AWARD EVENT
Nov. 23-25

Special Features

"The Internet Style of Learning," is a fascinating page about learning on the Web. One part deals with building relationships through the Web. To demonstrate this idea, there's a link to Philadelphia's Franklin Institute Science Museum. As the page says, "Here, six classes in grades 2 through 6, all from different schools, collaborated on a project about wind. Each class evolved a different approach to building windmills and fans. By sharing their individual approaches over the Web, classes were able to build on one another's work, creating sophisticated experiments to define the shape of the best windmill blades."

By collaborating on a project, not only with fellow students in the same school, kids pool their knowledge and discoveries to create a whole, bigger than the sum of its parts.

Welcome to The Franklin Institute Science Museum. We bring the exhibits, resources, and fun of a museum visit right to your desktop.

Begin your visit by touring our online exhibits. Our educational hotlists point to educational hotspots on the Internet. The online exhibit hotlist will help you find educational experiences online.

NEWS *The Philadelphia Inquirer's Health & Science Magazine*

Visit our publications library, where you'll find other science news, activities, and resources. Use our units of study to support your science curriculum. Sample some interesting science programs and demonstrations.

Wander through the museum. Preview "Street Machines," our current feature exhibit. You can stay as long as you like and you don't even have to travel. However, if you do plan to travel to The Franklin Institute, visit planning information is available. Brief exhibit summaries describe what you'll see while you're here. Check out our visitor services.

It's not quite the real thing, but a visit to our online museum should satisfy your yearning for learning about science. Wander, wonder, and just have fun!

Visit our partner school: Levering Science Magnet School.

Meet Amy, our resident science student.

Visit the Online Schools that have been "Caught In The Web."

Find out what's new at The Franklin Institute by reading our monthly online magazine for "inQuiring" minds:

"inQuiry Almanack"

If you need to learn the basic skills for exploring the Web, use our beginner's guide:

"World Wide Web Workbook"

Our table of contents will help you find your way through the museum.
Or, you can search for information anywhere you see the Search icon. SEARCH

If this is your first visit, please read our disclaimer & copyright statement and our explanation of who we are. Consult our online user services page to answer technical questions and to communicate with us.

The Franklin Institute Science Museum
222 North 20th Street
Philadelphia, Pennsylvania 19103

The Franklin Institute Science Museum is a member of The Science Learning Network and other outreach projects.

UNISYS
Made possible through generous support from Unisys Corporation.

© 1995, 1996, The Franklin Institute Science Museum, All rights reserved.
[illegible]@www.fi.edu

http://www.csi.ad.jp/suzuhari-es/1000cranes/index.html

1000 Cranes Project

Hiroshima, Japan

"We believe that your hope will spread in the hearts of people around the world as cranes fly in the sky. From now, we promise to make efforts for the peace of the world with people around the world."

—STUDENTS OF NAGATSUKA ELEMENTARY SCHOOL

Each year on August 6—International Peace Day—children from all over the world send paper cranes, made in the Japanese paper-folding tradition of origami, to Hiroshima, Japan. In the Hiroshima Peace Park, these cranes decorate the statue of Sadako Sasaki. This 12-year-old girl's death from leukemia came as a result of the atomic bomb dropped on that city during World War II. Sadako believed in the legend that if a sick person folds 1,000 paper cranes, the gods will restore his or her health. Hoping for life, she folded 644 before she died in 1955; her classmates completed the rest.

Hiroshima is a large port city on the island of Honshu, Japan. It was the target of atomic bombs during World War II; they left the poisoning effects of radiation that continue to this day.

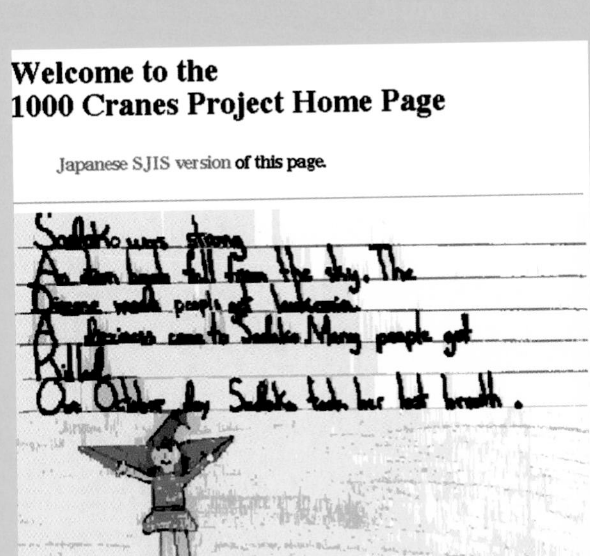

Welcome to the
1000 Cranes Project Home Page
Japanese SJIS version of this page.

This story is the inspiration for this Web site, developed by Shinichi Someoka, a professor at the Yasuda Women's University in Hiroshima. The site—in English and Japanese—is maintained by a group of university, elementary, and high school teachers for children who want to be make cranes for the project.

This site is a dramatic example of how the Web can be used to promote a sense of global community. The project site links to schools in Hiroshima, as well as in other parts of the world. Its "e-mail Exchange," maintained at the Nagatsuka Elementary School's site, showcases an ongoing exchange of ideas from all over the world.

1000 Cranes Project

E-mail is often the hottest page on a site. Make sure you use utilize this ability to communicate with the world.

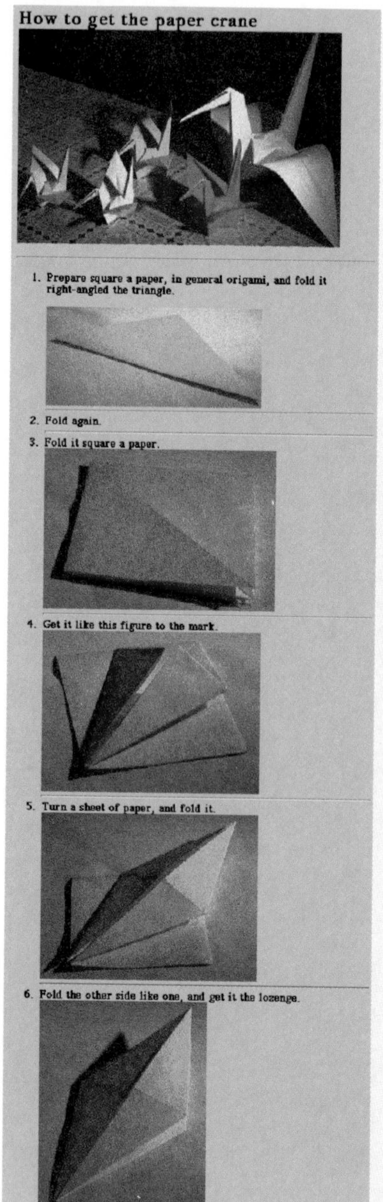

How to get the paper crane
1. Prepare square a paper, in general origami, and fold it right-angled the triangle.
2. Fold again.
3. Fold it square a paper.
4. Get it like this figure to the mark.
5. Turn a sheet of paper, and fold it.
6. Fold the other side like one, and get it the lozenge.

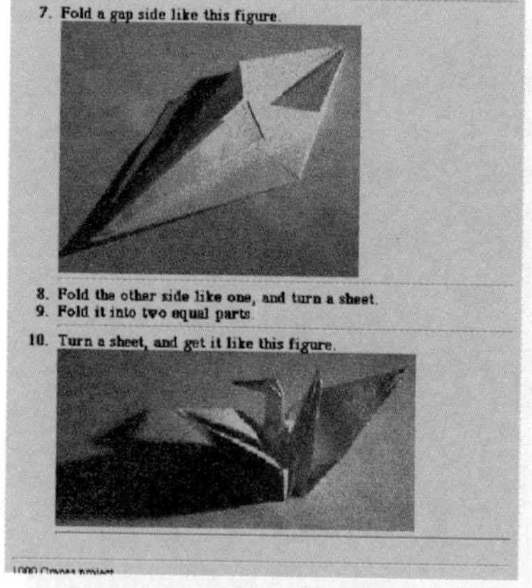

7. Fold a gap side like this figure.
8. Fold the other side like one, and turn a sheet.
9. Fold it into two equal parts.
10. Turn a sheet, and get it like this figure.

Among several schools linked to the Project is Suzuhari Elementary School in Hiroshima. This page is reached from the 1000 Cranes home page and features great student artwork.

A link off the home page leads to a page with big, colorful step-by-step instructions in the paper-folding art of origami. Again, the images are compressed GIF files.

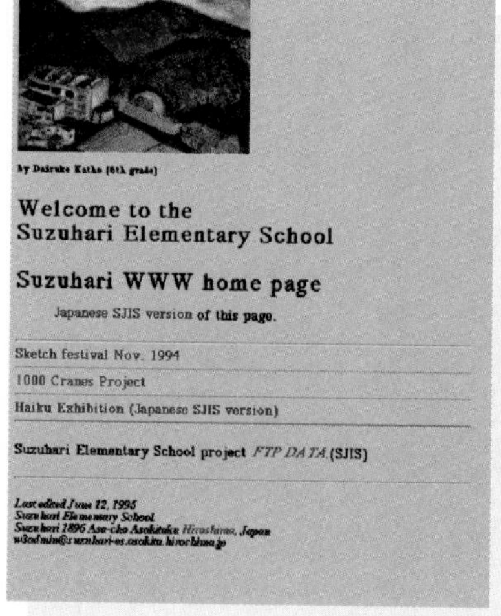

The home page also leads to other Hiroshima schools. Nagatsuka Elementary School's site features a large e-mail section, which records all of the peace messages they've received. Mail from Margaret Crayton's 5th grade class at Barnet Elementary in Vermont is a great example of communication through the Web. The exchange of e-mail letters between her class and teacher June Tahara's at Nagatsuka Elementary can be read, as the schools plan the making and mailing of 1,000 cranes.

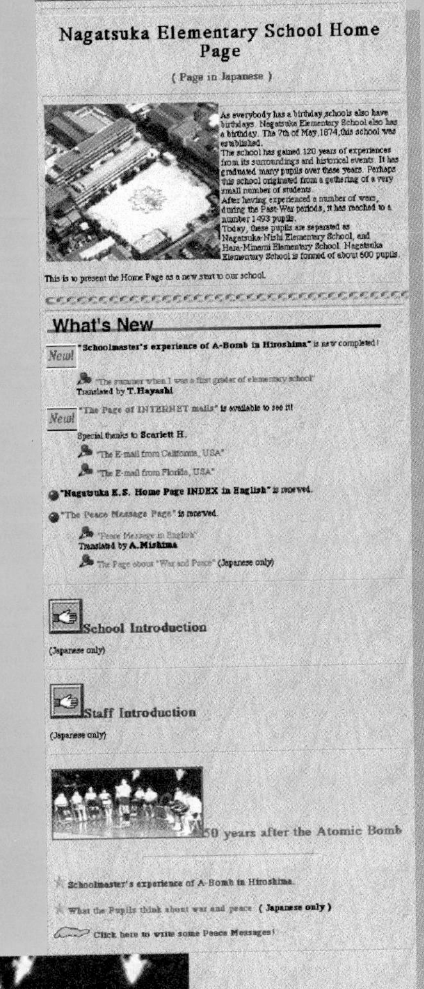

Nagatsuka Elementary School Home Page
(Page in Japanese)
As everybody has a birthday,schools also have birthdays. Nagatsuka Elementary School also has a birthday. The 7th of May,1874,this school was established.
The school has gained 120 years of experiences from its surroundings and historical events. It has graduated many pupils over these years. Perhaps this school originated from a gathering of a very small number of students.
After having experienced a number of wars, during the Past-War periods, it has reached to a number 1493 pupils.
Today, these pupils are separated as Nagatsuka-Nishi Elementary School, and Hara-Minami Elementary School. Nagatsuka Elementary School is formed of about 600 pupils.
This is to present the Home Page as a new start to our school.
What's New
New!
"Schoolmaster's experience of A-Bomb in Hiroshima" is new completed!
"The summer when I was a first grader of elementary school"
Translated by T.Hayashi
New!
"The Page of INTERNET mails" is available to see it!
Special thanks to Scarlett H.
"The E-mail from California, USA"
"The E-mail from Florida, USA"
"Nagatsuka E.S. Home Page INDEX in English" is renewed.
"The Peace Message Page" is renewed.
"Peace Message in English"
Translated by A.Mishima
The Page about "War and Peace" (Japanese only)
School Introduction
(Japanese only)
Staff Introduction
(Japanese only)
50 years after the Atomic Bomb
Schoolmaster's experience of A-Bomb in Hiroshima.
What the Pupils think about war and peace (Japanese only)
Click here to write some Peace Messages!

In the last letter we learn that the cranes were mailed to Hiroshima; there's a photo of them delivering the cranes to the memorial. There's also a shot of the 5th grade classroom, the ceiling alive with dangling paper cranes. "What a wonderful day today! We have received the package from you, in Vermont… When we examined each crane, it seems like we can see the smile of the teachers, children, and others who made them…We are very pleased!"

Special Features

Featured here are two schools that have special relationships with the 1000 Cranes Project. Alianza School is a bilingual (Spanish/English) elementary school in Watsonville, California. The kids at Alianza got involved with the Project because their Technology Coordinator, Fred Mindlin, saw it on the Web. He e-mailed this letter to the school: "Hello! I just found the Suzuhari School home page on the Web. I'm doing a project with my 3rd and 4th grade class in Watsonville, CA, and I would love to have a sister school in Hiroshima to exchange e-mail about Sadako and the 1,000 paper cranes. Please let me know if anyone at your school might be interested in participating." Mr. Tamai of Suzuhari wrote back, and that began the relationship.

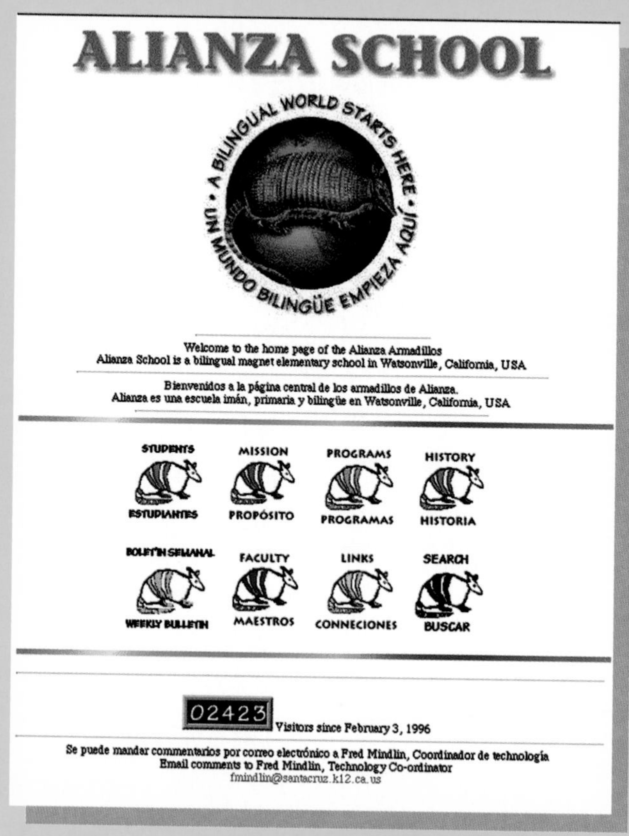

The home page features a drawing by Candy Silva, a student at Alianza School. Even though the GIF file appears large, it's compressed to 22k for quick building.

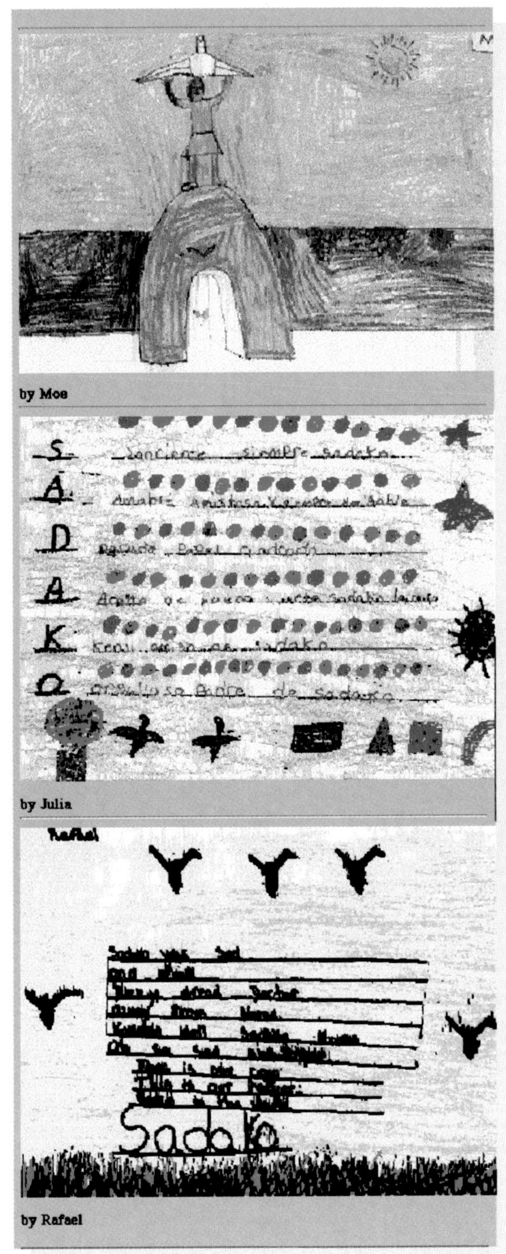

The 1000 Cranes Project site features an exhibition of pictures (all GIF images, about 15k each). These tell Sadako's story and its lesson of peace, drawn by several students from Alianza School.

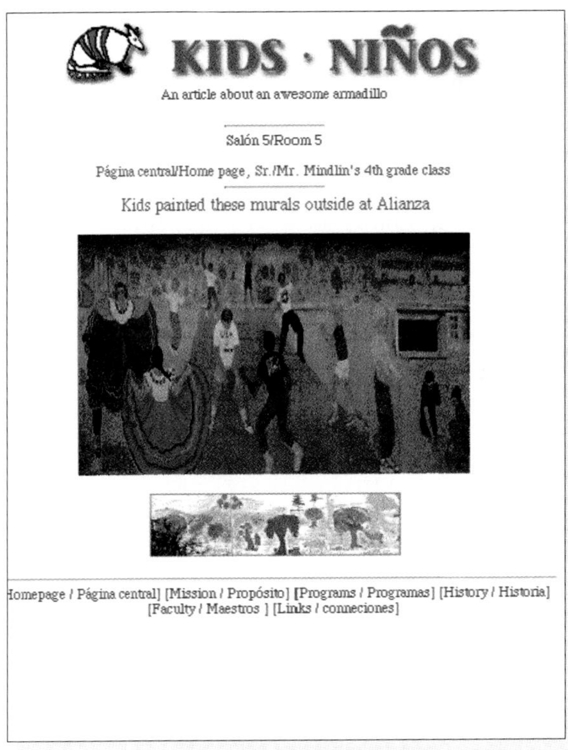

Creating an Animated GIF

Several of the sites profiled in this book feature animated GIFs (images in the Graphics Interchange Format that appear to move onscreen). To create animated GIFs, you need Adobe Illustrator 5.0 or later, Adobe Photoshop 3.0 (to convert Illustrator files to images), and a GIFBuilder program, available as shareware from GIFBuilder Home, North America, or Australia Mirror, or Info-Mac Mirror sites. You'll also need Netscape Navigator or another browser to test the GIF.

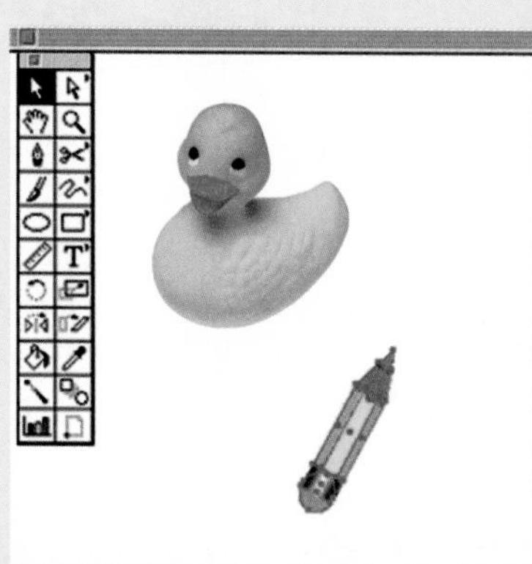

1 **Using Adobe Illustrator,** draw the elements of the animation, making sure to group together the elements that make up a single animation object. This example shows a pencil that will draw a duck.

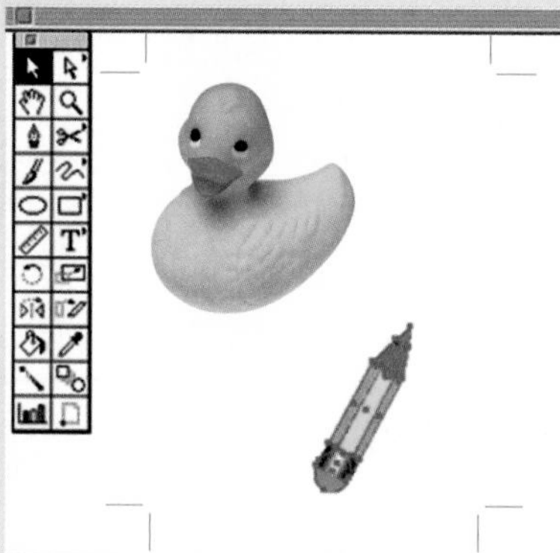

2 **Draw a rectangle around** the portion of the screen that you want to be the image. Select the rectangle, then choose Object>Cropmark. Mark to ensure that all the images will be positioned correctly when you open the Adobe Illustrator file in Photoshop.

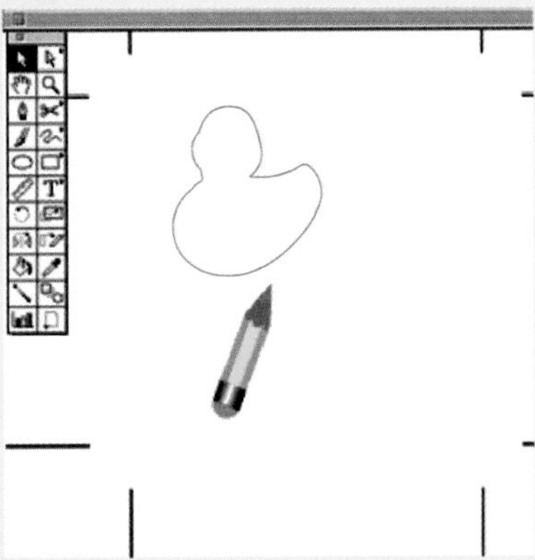

3 Select the duck and set its Object Paint attribute to "none." If you need to see the duck to position the pencil, then choose View>Artwork.

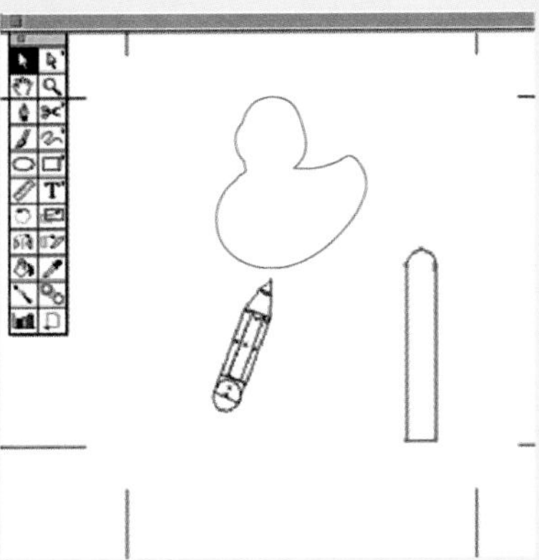

4 Now start moving the pencil around. Each time you move it, choose Save As to save a file for that position under a different name. (You are saving the individual frames of the animation as individual Illustrator files.)

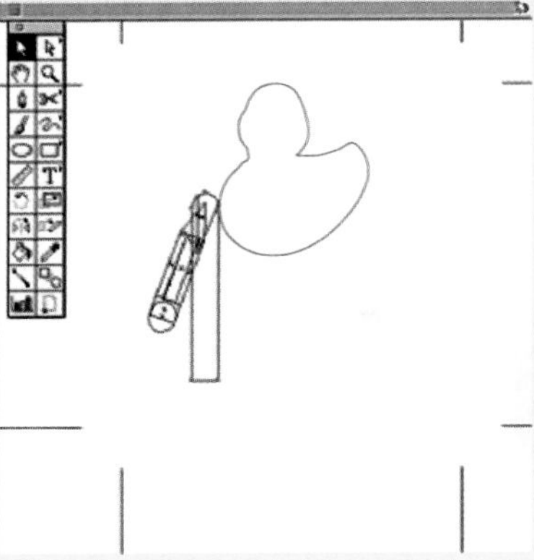

5 Off to the side, draw a pencil stroke. This will be combined with the duck in Step 6 to create a partial filling-in of the duck, so that in the animation it will look as if the pencil is coloring it in. *(continues on next page)*

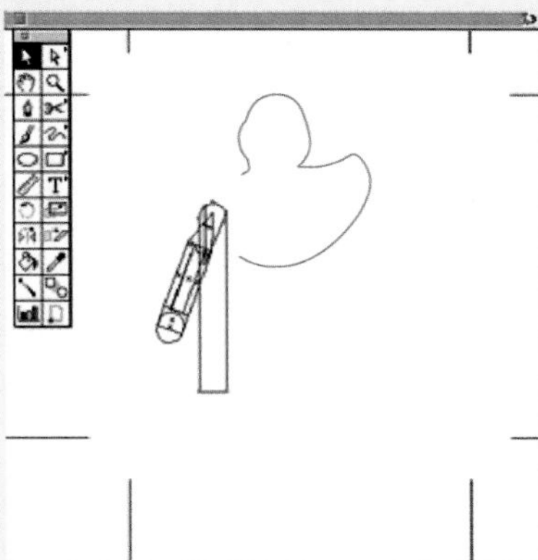

6 Move the pencil-stroke shape over the duck. Move the pencil into position. Select the duck and the pencil-stroke shape.

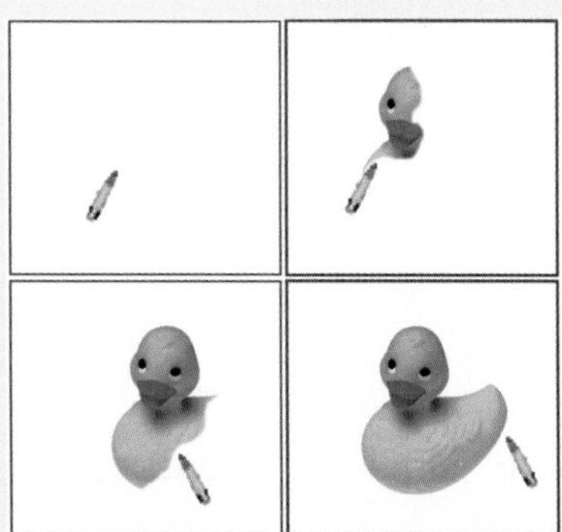

7 Choose Filter>Pathfinder>Intersect. Now the two regions intersect. Set the color of the region to yellow, bring the pencil to the front, and then save the file.

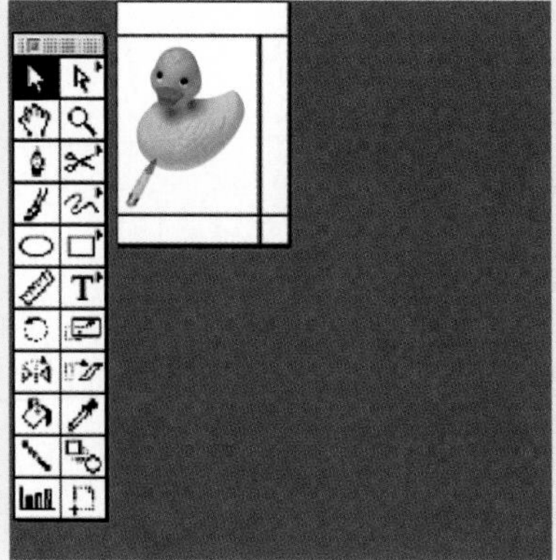

8 After saving the file, repeat the Undo command on the Edit menu until the pencil-stroke shape and the original duck are restored. Now move the pencil stroke and pencil and repeat the process for each frame.

9 Repeat Steps 7 and 8, building animation frames as described above. Each frame should have its own Illustrator file; store all these files in a single folder.

10 Open each Illustrator file in Photoshop. First choose Mode>RGB and then choose Mode>Indexed. This will convert the image from CMYK to RGB and then to Indexed color.

11 Now choose Save As and save the file into a folder PICT format. (The program GIFBuilder expects PICT files as input.)

12 Open the GIFBuilder and make sure the Frame window and Animation window are open. Drag and drop all of your PICT files into the Frame window.

13 GIFBuilder will let you adjust timing between frames, animation loops, and more. When you're finished experimenting, save the file as your final animated GIF.

http://www.telenaut.com/gst/

Global Show-n-Tell Museum

Palo Alto, California

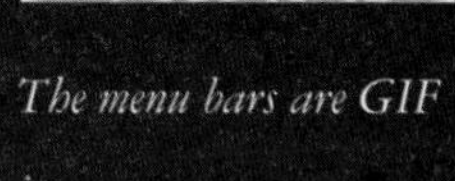

The menu bars are GIF images.

Global Show-n-Tell Museum is an award-winning showcase for children's art. Sponsored by Telenaut Communications and ManyMedia, this site solicits kids' art and publishes its choices on the Web.

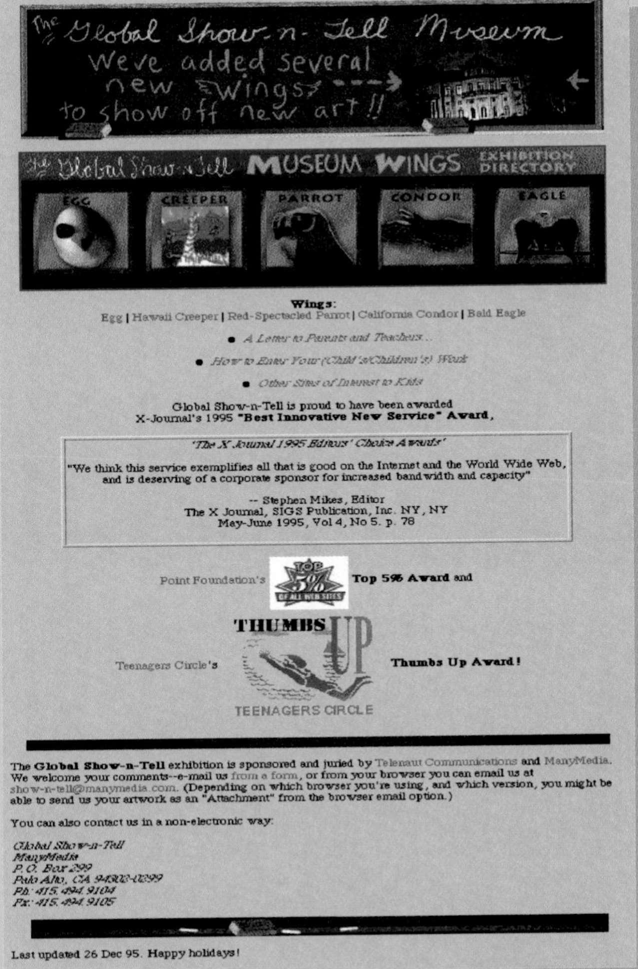

A play on words illustrates the museum "wing" idea with bird motifs. A great tool bar links to the Hawaii Creeper, Red-Spectacled Parrot, California Condor and Bald Eagle (all endangered birds).

Palo Alto, a town south of San Francisco that's part of Silicon Valley, is also the home of world-renowned Stanford University.

The best part of this museum-on-the-Web is its interactive aspect. The site creators have given kids who want to enter lots of help and advice. On a welcome page, entrants are taken almost step-by-step through the processes used to scan their artwork and send it in. Instructions are simple and easy to follow, even for young children.

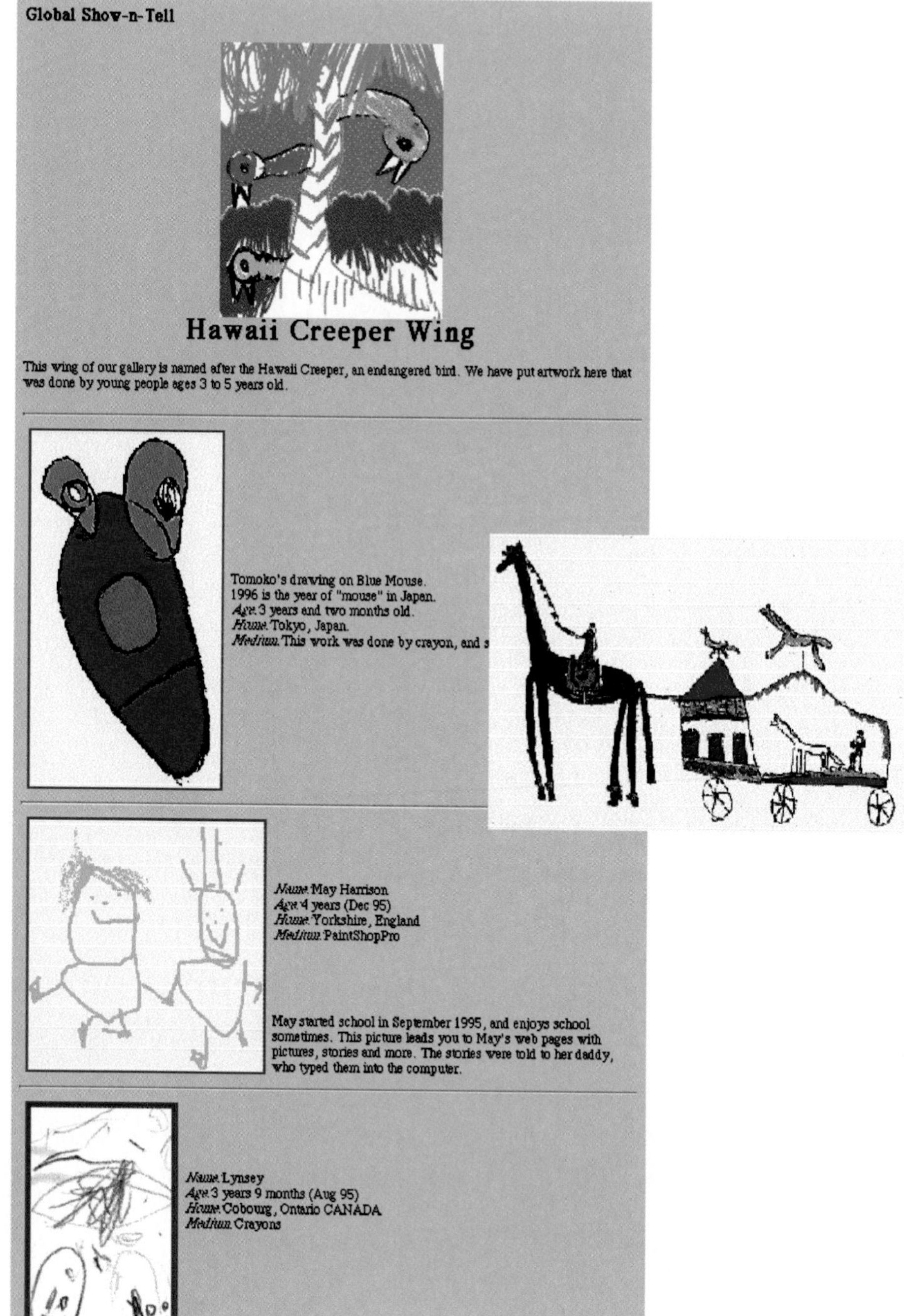

Global Show-n-Tell
Hawaii Creeper Wing
This wing of our gallery is named after the Hawaii Creeper, an endangered bird. We have put artwork here that was done by young people ages 3 to 5 years old.
Tomoko's drawing on Blue Mouse.
1996 is the year of "mouse" in Japan.
Age: 3 years and two months old.
Home: Tokyo, Japan.
Medium: This work was done by crayon, and s
Name: May Harrison
Age: 4 years (Dec 95)
Home: Yorkshire, England
Medium: PaintShopPro
May started school in September 1995, and enjoys school sometimes. This picture leads you to May's web pages with pictures, stories and more. The stories were told to her daddy, who typed them into the computer.
Name: Lynsey
Age: 3 years 9 months (Aug 95)
Home: Cobourg, Ontario CANADA
Medium: Crayons

Clicking on the Hawaii Creeper Wing allows visitors to view works by budding 3- to 5-year-old artists. All of the images are GIFs, compressed to 2–19k. By request of the site's creators, participants specify the medium they used and report how their work was scanned into digital form for use on the Web. Tomoko, a 3-year-old from Japan, drew a Blue Mouse in crayon; his parents scanned it into a GIF file. Five-year-old Eddie from Australia did his drawing of his bedroom using Windows Paintbrush.

Special Features

In the Red-Spectacled Parrot Wing, 7-year-old Garrett from California links visitors to his home page, which features stories he has written, as well as his pictures. Alex from Montana, 8 years old, says she "made this picture after looking at a girl's Web site from Chicago"—a good use of the Web for mutual inspiration. And Ekaterina from British Columbia, Canada, submitted a picture that is a link to her home page, where "The Parts of the Horse picture has two sound files on it!" (Her artwork shown here was done in felt tip on paper, scanned and reduced to a 10k GIF.)

Global Show-n-Tell

Red-Spectacled Parrot Wing

This wing of our gallery is named after the Red-Spectacled Parrot, an endangered bird. We have put artwork here that was done by young people ages 6 to 8 years old.

Name: Garrett Landon
Age: 7
Home Town: Santa Cruz, Ca
Hello. Please visit my homepage. I have a story and pictures titled Eggna and the Runaway Yokey. I will add more of my stories here from time to time.

Name: Alex
Home: Billings, MT
Comments: I am 8 years old and made this picture after looking at a girl's from chicago.

This picture will take you to Nicole's home page.

Name: Nicole
Age: 8 years
Home: Kaysville, Utah

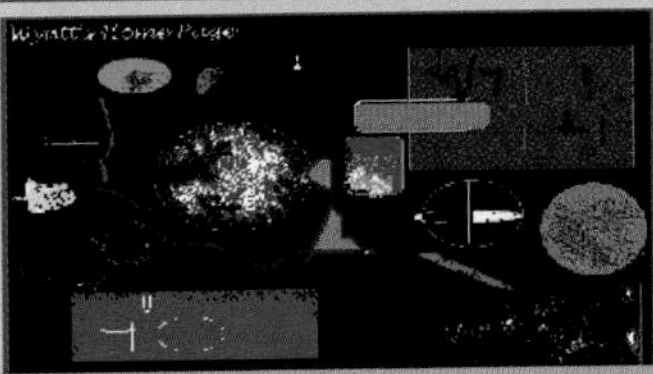

This picture will take you to Wyatt's home page.

Name: Wyatt
Age: 6 years
Home: Kaysville, Utah

Global Show-n-Tell Museum

http://www.seeusa.com/refrigerator.html

The Refrigerator

An Art Contest for Kids
Lenox Hill Station, New York

Welcome to the great refrigerator art contest! Every week, kids from all over the country send in art to The Refrigerator. The site creators then choose five contestants. Participants must be 18 years old or younger, and are asked to provide a title for their picture and an explanation of what the picture is and what it means to them.

This animated GIF of a drawing pencil is small (30k) and moves very quickly.

SeeUSA Communications, the creators of this site, have offices in Lenox Hill Station, New York.

Submit your art as a Photoshop file or on regular paper, where it will be scanned. The art is then posted as fast-loading GIF files (about 15k). Once up, visitors to the site view the choices and cast their votes (there's a box for voters' comments, too). Each week the winner's art is featured on the site. There's also a new writing contest called The Freezer.

The site's home page includes a cool animated GIF. Under the yellow refrigerator, a crayon draws a picture, then erases it and starts again . . . and again.

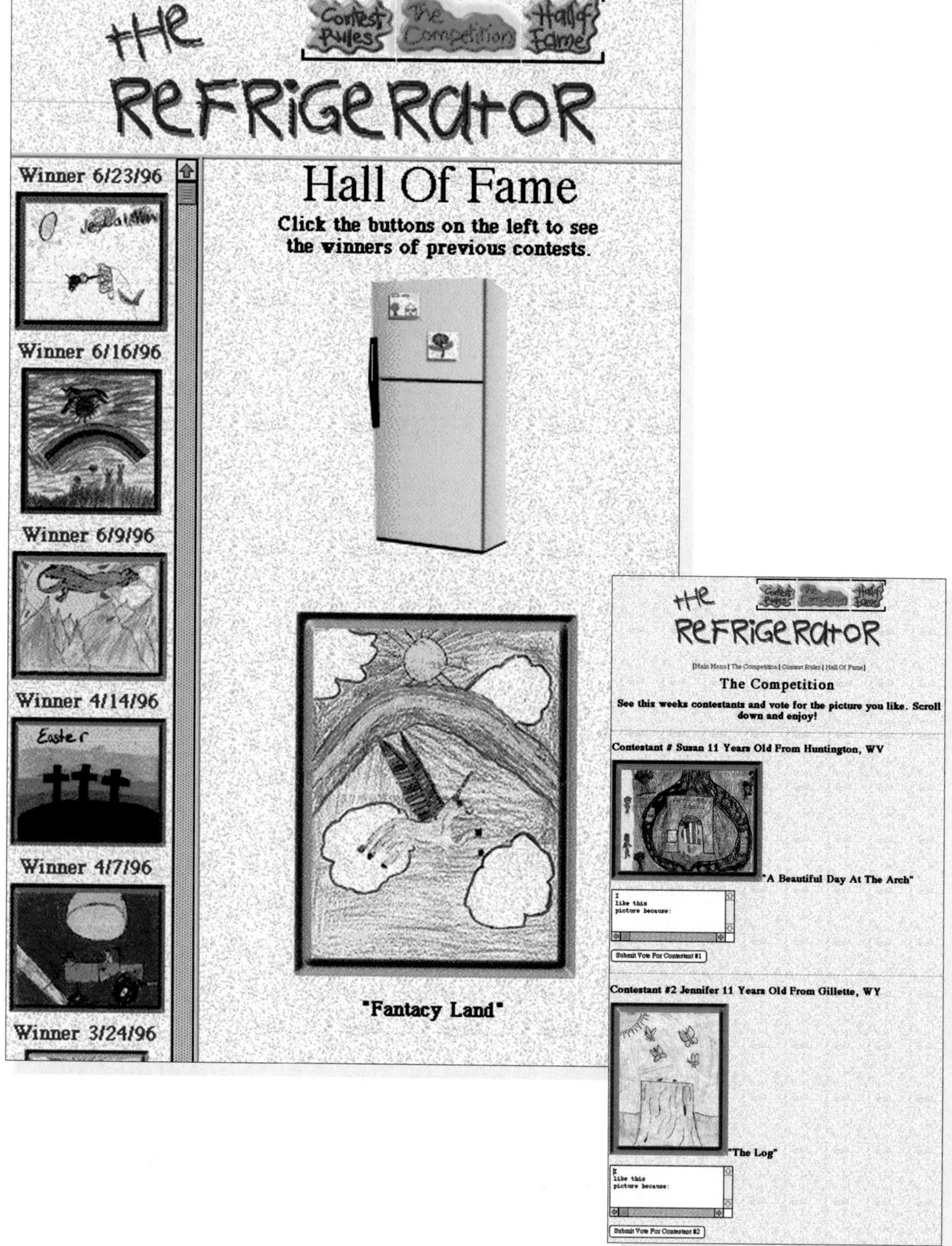

One winner, Jessica, 5 years old, says about her picture Nice Day For a Drink, "The bee is drinking nectar from the flower on a hot, sunny day. It means something special because I thought it up in my mind and just drew it. It makes me smile to see honey bees and beautiful flowers." Winner Mitchell, age 7, says of his picture Back in the Wild, "It's about dinosaurs at night."

Placing Images in Adobe PageMill

Use pictures to liven up your page design, and link to other pages, to maps with multiple links, or to buttons on forms. Note that Web browsers can display images in GIF or JPEG formats. Listed here are several ways to place images on your pages.

1 To move an image from another page, either drag and drop it or copy and paste it on the page where you want to use it.

2 To move an image from your files, use the Insert Image button on the Page View button bar. Click on this button to display the standard file dialog box. Locate the image you want to insert and click the Open button. (PageMill will insert a reference to it on your page if the image is already a GIF file. If the image is a PICT file, PageMill saves a copy and inserts a reference to the copy.)

3 To use an image from another application, Scrapbook, desktop patterns control, etc., drag and drop the image or copy and paste it.

4 Drag an image file icon into your page directly from the desktop. Make sure any images you place using this method are in the appropriate Web site folder; otherwise they will not be transferred to the server with the rest of your site.

http://www.whitehouse.gov/WH/kids/html/kidshome.html

The White House for Kids

Washington, D.C.

"This page is designed to keep you informed about some of the important issues being discussed in Washington, D.C., both at the White House and on Capitol Hill."

—President Clinton

Welcome to the White House site, this kid-friendly introduction to the White House features pages on history, government, personalities—and even presidential pets. Sections called Come Visit, Inside the White House, and Historic Moments of the Presidency highlight aspects of this United States landmark that are of special interest to children.

Design pages so that "Help" or "?" buttons are always easily available.

This site comes from—where else?—the nation's capital in Washington, D.C.

Clicking on the home page question mark brings up Frequently Asked Questions, such as "What is Welcome to the White House?" And what can you do with it? The answers inform visitors that the site allows users to link to all online resources made available by the government, provides an index and helpful search engine for access to White House documents, and provides e-mail service.

The White House for Kids

If visitors choose The White House for Kids, they find a home page with bright and cheerful graphics, presided over by Socks, the Clinton White House cat. Clicking on one of six stars brings up Location (a map and description); History (including a pictorial tour of the White House); Our President (biographical information); White House Pets; Write the President (how to reach him through e-mail); and, of course, White House Kids.

[Text version]

Children in the White House

Many Presidents have had children or grandchildren who lived with them or visited often at the White House. President Bill Clinton's daughter, Chelsea Victoria, enjoys spending time with her father. Chelsea is the first child to live in the White House since Amy Carter. An avid soccer player and ballet enthusiast, Chelsea's favorite subjects in school are math and foreign languages.

Amy Carter, President Jimmy Carter's daughter, moved into the White House at the age of nine. She has three older brothers, named Jack, Jeff, and Chip. Amy's mother, Rosalynn, once remarked, "Her brothers are so much older that it is almost as though she has four fathers, and we have had to stand in line to spoil her."

President Richard Nixon's children, Tricia and Julie, along with Julie's husband, David Eisenhower, enjoyed family dinners in the White House.

Lynda Johnson, President Lyndon B. Johnson's daughter, was married to Charles Robb in 1967 in the East Room of the White House. It was the first wedding to take place in the White House since 1914, when President Woodrow Wilson's daughter, Eleanor, married William Gibbs McAdoo.

President John F. Kennedy's children, John Jr. and Caroline, would often come to visit their father in the Oval Office. The President enjoyed their company and loved to watch them play. Caroline had a pony named Macaroni who roamed freely around the White House gardens.

Thomas (Tad) Lincoln was the youngest son of President Abraham Lincoln. Known for his antics around the White House Tad once discovered how to make all of the White House bells ring at the same time -- much to the surprise of the entire staff and residents of the building!

White House Kids profiles all the younger White House residents through history, using pictures and text. There are glimpses of Tad Lincoln, Amy Carter, and Chelsea Clinton, among others.

[Text version]

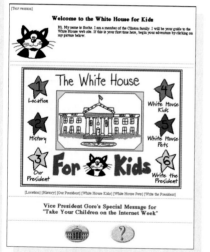

Welcome to the White House for Kids

Hi. My name is Socks. I am a member of the Clinton family. I will be your guide to the White House web site. If this is your first time here, begin your adventure by clicking on my picture below.

[Location] [History] [Our President] [White House Kids] [White House Pets] [Write the President]

Vice President Gore's Special Message for "Take Your Children on the Internet Week"

Hot Links in Adobe PageMill

The key to helping visitors navigate successfully through your site is to create links from one page (the source) to another (the destination). The destination can be on the same page or another page in your site, or anywhere else on the Web. Links can lead to the top of the destination page, or to a specific place on a page, called an anchor. Here's how to create a basic link in PageMill.

Select a source and a destination

1 Determine the destination for your link. If necessary, create an anchor as your destination. You can do this by dragging the page icon to somewhere within its own page. (Note: if there is no page icon, save the page; the icon will appear.) After creating an anchor, drag it to another page or to another location on the page. (Use the Show/Hide Anchor command from the Edit menu to see the anchors while you work with them.)

2 Select the source of the link—the text or image the reader will click to get to the destination.

Create a link

1 Drag something representing the destination (a page icon, image icon, anchor, etc.) to the text or image selected as the source and drop it; OR

2 Type the address of the link (URL) directly into the Link Location Bar; OR

3 Type the link address into the Text Attributes panel of the Attributes Inspector.

http://www.npac.syr.edu/textbook/kidsweb

Kid's Web

Syracuse, New York

The links on this page are represented by small GIFs. Here, Spock takes us to Drama.

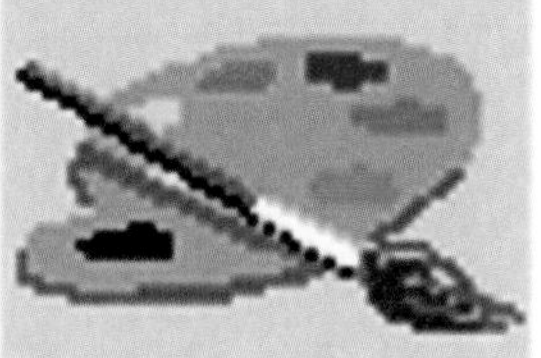

Here's the ultimate source for links to every imaginable category of information, from astronomy to pop music, to "fun and games." The site is part of Syracuse University's Living Schoolbook Project, which gives a glimpse into the classrooms of the future. Its goal is to apply high-performance computing and communications to education for grades K–12.

Syracuse, a city in upstate New York, is a college town and the home of Syracuse University, where this site got its start.

Kids Web

A World Wide Web Digital Library for Schoolkids

The documents accessed from this library are on Web servers all over the world. Links to these computers may be very slow or even temporarily inaccessible.

The Arts

 Art

 Drama

 Literature

 Music

The Sciences

 Astronomy and Space

 Biology and Life Sciences

Like any library catalog, the site's home page is divided into five broad subject categories: The Arts, The Sciences, Social Studies, Miscellaneous, and Other Digital Libraries. Under each heading, illustrated with cool thumbnail photos, is a list of subheads—Weather, History, Sports, etc.

To get an idea of how complete the coverage is on this site, click on History, which has five subheads, ranging from Europe to South America; on Drama, with film, television, and theater coverage; and on Fun and Games, for comics and online interactive games.

For researching any kind of class project, or just for satisfying curiosity about any topic under the sun, this site is the Web library of the future—available right now.

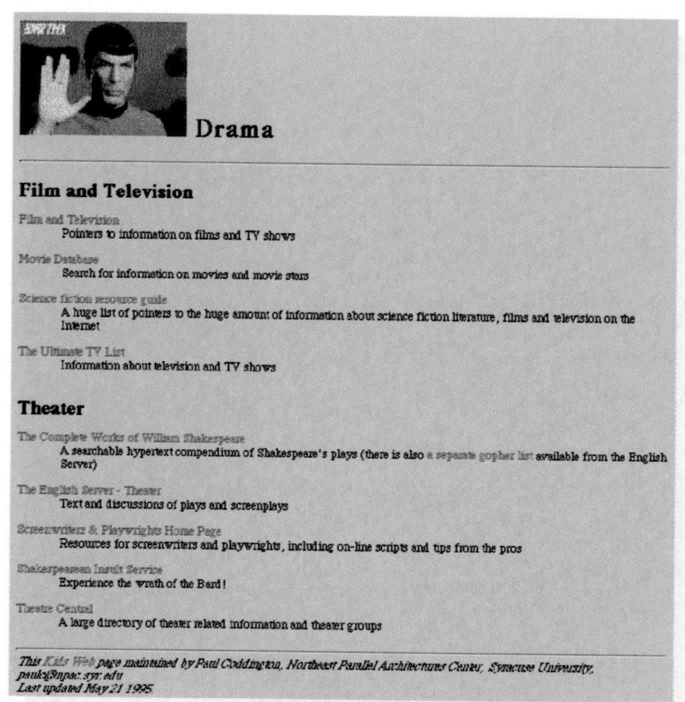

Drama

Film and Television

Film and Television
Pointers to information on films and TV shows

Movie Database
Search for information on movies and movie stars

Science fiction resource guide
A huge list of pointers to the huge amount of information about science fiction literature, films and television on the Internet

The Ultimate TV List
Information about television and TV shows

Theater

The Complete Works of William Shakespeare
A searchable hypertext compendium of Shakespeare's plays (there is also a separate gopher list available from the English Server)

The English Server - Theater
Text and discussions of plays and screenplays

Screenwriters & Playwrights Home Page
Resources for screenwriters and playwrights, including on-line scripts and tips from the pros

Shakespearean Insult Service
Experience the wrath of the Bard!

Theatre Central
A large directory of theater related information and theater groups

This Kids Web page maintained by Paul Coddington, Northeast Parallel Architectures Center, Syracuse University, paulc@npac.syr.edu
Last updated May 21 1995.

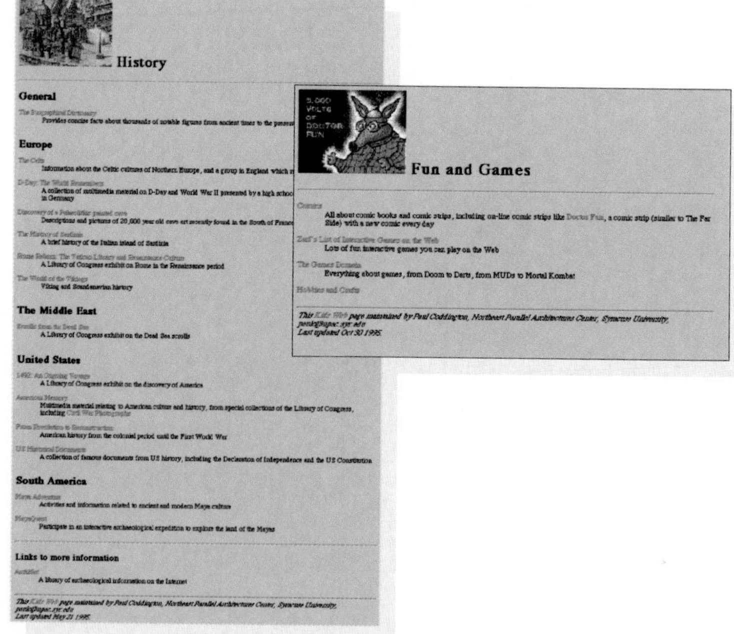

History

General

The Biographical Dictionary
Provides concise facts about thousands of notable figures from ancient times to the present

Europe

The Celts
Information about the Celtic cultures of Northern Europe, and a group in England which r

D-Day: The World Remembers
A collection of multimedia material on D-Day and World War II presented by a high schoo in Germany

Discovery of a Paleolithic painted cave
Descriptions and pictures of 20,000 year old cave art recently found in the South of France

The History of Sardinia
A brief history of the Italian island of Sardinia

Rome Reborn: The Vatican Library and Renaissance Culture
A Library of Congress exhibit on Rome in the Renaissance period

The World of the Vikings
Viking and Scandinavian history

The Middle East

Scrolls from the Dead Sea
A Library of Congress exhibit on the Dead Sea scrolls

United States

1492: An Ongoing Voyage
A Library of Congress exhibit on the discovery of America

American Memory
Multimedia material relating to American culture and history, from special collections of the Library of Congress, including Civil War Photographs

From Revolution to Reconstruction
American history from the colonial period until the First World War

US Historical Documents
A collection of famous documents from US history, including the Declaration of Independence and the US Constitution

South America

Maya Adventure
Activities and information related to ancient and modern Maya culture

MayaQuest
Participate in an interactive archaeological expedition to explore the land of the Mayas

Links to more information

ArchNet
A library of archaeological information on the Internet

This Kids Web page maintained by Paul Coddington, Northeast Parallel Architecture Center, Syracuse University, paulc@npac.syr.edu
Last updated May 21 1995.

Fun and Games

Comics
All about comic books and comic strips, including on-line comic strips like Doctor Fun, a comic strip (similar to The Far Side) with a new comic every day

Zarf's List of Interactive Games on the Web
Lots of fun interactive games you can play on the Web

The Games Domain
Everything about games, from Doom to Darts, from MUDs to Mortal Kombat

Hobbies and Crafts

This Kids Web page maintained by Paul Coddington, Northeast Parallel Architectures Center, Syracuse University, paulc@npac.syr.edu
Last updated Oct 30 1995.

Moving Adobe Illustrator Art into PageMill

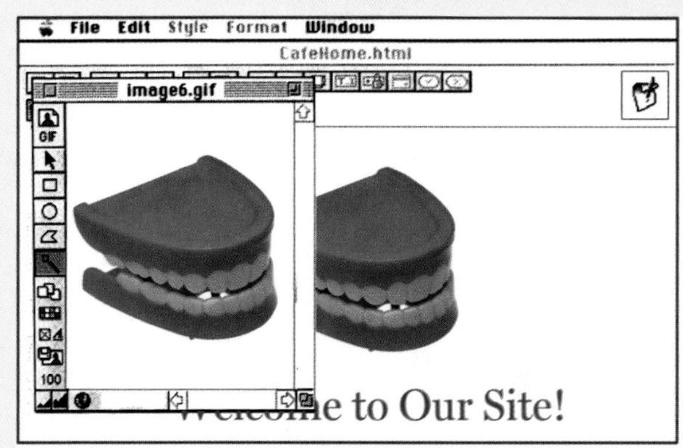

Adobe PageMill is one of the most popular HTML editing programs. It's easy to integrate your Adobe Illustrator art with PageMill. Here's how:

1 **Resize your artwork** to the actual size you want it to appear on the Web.

2 **Make sure the PageMill program** is open. Reposition your Illustrator artwork so you can see the PageMill blank window in the background. Select the artwork and drag and drop it into the blank PageMill window. PageMill automatically converts your artwork to a GIF image.

3 **When saving your work in** PageMill, the program will save the image in the GIF format, separate from your HTML pages. Also, it's always best to keep the file names short, with no work spaces, and lowercase, so all browsers can read them.

http://gagme.wwa.com/~boba/kids.html

Uncle Bob's Kids' Page

Chicago, Illinois

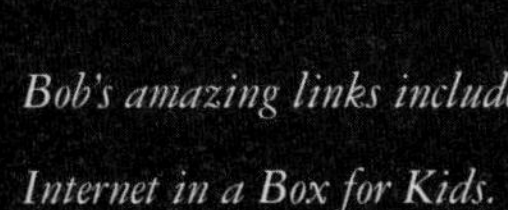

Bob's amazing links include Internet in a Box for Kids.

This site features an amazing list of pages for kids, grades K–12, as well as for their parents and teachers. Here, visitors can find links to a dizzying variety of sites. How about Unicycling, or a guided Journey to Beijing? Or tune into the Cool Word of the Day, or to the Origami page, where you can look at amazing examples of Japanese paper folding and then try some out using the step-by-step instructions on the screen.

Uncle Bob's Kids Page originates from Chicago.

KIDS' PAGE

WELCOME to Uncle Bob's Kids' Page. This page is a treasure chest of annotated links, with spotlights on special subjects. I hope you will enjoy yourself, as others have. Happy surfing.

A LITTLE INFORMATION

WHY DID I MAKE THE KIDS' PAGES?: Most of my pages contain a wide variety of links. Some go to pages which have materials that may not appropriate for children. So I decided to make a special set of pages just for kids.

WHO'S IT FOR?: These pages should be of interest to children, parents (the whole family), K-12 students, teachers and kids of all ages. Here's how to add this page to your bookmarks. Feel free to add a link to this page to your home page or hotlist.

IF AT FIRST: Always try a link a second time if it first fails to get a DNS entry, or to make a connection, or to receive data. If you are really interested in seeing the page, try it a third time if necessary.

NOTE: Many of the links on these pages benefit (and even require) the use of a graphical Web browser. There is further information available about Web browsers with links to the archive sites to obtain browsers. To find out exactly what browser (and version) you are currently using, you can get a browser check. And for further help, you can access info on configuring your browser.

WHAT'S NEW?: Yes, these pages need updating. I have enough links for two more sections. I hope to update these pages after I update and expand the Beatles page, some time in March or April. Yes, I know I keep pushing that time back, but things are busy around here.

WARNING: Because of the nature of the Net in general, and the Web in particular, it is possible to access a series of links that may take a child to almost anywhere. Parents should supervise children while they browse the Web. Below are some links on safe surfing.

HarperCollins Children's Books' Web site says Uncle Bob's is the best: "This site has great links for kids—links to games, virtual museums, entertainment sites, and much more." But here's what really makes this site useful: the links are annotated with brief, helpful comments on what to expect, so you don't waste a lot of time going to places you don't want to.

Uncle Bob's Kids' Page

Check to see if sites are "kid-safe." This is an important part of Bob's site, which also includes a testimonial by the President of ChildSafe Web Sites, and links to SafeSurf and Cyber Patrol.

WELCOME TO OUR ONLINE ACTIVITY CENTER for Theodore Tugboat, the TV series about a cheerful tugboat who likes to be friends with everyone. Life in his playful Big Harbour community is always changing, and whatever each new day brings, Theodore likes to do the things that friendly tugboats do.

There's lots to do and see here about Theodore and his many floating friends. (last updated Tuesday, July 2, 1996)

CHILDREN can help Theodore decide what to do next in an illustrated, interactive story created especially for the Internet. You can also download a page from our online coloring book or receive a postcard with Theodore's picture.

PARENTS and TEACHERS can review a synopsis of some episodes, find a description of our characters (we have more than 30 of them) or read about how The Big Harbour works. You can also participate in our email discussion list or reserve a Theodore Tugboat T-shirt. With any other thoughts, questions, or suggestions, please send email anytime to theodore@cochran.com.

FROM HERE you can also find over 300 links to other sites for children, researched and rated by our own Online Librarian, Berit Erickson. We hope to make this a consistently reliable starting point to help you find children's activities on the Internet.

PEOPLE WHO WORK IN TV ALL THE TIME (and anyone else who's interested) can find more information about the production. We also maintain a list of links to other sites of interest to TV professionals.

OUR SITE has been rated as one of the top 5% on the internet by Point Communications, and has also been selected for inclusion in the Internic's weekly Scout Report.

Scout Report SELECTION

Thanks for your visit. Have fun!

COCH INTERA

THEODORE TUGBOAT(TM) is a trademark of Cochran Entertainment Incorporated
All material © Cochran Entertainment Incorporated 1992-1996
all rights reserved
Theodore Tugboat's Online Activity Centre is operated by Cochran Interactive.
Last updated July 2 1996 by Andrew Hartlen, ajh@cochran.com.

This site provides links to things both silly and serious. One great link is the Exploratorium. Bob's annotation says, "Fun for kids of all ages. Has a digital library and FTP site with images and more." Another great link is the wildly popular Theodore Tugboat.

Mr. Edible Starchy Tuber Head

Eye
Ear
Nose
Mouth
Hair
Chin
Feet

At the other end of the spectrum, but equally cool is the Mr. Potatohead link. Says Bob's note, "It's no joke."

Backgrounds in PageMill

Backgrounds can add extra visual interest and even be a kind of "signature" for your Web site—a special look that is carried throughout your pages. Note that PageMill supports the Netscape extension that allows you to set the page background color. You can also use an image as a background for the page.

To change the background color:

1 **Open the Attributes Inspector** and click the Page icon to bring up the Page Attributes panel.

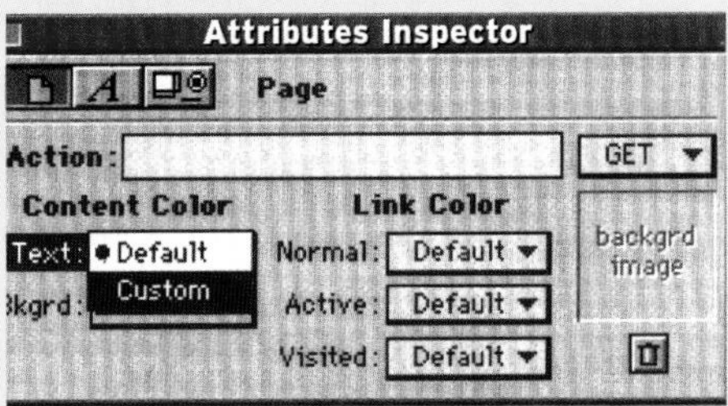

2 **Select Custom in the Background** (Bkgrd) pop-up, and then choose a background color from the Color Picker dialog box.

To use an image as a background:

1 **Open the Attributes Inspector** and click on the Page icon.

2 **Select the image you want** to use, remembering that an intensely colored or visually busy background can make the text on top of it hard to read. It's also a good idea to use a small image that downloads quickly for the reader.

3 **Drag an image into the image** well ("backgrd image") at the right side of the Attributes Inspector. The image is tiled, or repeated, to become the page background.

Kids do the Web

Appendix

Copyright questions

The ease with which text and images can be copied, manipulated, and distributed over the Web has raised a lot of questions about personal and public use of copyrighted material. While the Internet and the Web have introduced confusion into copyright issues, the copyright laws in the United States are fairly clear: "A copyright gives the *authors* of literary, dramatic, musical, artistic, and other intellectual properties limited exclusive rights to *reproduce* the work, create *derivative* works based on the original, distribute copies of the work, and perform or display the work in public."

As the author, no one can "steal" your work and use it, or profit from it, without your permission. Web ethics mean you don't take things from other sites, but create a totally unique site.

It should also be clear what it means to *reproduce*, or borrow, or grab the work over the Web and use it in your own site. It's against the law to copy images, movies, text, and animation that you've taken from another Web site and use them in your own site without permission. This could include something as simple as a button that you like or an icon you admire, whether the Web site you are "borrowing" from is authored by a group, a company, or an individual.

But what constitutes a *derivative* work? Does this mean that you can copy a piece of sky or grass if you don't show the main part of the photo or image? Does it mean that the piece you "borrow" must be recognizable in order to be a violation? Does it mean you can copy a paragraph of a larger story and incorporate it into your own text? Does it mean that you can use another's work as part of a collage? The answer to all these questions is NO. You are not allowed any unauthorized use of any part of copyrighted material, be it text, graphics, photos, or movies.

Another area of confusion in copyright law is the term "fair use." Fair-use privilege allows, in certain cases, a limited amount of copying for the purpose of commentary, news reporting, teaching, scholarship, or research. If your site is exhibiting any of these qualities, check first with your teachers, librarians, parents, or sponsors for direction and instructions. The safest practice is to always ask permission from the source—sometimes a simple e-mail can do the trick.

You are allowed to use art that is in the public domain. This is generally work for which the copyright has expired. Depending on the circumstances, copyrights can last for 100 years or more, so a work usually has to be quite old to be in the public domain. Note that this does not necessarily apply to photographs of old art. While the painting, sketch, or sculpture may be ancient, the photograph that you want to scan and use may be copyrighted. Even if you take the picture yourself, the piece of art is probably owned by a museum or collector who also owns the right to limit access to the art.

Are people public property? While you may have heard that photos of public personalities can be used to illustrate newspapers and magazines, these are done by professional publishing companies with established legal departments that can determine who is and who isn't a public personality. In terms of the original work you might do at home, work, or school, you might need a photo release from anybody in a picture that will be published on your Web site. While kids might love to have their photo published on a Web site, some parents might strictly object to such a public display of their children—establish a simple process when publishing on the Web, and check your local library for information about photo release forms, or ask a local photographer.

It all sounds confusing and depressing. But, really it isn't. When you create original sites, instead of copying or borrowing, your site will be protected by copyright law rather than breaking it. Browse other sites for ideas, or inspiration, but create something original that has meaning for your own site—the original sites are always the most popular.

This is an introduction to copyright issues. Don't rely on this discussion to determine whether or not use of an image, a graphic, text, a digital movie, or animation will violate a copyright. *When in doubt, don't use it.*

For more information write to the Copyright Office, Information and Publication Section LM-455, Library of Congress, Washington DC 20559. Or, perform a search on your favorite Web search engine using the words "Copyright Office." Readers in countries other than the United States should check with their country's copyright offices. Each country has unique applications and laws governing copyright. While the Web reaches around the world, pay attention to the laws within your country. Eventually copyright law will catch up with kids creating Web sites and make it much more simple.

Use quotation marks to define proper names, such as the book "Tom Sawyer" or the film star "Marilyn Monroe". In Alta Vista's search engine, type in the proximity operator NEAR in your query to search for a first word appearing close (or in proximity) to the second word: such as Africa NEAR Lilies. Each search engine usually has tips and ways to make your Web search more productive.

Tips for Web searching

The Internet has more information than dozens of libraries put together. Many homework assignments can be greatly embellished by using the almost limitless resources of the Web to conduct research, acquire graphics, and even create a URL, or Web, bibliography for further investigation. The trick is finding the right information quickly.

Your home page should always have links to four or five search engines. Consider each search engine to be a Web librarian that can assist in finding information.

1 Know what you need to search for. Don't approach the Web with a vague idea unless you want to spend hours and hours of idle browsing. Write down on a piece of paper exactly what you need, such as Map of Africa, description of the flower species of Lilies, and picture of African mountain lillies.

2 Go to a central Web site with an advanced Web searcher or links to one—YAHOO!, or Netscape's home page, or Digital's Alta Vista. Search engines are constantly being created and improved, but try one of these:

http://www.altavista.digital.com/
http://www.yahoo.com/search.html
http://www.dejanews.com/
http://www.excite.com/
http://www.lycos.com/

3 Type in the subject matter you want to search. Depending on your subject matter you might have anywhere from a handful to thousands of "hits," or Web sites, with the phrase you typed in. Try typing in a more precise search. For instance instead of African flowers, type in African mountain lilies. BE PRECISE. The goal isn't to get as many "hits" as you can, but to get a handful of the very BEST sites with the information you need.

Additional sites for kids

This book profiles just a few of the great Web sites especially by and for kids. Of course, there are thousands of them, and all of the good ones couldn't be included. Here's a list of additional recommended sites to get you started on further Web explorations.

INTERNET SITES FOR KIDS

http://www.sed.tcu.edu/www/sed/kids.html

This site lists links to lots of "fun" stuff, from movies to comic books to games.

YAHOOLIGANS!

http://www.yahooligans.com

A good all-around source for links to all kinds of kid-friendly sites, including sports, art, politics, science, computers, games, and entertainment.

B.J.PINCHBECK'S HOMEWORK HELPER

http://tristate.pgh.net/~pinch13

Developed by a nine-year-old (with help from Dad), this site has all the links every school kid needs, indexed under Search Engines, Reference, News and Current Events, Math & Science, Social Studies, English, History, Playtime, and Foreign Languages.

BERIT'S BEST SITES FOR CHILDREN

http://www.cochran.com/theosite/ksites.html

Prepared by Cochran Interactive Incorporated, this list of links is annotated and rated; each link listed is, in itself, a link-based site that leads to more sites especially for kids.

INTERESTING PLACES FOR KIDS

http://www.cre.ricoh.com/people/steve/k.

Stephen R. Savitzky has compiled this list of links for his daughter, Katy; it's an extensive compilation of educational and "fun" sites.

KIDS INTERNET DELIGHT

http://www.clark.net/pub/journalism/kid.html

John Makulowich started this page in 1994; now it features links to 116 sites worldwide (all arranged alphabetically) that are of interest to children and parents.

WWW.THEKIDS.COM

htt://www.thekids.com

This colorful site features Tales to Tell (illustrated stories from around the world) and Best of the Net (links to good educational sites), as well as Discussion Rooms, Kidstuff, and Parentstuff.

INFORAMP, INC. STUFF FOR KIDS

http://205.212.88.2/kids.html

This site is an interesting of mix of links for fun and games, schools, stories, reference sources, and museums.

CYBERKIDS

http://www.mtlake.com/cyberkids/

This highly acclaimed online kids' "magazine" showcases an ever-changing art gallery of kids' work; a magazine by kids featuring news, poetry, and stories; and a Young Composers section, as well as games and other features.

JUST FOR KIDS

http://a2z.lycos.com/Just_For_Kids/

The Lycos Web search engine (http://www.lycos.com/) has an area Just for Kids. Sorted alphabetically, from A to Z, it lists dozens of both independent and commercial sites. It also has an option to view the most popular sites, sometimes a neat way to browse and save time visiting worthwhile sites.

CRAYOLA

http://www.crayola.com/crayola/home.html

Home of the popular crayon company, this Web site is sure to please those kids who actively play and draw with crayons. Games, contests, and fun facts about the world of color.

KIDZONE

http://www.mckinley.com/browse_bd.cgi?KidZone

The Magellen Internet Guide search engine (http://www.mckinley.com/) has an area for kids divided into such categories as Clubs & Organizations, Computers & Internet Tools, Kids on the Net, and The Reading Room, among others. Features a 4-star rating system as well as a "greenlight" for kids rating system. Check out the Animals category if you have a pet dog or cat!

THE WHY FILES

http://whyfiles.news.wisc.edu/

Sponsored by the University of Wisconsin and funded by the National Science Foundation, this informative site focuses on "Science Behind the News" and how things work. Read about the "why" behind the news stories of today. Great for homework research and inquisitive minds. Expand your knowledge and understanding.

YOUTH CENTRAL

http://www.yc.apple.com/

A site for kids and teens sponsored by Apple Computer. Features a neat village metaphor similar to the defunct "e-world" user interface. Features a Pen-Pal Plaza, Entertainment, Sports, and Tech Triangle sections. Visit the Tech Triangle for links that are specific to Apple's Macintosh line of computers. Sophisticated content is more appropriate for teens.

THE ELECTRONIC ZOO

http://netvet.wustl.edu/e-zoo.htm

All things animal is the theme of this very graphic Web site sponsored by Washington University of St. Louis, Missouri. Great resource for household pets like dogs and cats, with detailed information on all the breeds and their history. Zoo animals and animals of the wild also featured. A wonderful resource for publications, organizations, and news groups about the wild kingdom. Heavily illustrated so be prepared to wait if you have a slow modem or net connection.

E-CARDS

http://www.e-cards.com/

E-cards—the postcards of the Internet are free to use. Send a postcard to anyone with an Internet address. Every sending generates a donation to the World Wildlife Fund. You send a card from the e-card site, then a mail message is delivered to the recipient with the above URL for them to pick up their greeting by logging on to the site and selecting "pick-up." Not quite as easy as sending a normal e-mail message, but then, it's different.

Glossary

ANIMATED GIF

A method of embedding several GIF images together into a single GIF file, so that an animation occurs when the GIF file is downloaded. See pages 170–173 for one method of creating these short animated special effects.

ANTI-ALIAS

This is a method of blending the edge colors of an object with colors of its background, to smooth out the jagged edges produced by the screen's low resolution. Computer generated images can be anti-aliased by their software, like Adobe Photoshop. Scanned images need to have their background removed, then a new one recreated with anti-aliasing on.

BROWSER

The computer application you use to view Web pages, such as Netscape Navigator. It needs either a network connection, or a modem, to connect to a Web server. Web sites are stored on individual Web servers that are accessed via the Internet by your browser.

COMPRESSION

The images you want to display need to be compressed so they can be stored, processed, and moved around the computer fast enough to produce good interactive performance. Some file formats do that by removing excess digital information in the file. What you don't want is to have files that are too large to be transmitted across the Web.

PICT

A graphic file format used for line-art and photographic-quality images and graphics. You may run into PICT files if you use art off of clip-art CDs.

HTML

The coding language used to create hypertext documents published on the Web (and other media). Since HTML is a coding language, a lot of attention is being paid to HTML formatting applications, like Adobe PageMill, which don't required any coding of the HTML language.

GIF

Short for Graphic Interchange Format, it is the most common graphic format on the Web.

GIFs are 8-bit images (256 colors or fewer) and are easily portable across common computer platforms without conversion.

E-MAIL

Shortened version of electronic mail. Used to relay text messages back and forth to other people using computers. Some Web browsers have e-mail capabilities built into them.

INTERNET

The worldwide network that connects computers. The Web is the graphic portion of the Internet.

INTRANET

A network that functions much like the Internet except access is limited to a specific audience, such as employees of a company or corporation.

JPEG

A highly-compressed, high fidelity, color-rich image file format. JPEG supports variable degrees of compression. JPEG and GIF are common file formats for images and photos on the Web.

LINKS

Often referred to as hypertext links, or hot links, this is the shortened version. A link is an area of a Web page that, when "clicked" on with a mouse, advances the view to a brand new destination. That destination can be somewhere on the same page, or somewhere on the same Web site, or an altogether different site half a world away. In HTML you assign the destination link with a URL.

NETWORK PROVIDER, OR INTERNET PROVIDER

A company with a direct tie to the Internet that can give you personal, company, or school-wide access to the Internet and Web, usually for a monthly fee just like a phone company. On-line services are companies like America Online which offer a mix of custom content as well as Web access. Different network providers often give subscribers 5 megabytes or so of free space to post their own personal Web page.

HOME PAGE

The first page one views when "arriving" at a Web site, or a single page a site might refer to as its "front door." The home page is often the most important because it needs to download quickly yet look compelling, offer lots of links into the site without looking confusing, and must create the identity and interface of the rest of the site.

PDF

Adobe's format for its Acrobat product, officially known as the Portable Document Format.

PLUG-INS

Add-on software that expand, extend, or alter the feature set built into an application. Think of plug-ins as accessories you might wear, such as a watch to tell time, or sunglasses to shade the sun, or a backpack to carry stuff.

URL

The address of a Web site, or Web page, on the Web. It stands for Uniform Resource Locator. Thus http://www.adobe.com stands for: "http" stands for hypertext transaction protocol, or the way digital documents are transmitted over the network; "www" stands for World Wide Web; and "adobe.com" stands for Adobe Systems, with the ".com" meaning the address is a commercial one, or a business (".org" usually means a non-profit organization, ".gov" means government, ".edu" means a school, and so on).

WEB

Shortened version of the World Wide Web, or WWW. The Web uses servers to hold information, the network to transmit it, and browsers on the users' end to read the information.

WEBMASTER

The person in charge of the technical workings of the Web site, often involving some programming in HTML as well as knowledge of networks, computers, software, and the like.

Kids and Web reality

This book has tried to inspire and stimulate its readers. Kids are creating Web sites. It's easy. If they can do it, you can do it.

Unfortunately, the whole story isn't this rosy. It has been estimated that only 4–5% of schools in the United States have their own Web sites. That leaves nearly 80,000 schools without the ability to participate in this exciting and educational technology. In many countries, the numbers are appallingly lower, and in some third world countries the percentage is 0%. Of schools lucky enough to have Web access, the computer-to-student ratio is often one computer to 25–35 students, or an average of 6–10 minutes per student per day. Barely enough to browse and read a Web page or two.

The 95% of schools that do not have Web access face myriad obstacles to get it. The first, and often the hardest, obstacle is the actual wiring of the school. Time, money, and sometimes even building codes are prohibitive for tightly budgeted schools and school districts. Lack of manpower, technical advice, and project organization can also stop the Web before it can even get in the school.

A second obstacle is the technology needed to set up and run a Web server. Although it is getting easier, teachers and educators are specialists with little time to master Web server set up and administration. Many schools blessed with network access often don't have the technical training to set up and maintain their Web site. With budgets everywhere being examined, schools will continue to find it hard to hire even a part-time Webmaster, although this is exactly what they need.

The third obstacle is computers and software. All the wiring and Webmasters in the world cannot help a school that only has three computers and 750 students. Software to run the computers and to create the Web sites is another issue, as well as the training to efficiently operate the software.

Money, expertise, and volunteer time—that is what the kids of the world need. Please volunteer your services to your local school or community organization. If you are Web-savvy, volunteer. Or donate a modern computer. Work with your company or corporation on local community grants. Organize a parental action committee to work with teachers and educators. And if you're lucky enough to be at a school with great Web access and a great Web site like the ones in this book, consider helping the schools nearby.

ORGANIZATIONS TO THE RESCUE

Two organizations come to mind that can help get schools and kids onto the Web. The first is NetDay96; the other is Web66. Both have Web sites, so if you don't have access, find someone who does and make these the first places you visit.

NETDAY96

http://www.netday96.com/

NetDay96 began in California by two parents, Michael Kaufmann and John Gage, who were concerned by the lack of communication infrastructure in the state's school system. Their efforts were to snowball to include the President and Vice President of the United States, 50,000 voulunteers, and national media coverage as they wired about 3,500 California schools in a single day.

NetDay96 is the outgrowth of that phenomenal success. The organiztion is active in almost all of the United States, and will probably go abroad soon. NetDay96 has set up a grass-roots, non-profit organization to wire the schools of the world together. All through the help of volunteers like you.

NetDay96 has already assembled the organizational material a school district or volunteer group might need. From "wiring" manuals and how-tos, to sample letters to government representatives and a how-to get press coverage guide, NetDay96 is one of the finest examples of community activism at work for kids and teens.

If your school district would like to participate in the Web, but it doesn't have network access, contact NetDay96. And look for NetDay96 activities in your local area as a great place to volunteer, if only for a day.

WEB66

http://web66.coled.umn.edu/

Made possible by the University of Minnesota and the 3M Corporation, "the Web66 project is designed to facilitate the introduction of this technology into K12 schools. The goals are: to help K12 educators learn how to set up their own Internet servers; to link K12 Web servers and the educators and students at those schools; and, to help educators find and use K12 appropriate resources on the Web."